Tell Me Everything

First published in 2005 by Bounty Books,
a division of Octopus Publishing Group Ltd.,
2-4 Heron Quays, London E14 4JP

Reprinted 2006 (Twice)

Material previously appeared in:
Tell Me About (Bounty Books)
Tell Me Why (Bounty Books)
Tell Me When (Bounty Books)
Tell Me What (Bounty Books)
Tell Me How (Bounty Books)
Tell Me Where (Bounty Books)

ISBN-13:978 0 753710 814
ISBN-10:0 753710 811

A CIP catalogue record for this book is available from
the British Library

Printed and bound in China

Tell Me Everything

Bounty Books

INTRODUCTION

Whether you're looking up information for a project or coursework, or just out of interest, *Tell Me Everything* has the answers! Here is a taster of what you will find in more than 400 information-packed pages and fascinating fact files on related subjects.

THE WORLD explores the planet we live on and the animals and plants with which we share it. Within this section, 'The Animal Kingdom' looks at how animals feed, why they use display and camouflage, why and when they migrate, hibernate or change colour during the year, why some animals are seen at night rather than during the day, how fish can breathe under the water and many other fascinating subjects. In 'The Plant World' subjects include how trees breathe, why leaves come in all shapes and sizes and how plants reproduce. In 'Earth & Space' we look at our planet itself: the shape of the ocean floor, how the continents were in different places millions of years ago, what glaciers and ice sheets are, what causes erosion, extreme weather, the effects that we are having on our planet, the atmosphere, the age of the Earth and the size of the universe. 'Prehistory' covers the development of life on Earth, fossils, the evolution and behaviour of dinosaurs, whether the dinosaurs were wiped out by an asteroid and how they were replaced by mammals.

In THE HUMAN BODY we look at the marvellous structure that we take for granted. In 'Bones & Muscles' subjects covered include what our skeleton does and how it works with the muscles to support us and allow us to move around, how bones and wounds heal, the structure of joints and what happens to muscles during exercise. 'Heart & Circulation' explores the vital role these play in our lives, how the heart pumps, what valves are, what blood is made of and what blood groups are. 'Brain & Nervous System' shows how messages are flashed to and from our brains, how we feel and how instructions are passed from the brain, the brain's structure, how memory works, why we feel hungry, why we dream and even why some people are left-handed. 'Genetics & Reproduction' looks at the nature of chromosomes, how our genes dictate what we look like, how we learn to talk and how babies develop.

The HISTORY section explores all aspects of recorded human history, from great leaders and empires, to inventors and inventions, daily life, warfare and great civilizations. 'Who...' looks at famous historical characters, such as Alfred the Great, Abraham Lincoln and Genghis Khan, as well as great peoples from the past, including the Franks and the Hittites. 'How...' explores historical events on a deeper level, asking such questions as 'How successful were the Viking attacks?' 'How did the American Indians lose their land?' and 'How did the United Nations begin?' 'What...' covers events, for example, the Russian Revolution, the Crusades, the signing of Magna Carta and Home Rule, as well as artifacts such as Stonehenge, hieroglyphs, and Stephenson's Rocket and movements like Communism and women's suffrage. 'When...' takes a look at important events in world history such as the abolition of the slave trade, the first explosion of an atomic bomb and the opium wars, and examines ancient developments including the first use of honey, the first houses and the stone age. 'Where...' explores events and places from around the world, including the locations of Persepolis and the Silk Road and the landing place of the Pilgrim Fathers, as well as the expansion of the Muslim Empire, and where the Romans bathed and held gladiatorial games.

SCIENCE & TECHNOLOGY explores geology, weather, life on Earth, human technological achievements, the Solar System and deep space. 'The Earth' looks at how our planet moves around the Sun, earthquakes, volcanoes and plate tectonics, monsoons, droughts, lightning and the structure of the Earth. 'The Natural World' examines how scientists like Darwin and Linnaeus learned about evolution and the classification of animals and plants, as well as about extinction, the colonization of the land by early plants, and answers fascinating questions such as 'How do bees make honey?' and 'How do glow worms glow?' 'Discoveries & Inventions' looks at inventions throughout history from paper to planes and gunpowder to glass. 'The Solar System' explores the Moon, planets and other smaller bodies, such as comets, that travel around our Sun, and discovers the nature of stars, the Milky Way, black holes, galaxies and supernovas.

The World

The Animal Kingdom

WHY DO MOSQUITO BITES ITCH?

The itchy welt that forms on the skin when a person has been 'bitten' by a mosquito is, in fact, an allergic reaction to the insect's saliva, which it injects into the skin in order to prevent its victim's blood clotting. A mosquito cannot actually bite because its jaws do not open, but the middle of its proboscis has six needlelike parts, called stylets. These are protected by the insect's flexible lower lip, or labium, most of the time. When a mosquito 'bites', the lip slides out of the way like a sleeve as the stylets puncture the skin. The channels made by the stylets allow saliva to flow into the wound, thus allowing the insect to sip blood more easily. Only female mosquitoes bite and only those of a few of the 3,000 or more species attack animals and people.

FACT FILE

Some of the worst diseases that people and animals suffer are spread by mosquitoes. Some species are carriers of such serious infections as Dengue fever, yellow fever, malaria and filariasis.

WHY DO MOTHS EAT WOOL?

Eyed hawk moth

Most people think that small moths, called 'clothes moths', make the moth holes in our clothes by chewing them. There are various species, including the webbing moth, the casemaking moth and the tapestry or carpet moth. It isn't the adult moths that cause the problem, because they don't eat, but the caterpillars that do the damage. The female moth lays her eggs on wool, or sometimes other fabrics, and after between 4 and 21 days, depending on the species, they hatch into tiny caterpillars. The casemaking moth caterpillar turns the wool it eats into a case, which it lines with silk and drags around with it. There it lives as a caterpillar until it turns into a pupa, and eventually emerges as an adult.

FACT FILE

When at rest, eyed hawk moths resemble a dead leaf. If alarmed, they open their forewings to reveal striking eye markings on the hind wings. This is likely to scare predators such as birds.

Death's head hawk moth

Poplar hawk moth

CAN ANIMALS UNDERSTAND ONE ANOTHER?

Howler monkeys

FACT FILE

Otters live in habitats where it's easier to use sound to communicate with each other rather than visual signals. As well as a warning growl, they have a repertoire of various chirps, chuckles, screams and squeals to express their feelings.

Although animals cannot actually talk to one another, they have means of communicating by using visual and noise signals. Just as we use expressions, sounds and gestures to indicate how we are feeling, many animals make noises and signs. Mute swans, particularly males, will raise their wings, swim towards an intruder and hiss to warn him off, and other birds sing both to attract mates and defend territory. Howler monkeys do actually howl to defend their territory, and this acts as a warning as it carries through the forested areas of Venezuela. Animals can also communicate by using smell, and many mammals mark their territories with scent.

WHY DO PEACOCKS HAVE SUCH BEAUTIFUL TAILS?

We often hear the expression 'proud as a peacock' or 'vain as a peacock,' and that is because the peacock seems to take great pleasure in displaying its beautiful feathers. The display is done solely by the male to attract a female bird. The female, the peahen, does not have these beautiful feathers. The most obvious thing about the male peacock is the trail of greenish feathers with bold eyespots, which aren't tail feathers,

but grow from his back. The male also has a shiny metallic greenish-blue breast and neck, greenish feathers on his back that lead to the train and dark purplish-blue underparts. During courtship, the male bird spreads his train into a gorgeous fan as he parades in front of the female. He practically goes through a dance as he tries to convince the peahen that he is very handsome.

FACT FILE

Indian peafowl, the correct name for this species of peacock, originate from India and Sri Lanka, where they can be seen roaming in the wild.

HOW DO BIRDS SWIM UNDERWATER?

Kingfisher

Gannet

Coot

FACT FILE

The spoonbill is a long-legged wading bird that has a spoon-shaped bill. The bird swings its bill from side to side in the water to search for food.

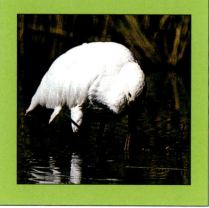

Some wildfowl and seabirds can swim under water, and they have various methods. Most, such as coots and cormorants kick from the surface, point their heads down and power themselves through the water with their strong legs, often emerging some distance from where they dived. Birds like the gannet can swim underwater as well as on the surface. Terns and kingfishers are among the birds that don't actually swim, but spot their prey from a height, plunge into the water and catch it, then float back up to the surface and take off. Gannets dive from heights of up to 130 ft (40 m) and chase fish through the water. The masters of underwater swimming are the penguins, who almost seem to fly through water and travel great distances.

WHAT ARE ARMY ANTS?

Wood ants

Army ants, which come from Africa and North and South America, are highly aggressive hunters and, like other ants, live in colonies of between 10,000 and millions of individuals. Their main victims are other insects and spiders, but some also capture, kill and eat other animals they come across, such as small mammals or baby birds, that can't escape. A few species inhabit permanent nests and make raids through tunnels, but most are nomadic and remain above ground all the time. Some of them hunt during the day, while others hunt at night.

Some kinds of army ant hunt and rest alternately for a few weeks. While active, they may cover great distances and take shelter in a new place every night. Once the queen has laid her eggs, however, they will stay in one place for safety. They take shelter in large bunches, perhaps in a hollow tree or log, or even hanging from a branch, with the queen, eggs and larvae protected in the middle.

FACT FILE

The black ant has a special relationship with aphids. They collect the sweet honeydew from the aphids and in return protect them from predators such as ladybirds.

WHAT IS A VAMPIRE BAT?

Whiskered

Geoffrey's   **Natterer**   **Bechstein's**

Several different bats in Central and tropical America are called vampire bats. At night, they bite warm-blooded animals such as cattle, horses and birds with their razor-sharp front teeth and drink their blood. Their saliva contains an anti-coagulant that prevents the victim's blood clotting. They do not, in fact, suck blood, but lap like cats. They are named after the fictitious monsters, such as Count Dracula, that suck blood from people, but although they have been known to attack sleeping humans, it is not common. One of the smallest of them is the common vampire bat, which is about 3 inches (8 cm) long and has reddish-brown fur on its body.

FACT FILE

Many species of bats live in colonies that may have thousands or even millions of members. Others live alone or in small groups. Most bats spend the day sleeping in their roost.

Long-eared bat

16

DOES A COW REALLY HAVE FOUR STOMACHS?

FACT FILE

Cows, sheep and goats have no front teeth in the upper jaw. Instead, the gums form a tough pad.

The simple answer to this question is no – cattle have only one stomach with four compartments, called the *rumen*, the *reticulum*, the *omasum* and the *abomasum*. This complex system enables them to bring partly digested, softened food back into their mouth to be re-chewed and then re-swallowed; this process is known as chewing the cud. Animals with these four-part stomachs are called *ruminants*. Micro-organisms in the digestive system allow the animals to break down the food to obtain as many nutrients as possible. In the fourth cavity, the 'true' stomach, gastric juices mix with the food, which then passes to the intestine for absorbtion.

WHAT IS THE LARGEST ANIMAL IN THE WORLD?

FACT FILE

The largest land mammal is the African elephant which can weigh up to 6.9 tons (7 tonnes).

The blue whale is the largest animal that ever lived on Earth. It is also the loudest animal on Earth. These enormous mammals eat tiny organisms, like plankton and krill, which they sift through baleen (a horny substance attached to the upper jaw). They live in pods (small groups). These grey-blue whales have 2 blowholes and a 2–14 inch (5–30 cm) thick layer of blubber. Blue whales are rorqual whales, whales that have pleated throat grooves that allow their throat to expand during the huge intake of water during filter feeding. Blue whales have 50–70 throat grooves that run from the throat to mid-body.

Blue whales

WHERE WOULD YOU FIND A COBRA?

Cobras can be found throughout the Philippines, southern Asia and Africa and are well known for their intimidating conduct and deadly bite. Cobras are recognized by the hoods that they flare when angry or disturbed; the hoods are created by the elongated ribs that extend the loose skin of the neck behind the cobras' heads.

The king cobra is the world's longest venomous snake. It averages 12 ft (3.7 m) in length but has been known to grow to 18 ft (5.5 m). It has olive or brown skin, with bronze eyes. The king cobra is found in the Philippines, Malaysia, southern China, Myanmar (formerly known as Burma), India, Thailand and the Malay Peninsula.

The venom of cobras often contains a powerful neurotoxin and acts on the nervous system. Venoms have some medicinal uses – for example, some are used as painkillers in cases of arthritis or cancer.

FACT FILE

The spotted salamander is one of the larger members of the mole salamander family reaching nearly 8 inches (20 cm) or more. They lay up to 200 eggs in a single mass in early spring, usually after the first warm rain.

Cobra

WHERE DO RHINOCEROSES LIVE?

Rhinoceroses are found in two regions of the world: Africa and Asia. The black rhinoceros and white rhinoceros live in Africa, while the Indian, Javan and Sumatran rhinos live in parts of Asia. Black, white and Sumatran rhinos have two horns, while the Indian and Javan species have only one. The horns are made of densely packed, coarse hair, and are used only in defence or in fights between males.

Rhinoceroses are vegetarians and have to eat vast amounts of grass and other plants every day to maintain their huge bodies and usually move about very slowly to avoid wasting energy. They are distantly related to horses, but instead of hooves, have three toes on each foot.

FACT FILE

Rhinoceroses are usually placid, but if they feel threatened, they will charge. Despite their stubby legs, they can run remarkably fast – at speeds of up to 38 mph (48 kmh).

WHAT IS A MUTE SWAN?

FACT FILE

Swans nest along the shores of rivers, waterways and the coast in the summer and move to large lakes in the winter. Mute swans feed mainly on underwater plants, but also graze on marshland during the winter.

Swans are waterfowl that are closely related to, and larger than, ducks and geese. The mute swan has an orange bill with a prominent black knob and swims with its neck held in a graceful S-shape. They aren't, in fact, mute, and make snorting noises and hiss when threatened. When they are flying, their wings make a throbbing sound with each wingbeat.

In summer, breeding pairs are territorial and the males can be very aggressive in defence of their nest and cygnets, but in winter they may feed in large flocks. They feed by upending and reaching down with their long necks to nibble underwater plants.

HOW DOES A KINGFISHER CATCH ITS FOOD?

Kingfishers are birds with large heads, heavy, pointed bills and stubby legs and tails. Some are brightly coloured like the common kingfisher, while others, for example the laughing kookaburra, are camouflaged.

A kingfisher may sit for hours on a branch beside water looking for fish near the surface. Then, after perhaps hovering for a moment in midair, the bird dives after a fish, either seizing it in or spearing it on its bill. It bobs back to the surface and uses the membranes between its middle and outer toes to launch itself back into the air. Back at its perch, it tosses the fish into the air and swallows it headfirst. Other sources of food that kingfishers exploit include crustaceans, frogs and insects.

FACT FILE

Kingfishers burrow in the walls of river banks or sandbanks, or between the roots of upturned trees. They dig a tunnel a good 3 ft (1 m) long with a hollow at the end where the eggs are laid on a nest of fish bones.

WHAT MAKES A MOLEHILL?

Molehills are small conical mounds of soft earth, often connected by slightly raised lines of earth. These are made by moles. Each mound lies above one underground room of a mole's complicated home and the raised lines are above the passages between individual rooms or runs where it is digging for food.

A mole is a small mammal with a stocky, well-muscled body. With its large, strong forelegs and wedge-shaped head, it is perfectly adapted for its life burrowing through soil. The mole is a fast, tireless digger, and its

front paws have long, broad nails and turn outward, which makes them ideal for shovelling earth. Moles don't need to see and they are almost blind, with tiny eyes, but they have excellent hearing, which enables them to locate their prey, such as earthworms and subterranean insects.

FACT FILE

The central chamber of a mole's home is larger than the other rooms and contains a nest of leaves and grasses. Moles are born naked, but they start to grow fur at the age of two weeks. They leave the nest after five weeks.

HOW DOES A FLAMINGO FEED?

A flamingo is a bird with long, stilt-like legs, a curved neck and large bill. When they feed, flamingos dip their heads under the water and scoop backwards with the head upside down.

The edges of the bill have tiny narrow crossways plates called *lamellae*. The large fleshy tongue pressing against the inside of the bill strains the water out through the lamellae, leaving behind the small invertebrates and the vegetable matter upon which these birds feed.

All flamingos live in colonies, and some of these have tens of thousands of individuals. They mate yearly. The nest consists of a mound of mud, built up to keep the egg from the water, with a shallow depression in the top. They build the mounds by scooping mud and smoothing it onto the pile with their bills. Each parent takes turns to sit on the single egg while the other feeds, keeping it warm in most areas, but keeping it cool in hot areas like the lakes of the Rift Valley in Kenya.

FACT FILE

Different flamingo species have slightly different colouring and within a species, colour varies according to geographic location and to what they eat. Flamingoes who eat large amounts of pink crustaceans have brighter feathers than those that don't.

WHY DO TIGERS HAVE DISTINCT COLOURING?

The tiger is one of the largest of the big cats. The base colour of the coat is fawn to red, becoming progressively darker the farther southwards you go. The Balinese tiger is the darkest. The underparts of the tiger are white. The coat is overlaid with black to brownish-black transverse stripes and these contrasting colours provide a wonderful camouflage in its natural habitat.

FACT FILE

A leopard is another member of the big cat family which has a remarkable coat. Did you know that the name leopard is from the Latin word leopardus, which means a 'spotted lion'?

WHAT IS NATURAL SELECTION?

Natural selection is a process through which animals and plants evolve. Successful individuals tend to be those that are best suited to their environment and if a mutation in the genes of, for instance, a giraffe gives it a slightly longer neck than others in its group, it will be able to reach more leaves and so will probably become stronger and be more likely to breed successfully and pass on its genes for a longer neck to its offspring, making them more successful in turn. But, on the whole, individual giraffes with genes that mutated to give them a shorter neck would be less able to find food, would go hungry, be less likely to breed and so the genes for short necks would eventually die out. The theory of natural selection is based on the great variation among even closely related individuals. In most cases, no two members of a species are exactly alike. Each has a unique combination of such traits as size, appearance and ability to withstand cold or other harsh conditions.

FACT FILE

In 1858, Darwin and another British naturalist, Alfred R. Wallace, presented similar theories of natural selection. Many biologists rejected the idea at first.

WHICH MAMMALS MIGRATE?

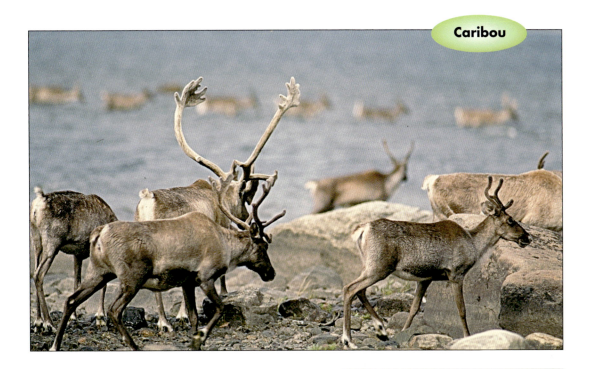

Caribou

Many animals migrate, including birds, some whales, sharks and butterflies as well as mammals, such as caribou and reindeer. Whether they are in the ocean or on land, they migrate to exploit available food and to breed. Humans and other animals have learned to exploit these annual cycle of movements. Crocodiles, for instance, lay in wait for the massive herds of wildebeest as they cross the rivers of the Great Plains of Africa.

Caribou live in herds in the cold northern regions of North America, feeding on grass and shrubs on the tundra in the summer. When snows bury their food supply, they migrate south to warmer forested regions where they eat lichen. They return north when the snows start to thaw.

FACT FILE

The lemming is a small rodent, whose populations vary over roughly four years. At the peak, food is scarce and they are forced to migrate. According to legend, great numbers of lemmings throw themselves off cliffs and drown, but it is more likely that they just starve.

WHERE DOES A CRICKET PRODUCE ITS SONG?

Crickets are jumping insects that are related to grasshoppers, and species include the European house cricket and the common cricket of the United States. They live in fields, meadows and in the grass alongside roads. Most songs are produced by the males, although females of some species do also sing. Unlike grasshoppers, which produce sounds using their legs, crickets do so by rubbing their front wings together. They don't have ears, but hear using organs in their front legs. Cricket songs are mating calls that are designed to attract females and usually consist of a series of chirps or a set of trills.

Cricket

Crickets differ from grasshoppers in several ways other than how they produce sound. Most crickets have wings that lie flat over each other on their backs, while those of grasshoppers are slightly raised, and most cricket antennae are longer than their bodies, unlike the short ones that grasshoppers possess. There are also wingless crickets and some that have only very small wings. Crickets eat plants and small insects.

Grasshopper

FACT FILE

A grasshopper is an insect that can leap about 20 times as far as the length of its body. If a human being had that same leaping ability, he or she could jump about 120 ft (37 m).

IS IT TRUE MALE SEAHORSES BECOME MOTHERS?

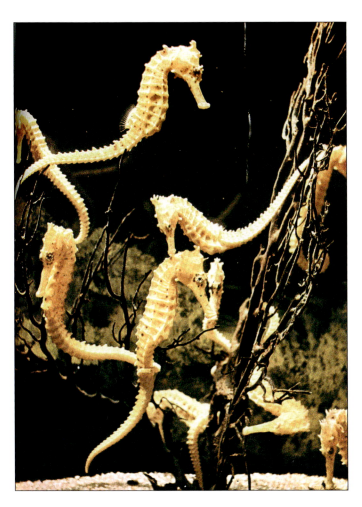

The seahorse is a small fish and acquired its name because its face looks horse-like. We are used to the idea that it is always the female that bear the offspring, but in seahorses it is the reverse. The female seahorse, when she lays her eggs, puts them into the broad pouch beneath the tail of the male. When the young have hatched and are ready to leave the pouch, the mouth of the pouch opens wide. The male alternately bends and straightens his body in convulsive jerks and finally a baby seahorse is shot out. After each birth the male rests, and when all the babies are born he shows signs of extreme exhaustion, including going very pale in colour.

FACT FILE

The seahorse has been described as having the head of a horse, the tail of a monkey, the pouch of a kangaroo, the hard outer skeleton of an insect and the independently moving eyes of a chameleon.

WHAT IS AN AMPHIBIAN?

The internal organs of an amphibian

kidney

heart

lung

stomach

FACT FILE

Some brightly coloured amphibians produce poison in glands on their skin. The bright colours warn birds and animals not to eat them. The poisons are among the most powerful known to humans. In South America, poison from the poison arrow frog is added to the arrow tips used by the Indians for hunting.

From an evolutionary point of view, amphibians are halfway between fish and reptiles. There are 4,400 living species of amphibian, including frogs, toads, newts and salamanders. Many live mainly on land, but most spend at least some of their lives in water.

Frogs and salamanders are able to breathe through their damp skins to a certain extent, both in the water and on land, but toads must rely largely on their lungs and cannot remain in water for long. Toads and frogs are similar in many ways, although toads usually have rougher, drier skins and may waddle rather than hop as frogs do. Some toad spawn is produced in strings, like necklaces, rather than the mass of eggs laid by a frog. The largest amphibian, the Chinese giant salamander, is 6 ft (1.8m) long.

1. Frog spawn hatches into larvae called tadpoles after about a week

Adult frogs often return to the pond in which they hatched

4.

2. At first, tadpoles feed on algae and breathe through feathery gills

The life cycle of an amphibian

3. By about 10 weeks the froglet has hind legs, internal gills and can eat small insects and its smaller brothers and sisters

HOW DO FROG EGGS HATCH?

Most amphibians lay their eggs in water. Frogs' eggs are called spawn. They are protected from predators by a thick layer of jelly. Inside this a tadpole develops. When it hatches out, it is able to swim, using its long tail, and breathes through gills. As a tadpole grows, first hind legs and then fore legs begin to grow. Lungs develop, and the young frog is able to begin to breathe with its head above water. Gradually the tail shortens until the young frog resembles its adult parents.

FACT FILE

The tree frog lives in the rain forests of South America and uses the pools of water in the centre of certain tropical plants. Although it can swim, it spends much of its life out of water, among the leaves of trees where there are plenty of insects for food. It has sticky toes that enable it to climb.

HOW DO BIRDS FLY?

The bodies of birds are specially modified to give them the power of flight. Their bones are hollow to keep them light. Their bodies are also extremely lightweight, allowing them to glide and fly with the minimum of effort. For example, an eagle has a wing span of more than 7 ft (2 m) and yet it weighs less than 10 lb (4 kg). Birds also have air sacs linked to their lungs to give them extra oxygen as they flap their wings.

However, flying is not just a matter of flapping wings up and down. It is a mixture of gliding and powered flight. When the wings are flapped they move in a complicated way, scooping air downwards and backwards. The wing actually twists so that the air is pushed back in the right direction to give lift. The wings are twisted again on the forward stroke so that they slide easily through the air without slowing down the bird's flight. A bird's feathers, which help to reduce wind resistance in flight, are ideal because they are very light, yet also strong and flexible.

FACT FILE

The falcon is a bird of prey which feeds on other birds and small animals. It is equipped with powerful talons and a sharp beak in order to kill and dismember its prey. When the falcon dives on its prey it closes its enormous wings and drops like a stone to pick up speed. Powerful muscles in the bird's legs help to cushion the huge impact of the strike.

The internal organs of a bird

lung

kidney

gizzard

intestine

cloaca

HOW FAST CAN BIRDS FLY?

The first question is: 'How do we measure how fast they fly?' They don't fly in straight lines and their speed will be greater if the wind is behind them or if they are diving. Figures have been published for some species, but not all experts agree with them.

In general, the heavier a bird is, the faster it needs to fly to stay in the air. One expert believes that the fastest recorded flight for a bird was that of a homing pigeon going at 94.2 mph (150.72 kmh).

A few speeds, however, are generally agreed. Some species of ducks and geese can go about 63 mph (100 kmh). Peregrine falcons can fly at up to 75 mph (120 kmh), while hummingbirds reach speeds of 56 to 60 mph (90 to 95 kmh). Starlings are thought to fly at about 45 to 50 mph (70 to 80 kmh). Swifts can achieve almost 60 mph (95 kmh) and swallows usually about 25 mph (40 kmh), which helps them to make their long migration flights quickly.

beak

gullet

crop

heart

liver

FACT FILE

Some birds cannot fly at all. Such birds include penguins, who use their wings in water, enabling them to swim very fast. The penguin shown below is a rare yellow-eyed species. There are only about 3,000 of them left in the world.

The sidewinder

HOW DO SNAKES MOVE?

Snakes have several ways of moving about. The most common way is to throw their body into loops and move forward by pressing against anything solid.

Another way in which a snake moves is by contracting its muscles, which pushes the body along rather like a concertina being squeezed open and shut.

The desert-living sidewinder moves by throwing a loop out to one side, then sliding its body towards the loop while throwing another loop sideways at the same time. The sidewinder looks like a spring rolling along the sand, but this is an effective way of moving on this soft surface. Most snakes are able to swim effectively by using a wriggling motion.

FACT FILE

Snakes and crocodiles are both reptiles. A reptile is an air-breathing animal with a body structure between that of an amphibian and a mammal. Living reptiles include crocodiles, tortoises and turtles, snakes and lizards.

HOW DO SNAKES INJECT THEIR POISON?

Some snakes have saliva glands that produce a toxin poisonous to their usual prey. This substance is called venom, so these snakes are described as being venomous. Some snakes' venom is so powerful it could kill an elephant. About 200 venomous snakes worldwide (there are 412 species) are thought to be dangerous to people.

Among the most famous of these are the cobras. Their fangs are at the front of the mouth, while the venom gland is farther back. The gland is surrounded by muscles that squeeze it when the snake bites and force the venom into the fang and down through the tip into the victim's flesh.

Another method of delivering venom can be seen in the African bird snake. These creatures have massive fangs, with grooves running down one side, at the back of their mouths. Just above the grooves is a hole that leads from the venom gland and when these snakes bite, venom drips through the grooves into the wound.

The cobra

FACT FILE

Giant snakes have been reported in many parts of the world. The largest recorded snake is the anaconda, which can reach a length of 30 ft (9 m).

HOW MANY KINDS OF FISH ARE THERE?

Fish have existed for millions of years and have evolved into thousands of different types. There were fish in the oceans before the dinosaurs walked on the land. There are around 40,000 different kinds of fish and they exploit every conceivable watery habitat on the planet.

Fish are divided into three general types: cartilaginous, bony and lungfish. The cartilaginous fish, whose skeleton is made of flexible cartilage rather than rigid bone, include sharks, skate and rays. Bony fish, as their name suggests, have a bony skeleton and are covered with scales of a similar substance. Members of this group of fish are the most common and account for over 90 percent of all fish. Lungfish are a special type of fish because they have two sets of breathing equipment, possessing both gills and lungs. This type includes mud skippers.

swim bladder

backbone

stomach

gills

heart

intestine

pelvic fin

Cross-section of a fish

FACT FILE

Salmon breed in small freshwater streams but spend most of their life in rivers and seas. To breed, they return to the stream where they hatched. They even leap up waterfalls in order to reach their spawning grounds.

How can fish breathe underwater?

Fish are able to breath underwater because they have special organs called gills. Gills are bars of tissue at the side of the fish's head. They have masses of finger-like projections that contain tiny blood vessels. Water goes into the fish's mouth and flows over its gills. The gill filaments take in oxygen (which is dissolved) from the water and pass it from there into the fish's blood. In this way the gills have the same function as the lungs of air-breathing animals. If water is contaminated, fish need to take oxygen from another source. Some attempt to come to the surface of the water and take in oxygen from the air. However, their gills are neither suitable nor adept at processing oxygen from the air.

Fish are able to smell, although they do not use their gills for this. They have two small nostrils on their heads which act as organs of smell. The sense of smell is much more developed in some fish than it is in others. Sharks, for example, use their keen sense of smell to hunt down and catch other animals to feed on.

kidney

dorsal fin

muscle

tail fin

FACT FILE

Piranhas are very aggressive fish and can be dangerous in large numbers. Piranhas are supposed to be able to strip all the flesh from a pig or cow in a few minutes, but they are probably not dangerous to humans unless attracted to blood.

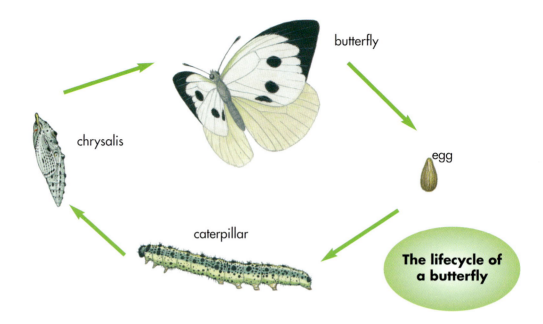

butterfly

egg

chrysalis

caterpillar

The lifecycle of a butterfly

HOW DOES A CATERPILLAR BECOME A BUTTERFLY?

A female butterfly can lay from hundreds to thousands of eggs, depending on her species. If her offspring will eat only one type of plant, she will lay her eggs on this. After days or weeks, the eggs hatch into tiny grubs (caterpillars), which begin to feed and grow immediately, shedding their skin several times as they outgrow it.

When a caterpillar is fully developed and large enough, it spins a little button of silk onto a plant and clings onto it with its rear end, dangles head down and shrugs off its skin. It then hardens to a pupa or chrysalis.

During the next weeks or months, the creature inside the hard shell changes completely, so that when it emerges, it is a butterfly. It spreads its wings so that they can dry and become firm before it will attempt to fly.

FACT FILE

This hover fly mimics a wasp, though it has no sting. It is an excellent flyer and can hover or fly backwards or sideways if necessary. It feeds on flower nectar.

HOW DO SPIDERS MAKE THEIR WEBS?

A spider lies in wait for insects

Spiders spin their web from silk, which is pumped out from tiny nozzles at the back of the abdomen, called spinnerets. As the silk is stretched by the spider into a thread, it hardens and becomes proportionately stronger than steel.

Some of these threads are quite sticky, while others simply support the web. The spider is able to feel the vibrations of the web when an insect flies into it and it then runs quickly across the web to capture its prey. Usually the insect is wrapped in silk before being eaten by the spider.

FACT FILE

Ants are called arthropods, which means they have a hard outer shell to protect their organs and joints to allow for free movement.

FACT FILE

Caribou usually live in relatively small numbers. However, when the time comes for them to migrate in search of food, they form herds of up to 3,000.

HOW DO BIRDS KNOW WHEN TO MIGRATE?

People have always been fascinated by why particular birds are present in summer but not in winter, and vice versa, even though they didn't understand it. Even just a few hundred years ago, some people thought that swallows hibernated under ponds during the winter. Even now, we still don't have all the answers.

What is migration? In this sense it is the movement of birds south from their summer breeding grounds to their winter feeding grounds in autumn and the return north in spring. Other forms of migration are moving from inland to the coast or between high and low ground.

Some go to warmer regions because they couldn't survive the cold. Others have to leave because their normal food is unavailable and they would starve if they stayed. But how do they actually know when to make this long flight? It is believed that birds can tell when the days get shorter (and longer in spring) and this acts as an 'alarm clock' to tell them that it is time to move along. Some birds, such as migrating swans or geese, seem to take the weather into account as well and stay at stopping-off points longer if conditions are suitable rather than move on.

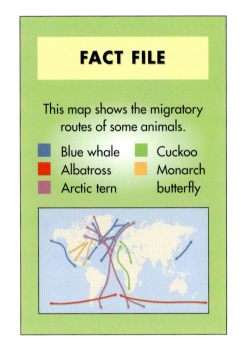

FACT FILE

This map shows the migratory routes of some animals.

- ▪ Blue whale
- ▪ Albatross
- ▪ Arctic tern
- ▪ Cuckoo
- ▪ Monarch butterfly

HOW FAR DO BIRDS MIGRATE?

Now we know why birds migrate, the next question is how far do they actually fly to find better conditions.

The champions among birds that migrate are the arctic terns. These amazing birds will travel as much as 22,000 miles (35,000 km) during the course of a year, going back and forth. It nests over a wide range from the Arctic Circle to as far south as Massachusetts. It will take this bird about 20 weeks to make its trip down to the antarctic region and it averages about 1,000 miles (1,600 km) a week.

Most land birds only make short journeys during their migrations. But there is one bird, the American golden plover, that makes a long nonstop flight over the open ocean. It may fly from Nova Scotia directly to South America, a distance of about 2,400 miles (3,800 km), without stopping.

We are not certain that birds start and end their migrations on the same day each year. But there is one bird that comes pretty close to it. It is said that the famous swallows of Capistrano, California, are thought to leave on October 23 and return on March 19, but of course their date of departure and arrival has been found to vary from year to year.

WHEN IS THE BEST TIME TO SEE A BAT?

FACT FILE

A bat called the pipistrelle has adapted to warm cavity walls or hanging tiles in our homes as their normal woodland habitat has been lost and natural roosts have become scarce.

Bats are most easily spotted on open ground near ponds and rivers at dusk. Insects hatch and fly from the water in large numbers, which attracts the bats. The bats catch the insects by a process known as echolocation. This is a technique in which an animal processes sounds and listens for the echoes reflected from surfaces and objects in the environment. From the information contained in these echoes, the animal is able to perceive the objects and work out exactly where they are. Bats change their roosting places from season to season. They choose caves, old ice houses and trees in which to hibernate. These give a constant temperature just above freezing.

WHEN DO BADGERS LEAVE THEIR SETS?

FACT FILE

Although foxes and rabbits have earths, badgers usually make the largest and most obvious entrances, with a faint musky scent on their air. You can see their footprints in the soil or snow.

Badgers have distinctive black and white faces, with broad bodies on powerful short legs. They live in colonies, underground (called sets), throwing out obvious heaps of soil at the entrances to their tunnels. They emerge from their sets at dusk to forage for food. They prefer hilly districts on the borders of woods or thickets with easily worked soils.

They feed on earthworms and other small animals, fruits, cereals and vegetables, using well-worn paths to their chosen pastures or clearings. Badgers take care to keep their sets warm and clean. Damp bedding is thrown out and fresh, dry grass or straw is scratched up and gathered in armfuls.

WHEN DO WHITE SEALS TURN DARK?

The common seal can be found on sandy estuaries, fjords and rocky inlets away from the full force of the open sea. Although they live and feed in the water, they still come to the shore to breed and to moult their hair. A seal pup is born with thick white fur but will lose this shortly after it is born and it will be replaced by a much darker, sleeker coat. Their diet includes all kinds of seafood: fish, shellfish, crabs and lobsters.

FACT FILE

The pup of a seal will suckle for ten minutes, five or six times a day. Their birth weight doubles in one week. After a month of rapid growth, the mother leaves to mate with another bull. The pup enters the sea to fend for itself.

WHEN DO ANIMALS HIBERNATE?

FACT FILE

Some mammals, like bears and squirrels do not really hibernate. They sleep more in the winter than in the summer, but do leave the den to feed when they can.

The word 'hibernate' derives from Latin and means 'winter sleep'. Certain animals, such as hedgehogs, dormice and some bats, hibernate during the winter to escape the severe weather conditions and because food is hard to find. Before they hibernate they eat as much as they can to get enough body fat for the winter. Hibernation is not like ordinary sleep: the body temperature of the animal decreases until it is only a little warmer than the air around it. As it isn't keeping itself warm, the animal burns body fat very slowly, so it needs less oxygen, its breathing slows and its heartbeat drops. When spring arrives, hibernating animals are awakened by increasing warmth and by hunger.

WHEN WILL WHALES BECOME EXTINCT?

Archaeological evidence suggests that primitive whaling, by Inuit and others in the North Atlantic and North Pacific, was practised by 3000 BC, and it has continued in remote cultures to the present. All whale species are becoming less common due to the fact that they have been regularly hunted for food and oil. Other factors are environmental pollution and drift net fishing. The grey whale was hunted almost to extinction by 1925 but was placed under complete international protection and since the 1940s has increased in numbers. Some of the larger species of whales can be seen in Europe as they pass by during migration.

FACT FILE

The humpback whale was also hunted almost to extinction, and its numbers dropped from 100,000 to 3,000 today. It is now generally protected.

The Plant World

WHAT ARE SUCCULENTS?

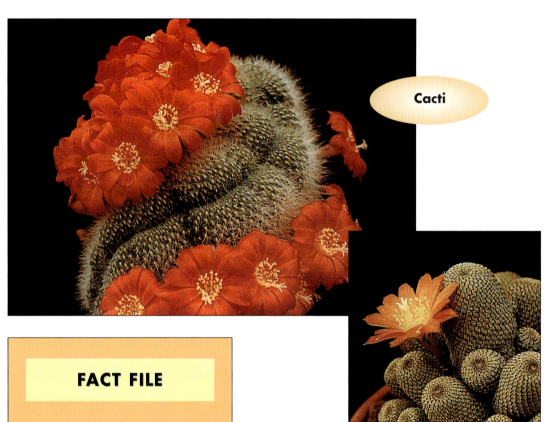

Cacti

FACT FILE

Cacti have many rare and beautiful features, developed during a long and slow evolutionary process. One of their principal characteristics is the ability to adapt to harsh conditions, which would cause most other plant groups to perish quickly.

Succulents are plants that have organs such as leaves, stems or roots that are capable of storing water in order to survive extended periods of drought. All the plants in the cactus family are considered stem succulents. During periods of moisture, the stem swells and then during droughts slowly contracts. Cacti that have ribs are particularly well adapted to this as the ribs fill in and contract like an accordion. Cacti get their name from the Greek word *kaktos* meaning thistle.

WHAT IS DODDER?

Dodder is a strange, totally parasitic plant. When its tiny seeds start to grow, they put up thin threads that begin to twist in ever-increasing circles. Most seedlings die, because they fail to find the right sort of plant to take their food from. But if one seed finds the right host, it quickly attaches itself and pushes absorbing organs into the plant. The root of the seed then withers and dies, since the dodder plant now takes all of its food from the host. The most popular host plants are alfalfa, clover and flax. Dodder has tiny pink leaves that have no need for chlorophyll, which enables most plants to make food from sunlight. In late summer, dodder produces small, pink flowers and then masses of tiny seeds.

FACT FILE

Once dodder has established itself, it produces a mass of pink threads which cover the host plant and weaken it severely.

CAN PLANTS FEEL?

Although plants do not have feelings in the same way that we do, they can certainly respond to different stimuli. They are able to grow towards a light source, even if turned upside down. Some plants have very sensitive leaves, which will fold up if touched. Others have leaves that open and close according to the time of day. The Venus flytrap has sensitive leaf tips. When an insect lands on tiny hairs on the leaf, the pairs of leaves snap shut, trapping the insect inside. Plants are even able to perspire. Although you can't see this happening, if you were to place a plant inside a plastic bag and fasten it, after a while you would see drops of

FACT FILE

Some plants have sensitive hairs on their leaves. If an unsuspecting insect lands on these sticky hairs, in no time at all it finds its legs hopelessly entangled.

water form on the inside of the bag. The moisture you can see comes from the leaves of the plant.

Lords and ladies

WHY IS HOLLY ASSOCIATED WITH CHRISTMAS?

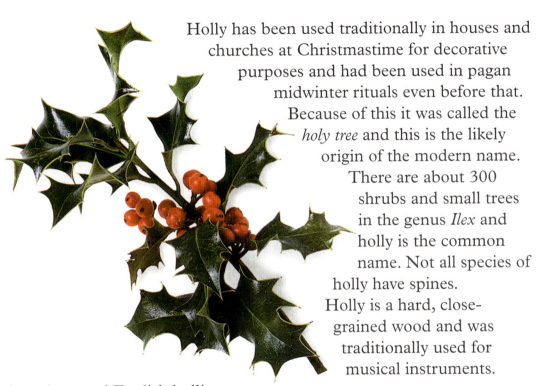

Holly has been used traditionally in houses and churches at Christmastime for decorative purposes and had been used in pagan midwinter rituals even before that. Because of this it was called the *holy tree* and this is the likely origin of the modern name. There are about 300 shrubs and small trees in the genus *Ilex* and holly is the common name. Not all species of holly have spines.

Holly is a hard, close-grained wood and was traditionally used for musical instruments.

American and English hollies are evergreen trees that have glossy green leaves and red berries that make colourful Christmas wreaths. However, the berries (which are actually drupes, i.e. fruits with stones) are poisonous to humans.

FACT FILE

The poinsettia is a popular houseplant also used as a Christmas decoration. What look like the bright red petals are actually a kind of leaf. The real flowers are the tiny green dots in the middle.

IS THERE REALLY A FOUR-LEAVED CLOVER?

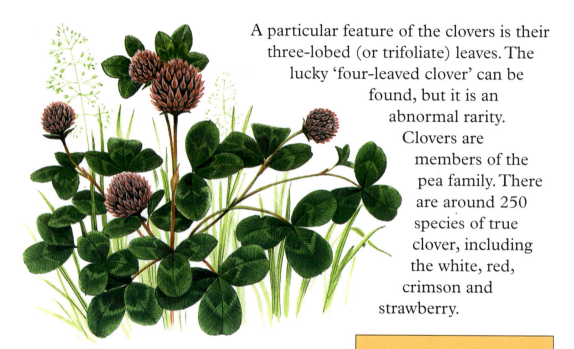

A particular feature of the clovers is their three-lobed (or trifoliate) leaves. The lucky 'four-leaved clover' can be found, but it is an abnormal rarity. Clovers are members of the pea family. There are around 250 species of true clover, including the white, red, crimson and strawberry.

Clovers are generally plants of grassland, but they are most common near the coast and on chalky or clay soils. Red clover has been used for centuries in crop rotation as it puts nitrogen back into the soil. Today, it is used extensively as an animal food and soil-improving crop throughout Europe and northern and central North America.

FACT FILE

The flowers of a clover are very rich in nectar and act as a means of attracting insects. The white base of the flower has a lovely taste of fresh honey.

DOES BINDWEED ALWAYS TWINE IN THE SAME DIRECTION?

It is a curious fact that all bindweed plants twine around their supporting plant in the same direction – anticlockwise – whichever way they start off. The Greater Bindweed, or Hedge Convolvulus, is a hedge plant found abundantly throughout England and Scotland. Despite the beauty of its flowers, bindweed is regarded as a pest by both the farmer and the gardener. Its roots are long and form a dense mass that exhausts the soil. Its twining stems extend in masses over all other nearby plants, consequently strangling them.

FACT FILE

If a gardener were to turn it in another direction, the bindweed, if unable to disengage itself and assume its natural direction from right to left, will eventually perish.

WHAT ARE CHANTERELLES?

Chanterelles are mushroom-like fungi with funnel-shaped caps. The delicious and fragrant golden chanterelle is a delicacy prized by gourmets. Chanterelles are characterized by the form of their spore-producing surface, which is smooth and veined.

Mushrooms are important to our environment as they help keep soil fertile for the growth of plants. As mushrooms grow, they break down the dead material that they are feed on, such as old leaves, and release nutrients back into the soil that the plants can use again in future.

Many insects and small mammals eat mushrooms as they are an important source of nutrients in themselves.

Golden chanterelle

Trumpet chanterelle

FACT FILE

The term tooth-fungi covers a range of unrelated species which all have spines or teeth on which spores are produced. Because of pollution, many of these are becoming rare.

WHICH IS THE LARGEST KNOWN FUNGUS?

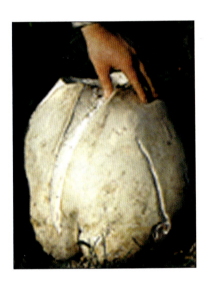

The giant puffball is the largest known fungi. It can grow as large as 4½ ft (150 cm), although an average fruitbody is the size of a football. Just one fruitbody will produce about 7,000,000,000,000 spores. The puffballs are ball-shaped fungi, and are any shade of white to tan. They range in size from smaller than a golfball to larger than a basketball. When a puffball matures, its spores become dry and powdery. If touched, the puffball breaks open and the spores escape in a smokelike puff.

Black Bovista

Scaly Meadow Puffball

FACT FILE

Flies and other insects are attracted to the stinking, slimy spore mass of the common stinkhorn. When they fly off after feeding, they carry away spores stuck on to their bodies. This is the way in which the stinkhorn spreads to new locations.

WHICH PLANT IS USED TO THATCH A ROOF?

The material normally used to make roofing thatch is common reeds, which are tall grass-like plants. They grow in almost all temperate and warm regions. They are found in a variety of habitats, from low upland meadows to wet lowlands and shallow lakes and ponds. Reedmarsh is a valuable wildlife habitat if managed properly. The reeds are usually cut in the autumn, arranged into dense bundles and laid in layers on roofs. The thatch is waterproof and provides good heat insulation for the house. If laid and maintained correctly, a thatched roof should last for up to 40 years. Traditionally, the bundles are held in position with pegs made from strips of willow, although chicken wire is commonly used now to help keep the reed in place.

Common reed

FACT FILE

In many wetland areas, reeds spread rapidly, crowding out other types of marsh grass. For this reason it has to be regularly cut down. Reed grass has been used in the production of paper.

56

WHAT IS THE FRUIT OF THE OAK?

Oaks mature slowly and will not usually flower until they have reached 20. But they live a long time and many oaks live between two and four centuries. The fruit of the oak tree is called the acorn and is an ovoid nut in a small cup. In spring, oaks produce small, yellowish-green flowers. Copious amounts of windborne pollen are produced by the male catkins. The fertilized female flower will become an acorn that will start off green and go brown by the autumn. Depending on the exact species, acorns range from under $\frac{1}{2}$ inch (13 mm) to more than 2 inches (51 mm).

FACT FILE

The Oak Leaf Roller Moth lays small groups of eggs on oak twigs. In spring, the caterpillar feeds on oak leaves, which they roll up with silk.

WHY DO PLANTS NEED ROOTS?

Roots are not pretty and bright like leaves and flowers, but plants could not do without them. Anchored in the soil, they hold plants upright against wind and weather. They also grow out and down in search of water and minerals, which are drawn all the way up to the leaves. Because trees grow to such

enormous heights, the roots need to grow outwards to balance the spread of the branches above. Most roots grow in the top 1 ft (30 cm) of soil. This part contains most of the minerals the tree needs to survive. Every single root grows a mass of tiny hairs near its tip to enable it to absorb water from the soil. There are little pockets of air in the soil. Without these, roots would simply wither and die.

FACT FILE

There is one plant that does survive without any roots at all, and that is called Spanish moss. It grows in subtropical climates where the air is very wet. It absorbs all the moisture it needs through its fine, thread-like leaves.

WHICH PLANTS HAVE NO TRUE ROOTS?

Liverwort

Liverworts, hornworts and mosses do not have true roots. They are anchored to the ground by hair-like structures called rhizoids that resemble roots. A liverwort absorbs water over its entire surface and dries out quickly, so most grow in damp, shady environments.

Moss has a short stem which grows from the rhizoids. It is covered by tiny leaves in a spiral pattern. The leaves contain chlorophyll, a green substance the plant uses to make food. In many cases, a vein runs the length of the leaf from the stem to the tip. This vein, called the costa or midrib, strengthens the leaf and transports food and water. Many mosses grow in moist or aquatic environments. However, certain mosses can survive extremely dry conditions. Their need for water changes with the amount of water available in the environment.

Other plants that do not have roots include lichens and airplants. The latter cling to larger plants and absorb nutrients from rainwater.

Moss

FACT FILE

Lichens have no roots. They have an outer layer of fungal cells that are pigmented green, brown or yellow. This protective layer, called the upper cortex, covers a zone of green or blue-green algal cells.

HOW DO LEAF SHAPES VARY?

Pinnate

Palmate

Pinnate, with pinnately lobed leaflets

Simple

Palmately lobed

FACT FILE

Some plants have all their leaves in a ring at the base of the stem. This is known as a rosette.

The shapes of plant leaves vary considerably. The edges of leaves may be smooth or jagged. The leaf blades may be undivided (simple), or they may be divided (lobed) in various ways. Some leaves may be made up of separate leaflets. The commonest types of leaf shape are shown above.

The leaves themselves may be arranged on the plant in different ways, and this is usually standard for any given type of plant. A leaf arrangement which has single leaves at each level is called alternate. Leaves arranged in pairs are known as opposite. Opposite leaves may all face the same way, or each pair may be at right angles to the pair below.

WHERE DID THE FIRST WILD STRAWBERRY GROW?

FACT FILE

Strawberries grow wild or are raised commercially in almost every country. Plant breeders have developed hundreds of varieties of strawberries that are suited for different growing conditions.

Wild strawberries are first recorded in ancient Rome. They have been grown ever since, but the first known hybrid was not developed until the eighteenth century, in France, by crossing varieties from different regions of the Americas.

Strawberries are members of the rose family and are low-growing plants that usually propagate by means of their extensive runners, from which roots extend into the soil. They are not in fact classed as true berries as each of the small yellow 'seeds' on the outside of a strawberry is, in fact, a separate fruit. The 'berries' are pale green when first formed and slowly turn red once they are fully grown.

WHERE DOES THE WORD LAVENDER COME FROM?

The name lavender derives from a Latin word for 'to wash'. It is believed that this name may have been used because the ancient Romans scented their bathwater with it. The plants are native to Mediterranean countries and are members of the mint family.

The pale-purple flowers grow in clusters around the top of the rigid stem. Lavender has long, narrow, grey-green leaves. Cultivated types of lavender include white and French, which has two little tufts at the top of the flower and is a deeper purple. Dried lavender retains its scent for a long time and is used in both pot pourri and herbal pillows, where it is thought to aid sleep.

Pot pourri

FACT FILE

The petals of certain flowers contain sweet-smelling oils. Such flowers include jasmines, mimosas and roses. The oils obtained from the petals of these flowers supply the fragrances for many high-quality perfumes.

WHAT ARE THE OLDEST PLANTS ON EARTH?

Ferns are among the oldest kinds of plants that live on land. Scientists believe that ferns appeared on earth more than 350 million years ago. They do not have seeds, but undergo a two-stage reproduction method. First, microscopic spores are produced on the underside of a mature plant's fronds, and once they are ripe, they drop off the frond and are carried by the wind. If they land in a damp area, they sprout and grow into minute flat plants with small reproductive structures. Sperm fertilizes the egg cell and as that grows the tiny plant shrivels and dies, and a new fern begins to develop.

FACT FILE

Tree ferns are among the oldest types of plants existing. Many of them have no root systems and absorb moisture through the top of their trunks.

WHAT IS MADE FROM THE WILLOW TREE?

Willow trees usually live in moist habitats and in floodplains and riverbanks where they grow very rapidly. Their wood is used in many ways, and their leaves supply food for wildlife. Twigs of the common osier are grown for use in basketmaking, and the light but dent-resistant wood of other willows is used for artificial limbs, wooden shoes and cricket bats.

Willow bark contains the active compound salicin, used in many folk medicines. Aspirin is a derivative of salicylic acid, which was first synthesized from derivatives of willow bark.

FACT FILE

Willow-pattern china originated in Staffordshire, England, c.1780. Thomas Minton, then an apprentice potter, developed and engraved the design, taken from an old Chinese legend.

WHAT IS BARK?

Bark is the outer covering of the stem of woody plants, composed of waterproof cork cells. This protects a layer of food-conducting tissue called the *phloem* or inner bark (also called *bast*). As the woody stem increases in size, the outer bark of dead cork cells gives way – it may split to form grooves, shred, as in the cedar, or peel off, as in the sycamore. A layer of reproductive cells called the cork cambium produces new cork cells to replace or reinforce the old ones. Trees are sometimes damaged by animals that eat the outer bark by cutting through the phloem tubes, this can result in starvation of the roots and, ultimately, the death of the tree. The outer bark of the paper birch was used by Native Americans to make baskets and canoes.

FACT FILE

Bottle corks are made from the thick, spongy bark of the cork oak, which occurs in the Mediterranean region. Oaks produce durable, tough wood and are important lumber trees.

WHAT IS PEAT?

In swamps and marshes, particularly in cold or temperate climates, matter that has fallen from dead plants decays, only very slowly, as there is very little oxygen. Peat is partly decayed plant matter made up of layer upon layer of plants such as reeds, rushes and sedges.

In Ireland, peat is used to generate electricity because other sources such as coal are scarce. Depending on its state of decay and the plants involved, dried peat ranges from a light yellow-brown tangle of plant matter to deep layers of dark brown, compact material that looks like brown coal. Commercially dug peat is removed by machine and used for various purposes – black peat as a fertilizer and light brown peat as bedding for cattle and sheep. Moss peat, which is derived mainly from sphagnum moss is used in agriculture as litter for poultry and horses, as well as a mulch and a soil conditioner. Efforts are being made to find alternatives because of concerns that too much of the peat bogs is being destroyed.

FACT FILE

Peat is the earliest stage of transition from compressed plant growth to the formation of coal. The oldest coal was formed 350 million years ago, and the process still continues in swamps and bogs.

Sphagnum moss

66

WHY DOES A PINE TREE HAVE CONES?

A pine tree has cones in order to reproduce. The pine cone is actually a highly modified branch which takes the place of a flower. Separate male cones and female seed cones are borne on the same tree. Each of the numerous scales of the male cone bears pollen, while each female cone scale bears ovules in which egg cells are produced. In the pine the male cones are small and short-lived and are borne in clusters at the top of the tree. At the time of pollination, enormous numbers of pollen grains are released and dispersed by the wind. Those that land accidentally on female cone scales extend pollen tubes part way into the ovule during one growing season, but usually do not reach the stage of actual fertilization until the next year. The cones that are usually seen are the seed cones, which are normally hard and woody.

FACT FILE

Scots pine trees need to be tough to survive long, cold winters. They have thousands of tiny, needlelike leaves. The needles have a waterproof coating to protect them from the rain and snow.

WHAT ARE STOMATA?

Stomata are tiny holes in leaves, which the plant can open and close. When the stomata are open, they let air in and out, and water out. When the stomata are closed, water cannot escape from the leaves.

Plants absorb water from the soil through their roots. This water moves up the stem to the leaves, where about 90 percent evaporates through the stomata. Large trees lose more than 200 gallons (800 litres) of water from their leaves each day. This loss of water from leaves by evaporation is called transpiration. Other plant processes that involve water include photosynthesis, which uses water to make food, and respiration, in which water is produced. When it is dark, plants shut down for the night by closing stomata.

FACT FILE

Every day, a large tree loses enough water for you to take eight long showers. About 90 per cent of the water absorbed by the roots is lost by the leaves in transpiration.

WHICH IS THE BIGGEST FLOWER OF ALL?

FACT FILE

Green algae are the smallest plants. They form, for example, a greenish film often found on the bark of trees. Millions of cells of algae are needed to cover the tree trunk.

The biggest flower of all is called the *rafflesia*, a parasitic plant that does not photosynthesize. It grows in the rainforests of southeast Asia. The plant actually grows underground and is not visible until a huge bud appears, somewhat like a cabbage. This opens up into a leathery flower which is approximately 3 ft (1 m) across and weighing up to 22 lb (10 kg). The flower is not a pretty sight. It looks and smells just like a huge lump of rotting flesh. It attracts thousands of flies, which pollinate the flower as they walk on it.

HOW DO TREES GROW ?

Tree trunks consist of a number of structures. On the outside is the bark, which is itself divided into two layers, an outer layer called cork and an inner layer known as phloem. The middle of the tree is the wood, or xylem. Between the wood of a tree and the inner bark, there is a thin band of living cells called the cambium, which is where two layers of new cells are formed as wood on the inside and as bark on the outside. In this way, as the tree grows older it increases in diameter.

More living cells grow at the ends of twigs and branches and each year they extend farther, as well as forming leaves and sometimes flowers in the growing season.

When a cross section is cut through a tree alternating bands of light and dark wood are revealed. The lighter bands were formed in the spring and have bigger cells; the dark bands were laid down in the autumn and consist of small, tightly packed cells. Scientists can match tree rings with large databases of similar trees and use these to work out the age of a tree.

FACT FILE

Trees are the largest living organisms on Earth. The biggest tree, the Californian giant redwood, is nearly 300 ft (100 m) high and has a trunk that is 35 ft (11 m) thick. These ancient trees have very few branches and leaves, and are often scarred by forest fires and lightning strikes.

HOW DO LEAVES GROW?

Most green plants, including trees, have to manufacture their food. They do this in their leaves (and in some plants the stems as well) through a process called photosynthesis.

The roots of a plant or tree take water from the soil by capillary action and it eventually reaches the veins of the leaves. Carbon dioxide enters the tree's cells through the stomata in the leaves and when the sun is shining, cells there, called chloroplasts, which contain the green pigment chlorophyll, manufacture sugar, starches and cellulose.

The sugar, starch and cellulose are transported throughout the tree to where they are needed to produce new cells and add sweetness to the fruit.

Oxygen is a by-product of the process and exits the tree through the stomata, together with most of the water that was absorbed by the roots.

FACT FILE

Energy from the Sun evaporates water from the leaf surface, through the stomata. This reduces pressure in the channels carrying water from the roots, so more water is drawn up the stem.

Water evaporates from the leaf surfaces into the surrounding air

More water is taken up by the roots from the soil

HOW DO FLOWERS DEVELOP THEIR SCENT?

Fragrant flowers contain substances called essential oils in their petals. There are thousands of different types and they are very complex. When these substances are broken down or decomposed, which is a natural process and in the wild is aimed at attracting pollinators, the essential oils become volatile oils, which evaporate, and when this happens we can smell the fragrance the flower gives off. Some plants also have essential oils in other places, for example, citrus fruits contain essential oils in the pith of their fruits and give off strong scents if scratched. Others contain scents in their nuts, bark or roots, such as ginger.

A flower's scent depends on the different chemicals in the volatile oils. Various combinations produce different fragrances.

The Arabians were the first to distil rose petals with water to produce rose water. This was 1,200 years ago, and we still extract perfume from flowers today.

FACT FILE

The hummingbird is the world's smallest bird. It can hover backwards as it feeds on flower nectar.

petal

pistil:
stigma
style
ovary

stamen:
anther
filament

sepal

Cross-section of a flower

WHAT HAPPENS IN FLOWERS?

Flowers come in many different shapes and sizes, but most contain the same four main parts, although these may not look the same in different flowers. In a 'normal' flower the sepals make up a green outer cup, and within the sepals are the petals, which are often coloured. In the middle of the flower are one or more pistils, which form the female part of the flower. The bottom of this area is enlarged to form the ovary, which contains little round ovules, which will later form into seeds if they are fertilized by the contents of a pollen grain from another flower. Pollen is produced by the stamens, the male organs of the flower and to fuse with an egg cell a grain must land on the stigma and develop into a tube to reach the ovules at the bottom of the pistil. Pollen can be carried by wind or by insects feeding on nectar and moving from plant to plant.

FACT FILE

Pollen is the plant's equivalent of an animal's sperm. It carries the male reproductive genes. Pollen grains have a pattern, allowing the plant to be identified.

WHY DO PINE TREES STAY GREEN ALL YEAR?

In most trees, leaves give off enormous amounts of water. In fact, in some, more than 90 per cent of the water absorbed by the roots and transported to the leaves is lost through evaporation. For most broad-leaved trees, such as oak, chestnuts, ash and maples this would be impossible to sustain in winter when the ground is frozen and they would die through lack of water. So these deciduous trees drop their leaves in autumn to protect themselves. Certain trees, however, like pines and firs have developed another strategy to avoid drying out. Their leaves are needlelike and covered in a waxy layer that prevents evaporation. They do not need to drop their leaves in autumn because their water requirements are low. When individual leaves do fall, new ones replace them and the branches never look bare.

Corsican Pine

Norway Spruce

FACT FILE

Fertilizers are used to make crops grow larger and faster. Crops are also regularly sprayed with pesticides and herbicides. There are fears that the chemicals could cause health problems.

WHAT ARE PERENNIAL PLANTS?

Daffodil

Perennial plants survive from one year to the next. They usually grow quite slowly, and can afford to build up their strength before they need to produce seeds. The parts of perennial plants that are above the ground are generally killed by frost in the autumn, but the roots and/or underground parts live through the winter. Growth is renewed and the cycle begins anew in the spring.

Perennial plants that grow in arid or desert conditions commonly survive dry times by becoming physiologically inactive. In some cases they remain alive but are dehydrated until water becomes available, at which time they rapidly absorb moisture through above-ground parts, swelling and resuming physiological activity. Some plants can absorb dew, which for many is the main water source. Mosses and lichens adopt this strategy, as do some flowering plants, which are sometimes called resurrection plants.

FACT FILE

As well as looking very like small bees, the flowers of bee orchids actually produce a female bee 'smell'. They are therefore highly attractive to male bees.

WHAT IS POISON IVY?

Poison ivy is a harmful vine or shrub, which is a member of the cashew family. It is widespread in southern Canada and parts of the United States. The plant's tissues contain a poisonous oil, which is similar to carbolic acid and highly irritating to the skin. Although poison ivy usually grows as a vine, climbing up trees or wandering across the soil, it will form a shrubby habit if there is no support available.

In early spring, the leaves are red, and by late spring, they change to shiny green. Then, in autumn they turn back to red or orange. Each leaf is composed of three leaflets with notched edges. Later in the season, clusters of whitish, waxy drupes that resemble berries form. These are just as poisonous as the leaves.

FACT FILE

Ground ivy is a member of the mint family and is not closely related to true ivies or poison ivy. It has a trailing habit and sends creeping stems across the ground, and forms mats of leaves where it takes hold.

Earth & Space

HOW CAN A DAY BE DEFINED?

For early peoples, the only changes that were truly regular, were the motions of objects in the sky. The most obvious of these changes was the alternate daylight and darkness, caused by the rising and setting of the Sun. Each of these cycles of the Sun came to be called a day. Another regular change in the sky was the change in the visible shape of the Moon. Each cycle of the Moon's changing shape takes about 29½ days, or a month. The cycle of the seasons gave people an even longer unit of time.

There is no regular change in the sky that lasts seven days, to represent the week. The seven-day week came from the Jewish custom of observing a Sabbath (day of rest) every seventh day. The division of a day into 24 hours, an hour into 60 minutes, and a minute into 60 seconds probably came from the ancient Babylonians.

FACT FILE

Some clock faces are divided into 24 hours. On such a clock, 9 a.m. would be shown as 0900 and 4 p.m. would be 1600. This system avoids confusion between the morning and evening hours.

21 JUNE

North Pole: 24 hours daylight

13.5 hours day

SUN'S RA

12 hours day

10.5 hours dayli

South Pole: 24 hours darkness

WHAT IS A HEMISPHERE?

FACT FILE

The equator is an imaginary line drawn around the outside of the Earth. It divides the Earth into two halves, called hemispheres. It was invented by mapmakers because it makes a convenient point from which to measure distances north and south.

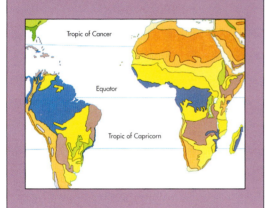

Tropic of Cancer

Equator

Tropic of Capricorn

A hemisphere is the name given to any half of any globe, including the Earth. It is derived from the Greek for half a sphere.

For convenience, geographers divide the Earth into hemispheres with the equator as a boundary. Everything north of the equator is in the Northern Hemisphere, while everything to south lies in the Southern Hemisphere. The equator lies at an equal distance from the geographic north and south poles.

Because land is not distributed evenly across the surface of the Earth, the globe may also be divided into land and water hemispheres, the former centred near London and the latter near New Zealand.

HOW DEEP IS THE PACIFIC OCEAN?

The Pacific Ocean, the largest and deepest of the world's four oceans, covers more than a third of the earth's surface and contains more than half of its free water. The floor of the Pacific Ocean, which has an average depth of around 14,000 feet (4,300 m), is largely a deep-sea plain. The name Pacific, which means peaceful, was given to it by the Portuguese navigator Ferdinand Magellan in 1520. The Pacific is the oldest of the existing ocean basins, its oldest rocks having been dated at 200 million years.

The Pacific Ocean is bounded on the east by the North and South American continents; on the north by the Bering Strait; on the west by Asia, the Malay Archipelago, and Australia; and on the south by Antarctica.

360 million sq km of Earth's surface is covered by water

FACT FILE

The Pacific Ocean contains more than 30,000 islands; their total land area, however, amounts to only one-quarter of one percent of the ocean's surface area.

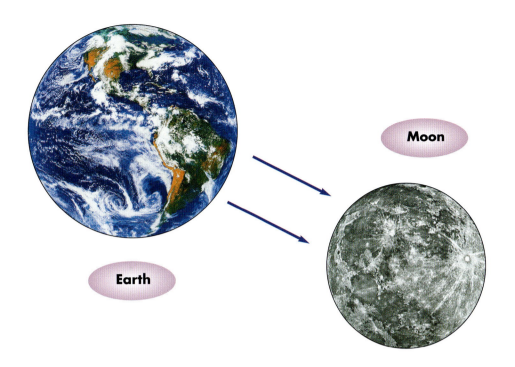

Moon

Earth

WHAT CAUSES TIDES?

The daily rise and fall of the ocean's tides occur because of the pull of gravity of the Moon. As the Earth spins round, the water in the oceans is 'pulled' towards the Moon slightly, making a bulge. There is a corresponding bulge on the other side of the Earth. Wherever the bulges are positioned it is high tide. In between, the water is shallower and so it is low tide. High tides occur every 25 hours, because at the same time that the Earth is spinning on its axis, the Moon is travelling around the Earth once every 27½ days. This means that high tides are about one hour later every day.

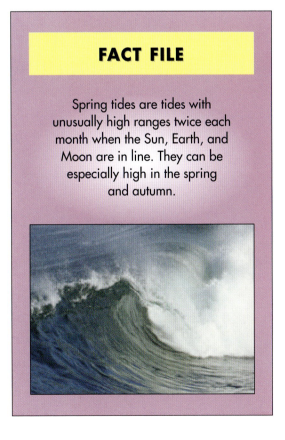

FACT FILE

Spring tides are tides with unusually high ranges twice each month when the Sun, Earth, and Moon are in line. They can be especially high in the spring and autumn.

WHAT ARE OCEAN TRENCHES?

FACT FILE

For centuries, most people assumed that the cold, black depths of the ocean supported little or no life. Scientists have since discovered a great variety of living things in the deep sea.

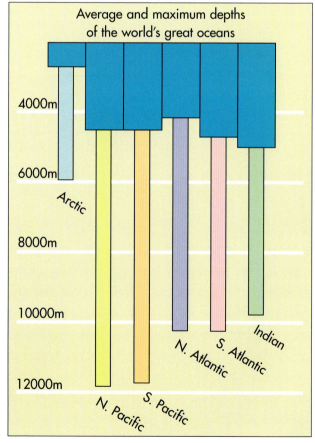

Trenches are the deepest parts of the ocean. Many trenches occur in the Pacific Ocean, especially in its western portion. Most trenches are long, narrow, and deep, 2 to 2.5 miles (3 to 4 km) below the surrounding sea floor. The greatest depth anywhere in the ocean is found in the Mariana Trench southeast of Japan. It plunges more than 6.8 miles (11 km) below sea level. Frequent earthquakes and volcanic eruptions occur along the trenches because they are where oceanic crust is being forced underneath continental crust.

Deep-sea fish are very different from those found in shallow waters

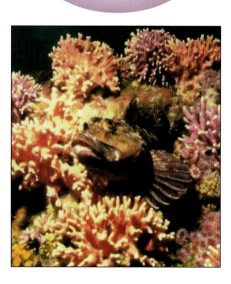

Average and maximum depths of the world's great oceans

4000m
6000m
Arctic
8000m
10000m
N. Atlantic
S. Atlantic
Indian
12000m
N. Pacific
S. Pacific

WHAT ARE CURRENTS?

The oceans are moved by the wind on their surface and from the movement inside the ocean. Ocean currents can move a large amount of heat around the Earth and can control the climate. The way the water circulates depends on the spinning of the Earth. The water in the northern hemisphere spins clockwise and the water in the southern hemisphere spins anti-clockwise. The ocean currents are different in summer and winter. The wind direction can change which ocean current will be influencing the weather in a country. A cold ocean current can make the weather cold, while a warm ocean current can make the weather warm.

FACT FILE

A whirlpool is a mass of water which spins around and around rapidly and with great force. It may occur when opposing currents meet, or it may be caused by the action of the wind.

Ocean currents

Summer in Northern Hemisphere

Cold currents are shown in blue, warm currents in red

200 million years ago

135 million years ago

Present day

150 million years' time

HOW DID THE CONTINENTS USED TO LOOK?

When the Earth formed, the lighter elements floated to the surface where they cooled to form a crust. Although the first rocks were formed over 3,500 years ago they have not stayed the same. They have been changed from forces on the inside and the outside of the Earth. The coastlines on each side of the Atlantic appear to have a jigsaw fit. It is thought that all the land masses were once joined together, forming a super continent called Pangaea. This split up to form the continents we know today.

FACT FILE

Movement of the land is still taking place as India and Asia are colliding, forming the Himalayas. This is called continental drift.

WHAT IS PLATE TECTONICS?

EURASIAN

AMERICAN

EURASIAN

IRANIAN

ARABIAN

PHILIPPINE

PACIFIC

CARIBBEAN

AFRICAN

INDIAN

NAZCA

AMERICAN

INDIAN Major plates

Plate boundaries

Direction of plate movements

ANTARCTIC

Plate tectonics theory explains the major features of the Earth's surface, both on land and under the oceans – how mountains are formed, what is happening in deep-sea trenches and why earthquakes and volcanoes occur where they do. The Earth's crust is broken into fragments, called plates, of varying sizes and these are moving in response to currents in the slowly flowing, but solid, mantle rock beneath. The plates move at different speeds, ranging from ½ to 4 inches (1 to 10 cm) a year. Scientists make these measurements by bouncing lasers from various points on the earth from reflectors left on the Moon by Apollo astronauts and work out the relative difference and direction of motion.

FACT FILE

The plates have been moving about slowly on the Earth's surface for hundreds of millions of years and will continue to do so, building mountain chains and creating new oceans, both forming and destroying land as they go.

WHAT SHAPES THE SEA-FLOOR?

The bottom of the ocean has features as varied as those on land. Huge plains spread out across the ocean floor, and long mountain chains rise toward the surface. Volcanoes erupt from the ocean bottom, and deep valleys cut through the floor. In the early 1960s, a theory called sea-floor spreading provided an explanation. According to the theory, the circulating currents deep within in the mantle pull the the sea-floor apart, carrying the continents with it. Molten magma is forced by pressure up into central valleys of the mid-ocean ridges. The magma cools and hardens to form new sea-floor and pushes older floor away. At the edges of the plate, some of the old oceanic crust dives under the continents.

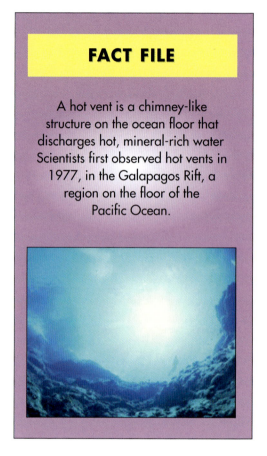

FACT FILE

A hot vent is a chimney-like structure on the ocean floor that discharges hot, mineral-rich water Scientists first observed hot vents in 1977, in the Galapagos Rift, a region on the floor of the Pacific Ocean.

Peru–Chile Trench   Andes   Brazilian Plateau   Atlantic Ocean   Mid-Atlantic Ridge   Constructive plate margin

South America

AMERICAN PLATE

NAZCA PLATE

Upwelling magma

WHAT ARE CONTINENTAL SHELVES?

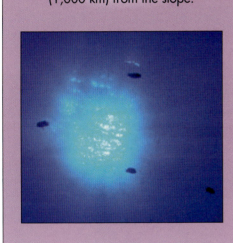

The continental margin is the area that separates the part of a continent above sea level from the deep sea floor. It consists of three parts, the continental shelf, the continental slope, and the continental rise.

The continental shelf begins at the shoreline and gently slopes underwater to an average depth of about 440 ft (135 m). The width of the continental shelf averages 47 miles (75 km), although in some places it is thousands of miles across and in others only a few feet. Valleys of varying depths cut through the shelf. At the edge of the continental shelf, there is an abrupt change in steepness, and the continental slope plunges down to the continental rise or, in some cases, to ocean trenches.

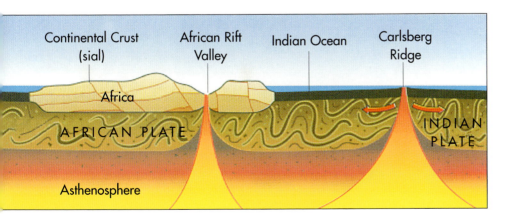

Continental Crust (sial)
African Rift Valley
Indian Ocean
Carlsberg Ridge
Africa
AFRICAN PLATE
INDIAN PLATE
Asthenosphere

WHY DOES LAND EROSION OCCUR?

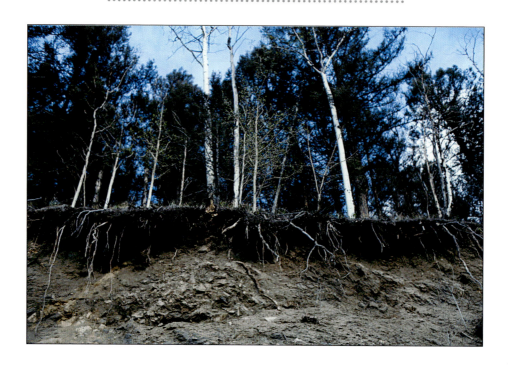

Erosion is a process through which rock and soil are broken loose from the earth's surface in one place and moved elsewhere. Natural erosion alters the shape of the land by wearing down mountains, filling in valleys and rivers with sediment. It is usually a slow process that makes little difference in thousands of years. Erosion begins with weathering, through the action of rain and snow, rivers, wind and ice, including glaciers. Sediments are eventually carried down from the mountains to the plains below, creating fertile land. If soil is left bare, rain and wind will wash it into streams and rivers and it will eventually be washed out to sea and end up on the ocean floor.

FACT FILE

Erosion can be speeded up by such human activities as farming and forestry. Landslides are one catastrophic result of too much supporting vegetation being lost.

Desert erosion

① ②

③

④

WHAT ERODES THE DESERTS?

A dry desert landscape includes surface features that have been created over thousands of years through erosion by wind and the ensuing deposit of silt and sand. After rain, water fills usually dry stream channels called wadis ①. The rapidly flowing water cuts into the soft rocks of desert mountains and carries sediments down through canyons and deposits sediments in fan-shaped forms known as alluvial fans ②.

Sometimes, the streams carry large amounts of water out into low areas in the desert plains that form temporary lakes. The water that collects in these lakes either evaporates or seeps into the ground. Water erosion in deserts also creates big flat-topped hills known as mesas ③ and smaller flat-topped hills called buttes ④.

Sand dunes are not fixed features but move with the prevailing wind.

WHY DO GLACIERS FORM?

glacier

debris carried
by glacier

deposited debris

Glaciers begin to form on mountains when the winter snow fall outweighs the summer snowmelt and evaporation. The excess snow builds up in layers over years. The increasing weight of successive layers of snow compresses the crystals below the surface, eventually turning them into dense, blue glacial ice. The glacier becomes so massive that it moves down the mountain slope under the influence of gravity, gouging out rock from the sides and floor of the valley. The top of the glacier continues to be fed with fresh snow.

FACT FILE

Glaciers have shaped most of the world' highest mountains, carving out huge valleys. Lakes in mountain regions are formed from flooded glacial valleys that become dammed by debris as the glacier melts.

WHAT IS AN ICE SHEET?

Over 10,000 years ago about a third of the land surface was covered by ice. Today a tenth is still covered in ice. Ice sheets can cover very large areas and can be very thick. The world's largest ice sheet covers most of Antarctica and is very slow moving.

Antarctica covers about 5,400,000 square miles (14,000,000 square km). It is larger in area than either Europe or Australia. However, Antarctica would be the smallest continent if it did not have its icecap. This icy layer, which averages approximately 7,100 feet (2,200 m) thick, increases Antarctica's surface area and also makes Antarctica the highest continent in terms of average elevation.

FACT FILE

Glaciers and ice sheets sometimes give up their secrets centuries later. Thawing ice has revealed the bodies of people who fell into crevasses hundreds of years ago. The ice preserved their clothes and their internal organs.

WHAT SHAPES A RIVER?

V-shaped valley

Gorge

Waterfall

Tree line

Floodplain

Meanders

YOUTH

MATURITY

OLD AGE

Sediment

Man-made levee

Rivers start on the top of hills as small streams channelling the rainfall or as a spring releasing ground water. They begin to cut at and change the landscape on the way to the sea. In the highlands the water can move very quickly and has a lot of power. The river can cut deep gorges and V-shaped valleys in the softer rocks. In the harder rocks they can form waterfalls. The river moves rocks and pebbles along its bed by bouncing and rolling. The lighter sediments are carried or dissolved in the water. When they reach the more gentle slopes the river becomes wider and moves slower. Mud and sand is dropped when the river floods and forms ridges along the river bank. When the river reaches the low plains it begins to meander.

FACT FILE

The farther a river is from its source on a mountainside, the slower the water travels. This is because the river eventually reaches flatter ground and widens before it reaches the sea.

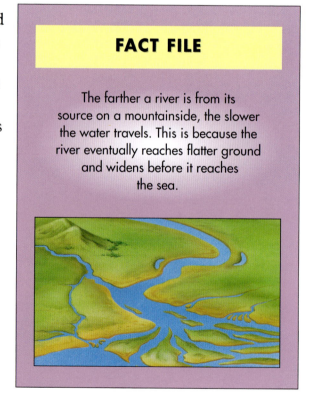

WHAT SHAPES THE COASTS?

FACT FILE

Many cliffs on the coast are made up of chalk. Chalk is formed from the skeletons of millions and millions of tiny animals called foraminifera. It is a sedimentar rock that formed millions of years ago beneath shallow seas.

Coastlines are constantly changing: they are either being eroded or built up. The waves are very powerful and can remove a large amount of material from a coastline, especially during a storm. The sand and pebbles removed from the coastline are carried by the sea and can be dropped farther along a coast or out at sea.

Many coastal features can be made by the steady erosion of the cliffs and headlands such as sand dunes, spits and salt marshes. A beach can make the waves less powerful and reduce the amount of erosion of the coast. Steep cliffs and wave-cut platforms can be formed in areas of hard rock. A bay can be carved out in an area where hard rock has soft rock between it.

SOFT ROCK

Cliff

HARD ROCK

Wave-cut platform

Wave-built terrace

HARD AND
SOFT ROCK

Cove

Headland

Arch

Stack

WHAT IS CLIMATE?

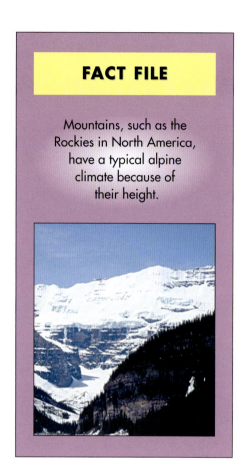

FACT FILE

Mountains, such as the Rockies in North America, have a typical alpine climate because of their height.

Climatic zones

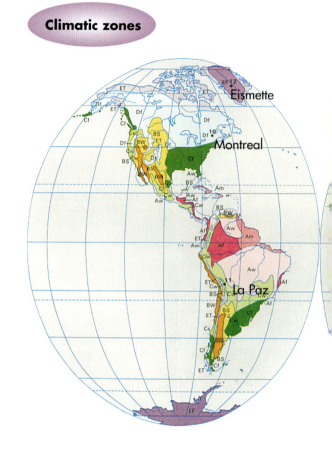

Af	Am	Aw	BS	BW	Cw	Ca

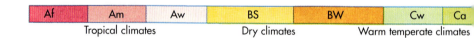

Tropical climates   Dry climates   Warm temperate climates

Climate is what the weather pattern is like over a long time. The seasonal pattern of hot and cold, wet or dry, is averaged over 30 years. The climate is different around the world as it is not heated evenly by the Sun. The equator gets most of the heat. Winds and ocean currents transport the heat around the Earth.

There are four types of climate: these are tropical, desert (dry), temperate, and polar.

Different areas of the world have different weather patterns. Some areas have a high level of rainfall while others remain dry. Throughout a year the weather in a country may change with the seasons.

WHAT IS A SAVANNA?

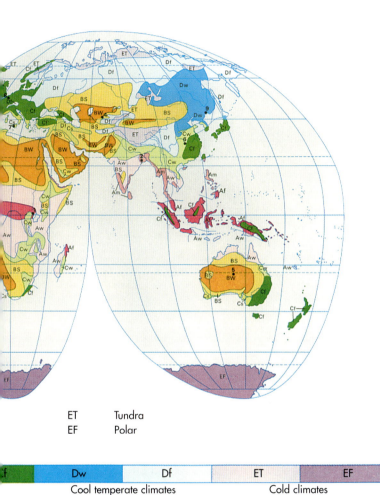

ET Tundra
EF Polar

Cf	Dw	Df	ET	EF
	Cool temperate climates		Cold climates	

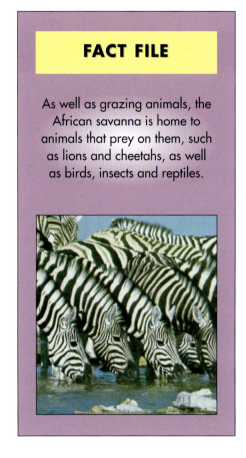

FACT FILE

As well as grazing animals, the African savanna is home to animals that prey on them, such as lions and cheetahs, as well as birds, insects and reptiles.

Savannas are grasslands in areas that have both dry and rainy seasons, and tend to lie between rain forests and deserts, with widely scattered trees and shrubs. Most savannas are in the tropics and they cover more than 40 per cent of Africa as well as large areas of India, central South America and northern Australia. Trees and shrubs are widely scattered on savannas and their growth is limited by the dry season, during which no rain may fall for nearly half a year. When the dry season begins, most trees drop their leaves to conserve water and the clumpy grasses die back. Grazing animals, such as zebras and wildebeest migrate across the savanna to follow the available water.

WHAT IS THE WATER CYCLE?

In nature, all the world's water circulates from the oceans to the sky, onto the land and then back to the oceans in what is called the water cycle or hydrological cycle. Heat from the sun evaporates water from the oceans, which gradually rises as vapour in the atmosphere. The vaporized water gradually cools and condenses to form clouds, which will deposit water back in the oceans or on the land as rain or snow. The majority falls directly back onto the oceans or seas, but some falls on the land and flows back to the seas, completing the cycle, sometimes after periods of thousands of years.

FACT FILE

Fresh water is obtained from two main sources, surface water and ground water. Streams, rivers and lakes provide surface water, while ground water may be obtained from springs or wells.

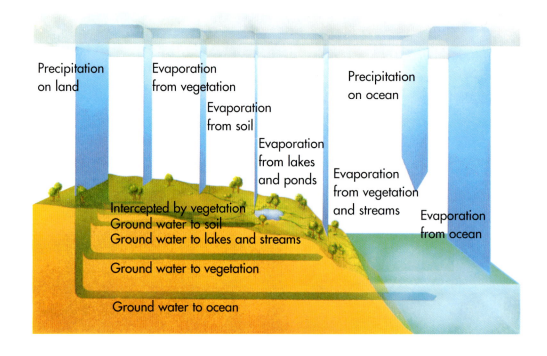

Precipitation on land

Evaporation from vegetation

Evaporation from soil

Evaporation from lakes and ponds

Precipitation on ocean

Evaporation from vegetation and streams

Evaporation from ocean

Intercepted by vegetation
Ground water to soil
Ground water to lakes and streams

Ground water to vegetation

Ground water to ocean

WHY DOES FLOODING OCCUR?

Flooding occurs when water cannot drain away fast enough in the rivers. In areas of non-porous rocks, water runs off the land very quickly and streams and rivers soon overflow. Flooding also happens when winter snows thaw in spring. Huge floods cover parts of Siberia every spring, when snow melts while the rivers are still iced up. Low-lying coastal lands are vulnerable to flooding, especially when gales and high tides cause water to flow inland. Low-lying Bangladesh is particularly liable to this kind of flooding. In addition, melting snow in the Himalayan mountains adds huge amounts of water to Bangladesh's rivers, increasing the flood risk.

WHAT ARE THE MOST EXTREME TEMPERATURES EVER RECORDED?

FACT FILE

One of the animals that has survived Arctic conditions is the polar bear. In very cold climates, animals need excellent insulation to keep their body heat from escaping. This can be in the form of dense hair fur, or feathers, or by a thick layer of fat or blubber

Libya and the Antarctic have recorded the most extreme temperatures. The hottest shade temperature was in Libya in 1922, when the temperature in the Sahara desert reached 58°C. Temperatures nearly as high as this were recorded in Death Valley in the USA in 1913. The coldest ever recorded temperature was in Antarctica in 1983, when Russian scientists measured a temperature low of –89.2°C. The longest heatwave recorded was in Marble Bar, Australia when the temperature stayed above 38°C. It lasted for 162 days from 23 October 1923 to 7 April 1924.

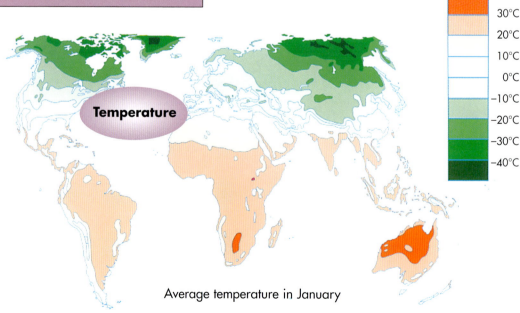

	30°C
	20°C
	10°C
	0°C
	–10°C
	–20°C
	–30°C
	–40°C

Temperature

Average temperature in January

WHY DO DROUGHTS OCCUR?

FACT FILE

An oasis is a fertile area found within a desert. It is a water source in the middle of often vast, dry land.

Drought is a prolonged period, sometimes lasting for years, when less-than-average amounts of rain fall, usually accompanied by higher temperatures than normal. In agricultural areas, the lack of rain and increased heat kills crops. Because the plants are dry, forest and grass fires are more frequent, spread more rapidly and cover wider areas, sometimes leaving the soil bare and prone to erosion so that even if the rains come again, it is difficult to grow crops. Streams, ponds, and wells often dry up during a drought, and animals suffer and may die because of the lack of water. Severe, prolonged droughts, such as those that have occurred in eastern Africa during the past twenty years and more, cause widespread hardship and famine for millions of people.

Rainfall

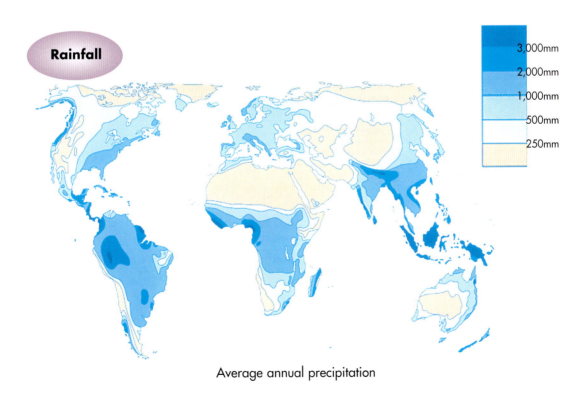

	3,000mm
	2,000mm
	1,000mm
	500mm
	250mm

Average annual precipitation

WHAT IS A TSUNAMI?

Earthquakes on the ocean floor can give a tremendous push to surrounding seawater and create one or more large, destructive waves called tsunamis, also known as seismic sea waves. Some people call tsunamis tidal waves, but scientists think the term is misleading because the waves are not caused by the tide.

Tsunamis may build to heights of more than 100 ft (30 m) when they reach shallow water near shore. In the open ocean, tsunamis typically move at speeds of 500 to 600 mph (800 to 970 kmh). They can travel great distances while diminishing little in size and can flood coastal areas thousands of miles or km from their source.

FACT FILE

Probably the best-known gauge of earthquake intensity is the local Richter magnitude scale, developed in 1935 by United States seismologist Charles F. Richter.

Another form of tsunami is called a storm surge, in which giant waves are whipped up by a storm. In 1970 a storm surge and cyclone hit Bangladesh, killing 266,000 people. Another surge in 1985 killed a further 10,000 people. In 2004 an earthquake off the coast of Indonesia triggered a series of deadly waves that killed at least 150,000 people in coastal areas from Somalia to Sumatra. Many millions of people were left destitute.

WHAT IS AN EYEWALL?

TELL ME ABOUT THE WORLD : EARTH & SPACE

FACT FILE

The end of a hurricane comes quickly if a hurricane moves over land, because it no longer receives heat energy and moisture from warm tropical water.

A tropical storm achieves hurricane status when its winds exceed 74 mph (119 kph). By the time a storm reaches hurricane intensity, it usually has a well-developed eye at its middle. Surface pressure drops to its lowest there. In the eyewall of the storm, warm air spirals upwards, creating the hurricane's strongest winds, the speed of which is related to the diameter of the eye. Just as ice skaters spin faster when they pull their arms in, a hurricane's winds blow faster if its eye is small.

Heavy rains fall from the eyewall and from bands of dense clouds that swirl around the eyewall. These bands, called rainbands, can produce more than 2 inches (5 cm) of rain per hour.

Tornados are violently rotating columns of air that descend from the base of a thunder cloud to the ground. The windspeeds can reach 250 mph (400 kph) and the path of damage caused by a tornado can be as much as 1 mile (2 km) wide.

WHAT IS ACID RAIN?

FACT FILE

Attempts have been made to neutralize the acidity of some lakes by adding lime, but it is not known whether this may have harmful side effects.

Acid rain is rain, snow or sleet that has been polluted by acids. Increased acidity upsets the delicate pH balance of fresh water and kills insects, fish and other wildlife that depend on lakes, rivers and streams. High concentrations of acid rain can harm forests, burning the trees leaves and changing the acidity of soil, making it difficult for plants to thrive. They become less resistant to disease and many die.

Acid rain is a problem of the industrial age, resulting mainly from the burning of fossil fuels in power stations and factories as well as cars and other vehicles. The resulting compounds, for example sulphur dioxide and nitrogen oxides, react with vapour in the atmosphere to create such compounds as sulphuric and nitric acid.

Large parts of eastern North America, central Europe, Scandinavia and parts of Asia are badly affected by the effects of acid rain. Acts forcing companies to reduce their emissions of such compounds have been in force in many western countries for some years now and the levels of acidity are beginning to drop. However, this improvement is not yet happening worldwide.

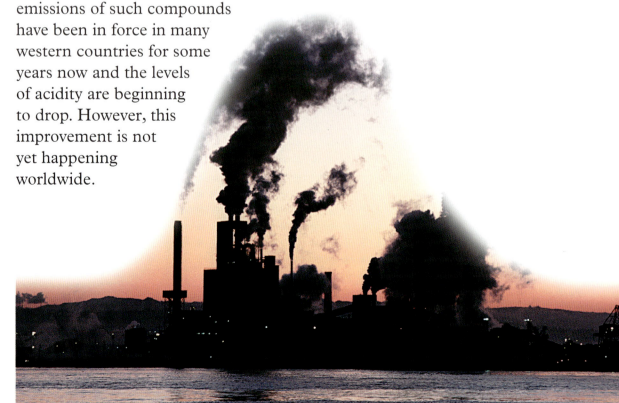

WHY DOES DEFORESTATION OCCUR?

The world's rain forests are disappearing rapidly. More than half of their area has been irretrievably destroyed by humans. The primary causes are land clearance for agriculture, commercial logging of tropical hardwoods and destructive open-cast mining for chemicals. Large areas have also been lost to hydroelectric projects.

FACT FILE

Rain forests benefit people in four major ways. They provide (1) economic, (2) scientific, (3) environmental, and (4) recreational value.

In the last few years of the twentieth century, forest clearance in Indonesia caused extensive forest fires; the smoke blanketed much of southeast Asia for some months.

Worryingly, rain forest species such as the orang-utan are in danger of extinction because of the destruction of their habitat. Most animals die when people clear large areas of forest, leaving only isolated patches that are not large enough for them to live in. More than 7,000 species, including insects, reptiles and mammals are thought to become extinct each year.

HOW BIG ARE ASTEROIDS?

Asteroids are small rocky or icy bodies that orbit the Sun. There are over 100,000 in orbit and some measure less than ½ a mile (1 km) across, while the largest known is 630 miles (1,000 km) in size and only a few of them have a diameter of more than 19 miles (30 km). They are sometimes called minor planets. Most asteroids are found in an orbit between Mars and Jupiter, called the asteroid belt, and more than 7,000 of these have been identified. The asteroid belt may be the shattered remains of a planet destroyed by Jupiter's enormous gravity, or perhaps one that was prevented from forming. There are also asteroids in orbits near the Earth, as well as in the same orbit as Jupiter.

One asteroid, called Ida, has a tiny moon of its own, Dactyl, and is the smallest known body in the solar system to have a satellite. Astronomers believe that the asteroids were probably formed, at the same time as the planets, from the dust cloud that surrounded the Sun when it was young.

The Asteroid Belt

FACT FILE

Many asteroids have struck the Earth already, although the resulting craters have been covered by geological activity. Many scientists believe that such an impact off Mexico 65 million years ago caused the extinction of the dinosaurs.

HOW ARE METEORITES FORMED?

Meteorites are made of rock or metal. They may have been formed at the same time as the solar system, or may be debris from impacts between other small bodies and planets such as Mars. They enter the Earth's atmosphere at speeds of at least 6.9 mps (11 kms), which makes them glow as they vaporize. Several thousand meteoroids enter the Earth's atmosphere every year, but very few reach the ground. Technically, meteoroids are only called meteorites if they actually hit the planet. The largest known meteorite is made of iron and weighs 65 tons (66 tonnes). It probably fell to the Earth in prehistoric times in Namibia, southwest Africa.

It is very hard to find meteorites. Recently, researchers have been finding them on the ice sheets in the Arctic and the Antarctic, where they are easier to locate.

On planets and moons with no atmosphere, huge numbers of meteorites strike with enormous power. Our own Moon is estimated to have 3,000,000 meteorite craters measuring 1 mile (2 km) or more in diameter. However, meteorite craters are rare on Earth because the atmosphere slows the meteoroid and usually burns it up.

FACT FILE

An enormous meteorite caused this huge impact crater at Wolf Creek in Australia. The amount of energy the impact released would have been equivalent to hundreds of nuclear weapons.

WHAT IS A FALLING STAR?

'Falling stars' appear as faint streaks of light in the sky. Today we know that they are not stars, but meteors. Meteors are small solid bodies, some only the size of dust particles, that travel through space and may hit the Earth's atmosphere.

Hundreds of thousands collide with the Earth's atmosphere daily and we see some of them because they leave fiery trains of light. If more than ¼ inch (8 mm) across they vaporize because of frictional heating and cause ionized trails in the upper atmosphere. Larger bodies may penetrate deeper and then blow up as a fireball.

Meteors may appear in the sky singly, which is why they are often mistaken for a 'falling star'. Meteor showers happen when the Earth is at specific places in its orbit, and are thought to be caused by material from the tails of comets.

The Milky Way

FACT FILE

Sometimes it is very difficult to see stars. The stars are still there, but clouds may be covering the night sky. Also there are so many artificial lights from our homes and street lighting, that it is often not dark enough to see the stars.

HOW DO STARS MAKE PICTURES?

For many thousands of years people all over the world have traced patterns in the stars and given them names. These groups are called 'constellations' which comes from the Latin for 'star' (*stella*) and 'together' although, in fact, the stars contained within them are unrelated.

Many of the constellations we know today are derived from those invented by the ancient Babylonians, who named some of their star pictures after animals and royal and mythological figures. Their knowledge was handed down to the Greeks and from them passed to the Romans, who both attached their own heroes and gods to the star patterns, and we still use their names for many of the constellations. For example, Ursa Major is the great bear, Cancer is the crab and Aries is the ram. Later on, astronomers added more constellations, mainly in the southern part of the sky, including Microscopium, the microscope, and Carina, the keel, and today they recognize 88 constellations.

FACT FILE

Halley's Comet returns to the inner solar system every 76 years after having travelled out close to the orbit of Pluto. Its last encounter with Earth was in 1986.

HOW MUCH DOES THE ATMOSPHERE WEIGH?

The Earth is surrounded by a thick blanket of about 20 gases, mainly nitrogen and oxygen, called the atmosphere. It also contains water vapour and dust particles. It is densest closest to the ground and thins progressively with increasing height.

Air, like all matter, has weight. Scientists have calculated that our atmosphere weighs 5,100,000,000,000,000 tons (5,170,000,000,000,000 tonnes)!

So why don't we feel the weight of all this air pressing down on us and against us? Something like a ton of air is pressing against you at this very moment, and yet you are not aware of this because your body is made to live with this pressure. Higher up in the atmosphere, pressure is less, which is why aircraft cabins have to be pressurized. Similarly, pressure increases rapidly with depth in the oceans, and divers can reach only the very top levels of the water without the protection of submarines.

The Earth's atmosphere is one of the most important things that allows it to support life. Chemicals in it protect us from the Sun's rays, it prevents all but the biggest meteorites hitting the surface, without it the oceans would evaporate and, of course, it provides oxygen for us to breathe.

FACT FILE

Beneath the land and water that cover the Earth's surface lie layers of rock and metal at very high temperatures. The deepest mines ever dug have not reached the bottom of the outer layer, called the crust. Under the crust is a layer of partly solid and partly molten rock.

HOW OLD IS THE EARTH?

The Earth began to form over 4.5 billion years ago, but for millions of years nothing could live here. About 3.6 billion years ago, scientists think that a body the size of Mars crashed into the young Earth, resulting in the formation of the Moon. Gradually, the Earth's crust and the oceans and atmosphere formed. But how do we know this? The Earth's geological record does not go back that far, so the answer is based on theory.

To find the age of the Earth it was necessary to find out how the Sun and all the planets came into being.

The first theory is the 'nebular hypothesis', which dates to the eighteenth century. In this theory a mass of white-hot gas whirled about in space getting smaller and hotter all the time, throwing off rings of gas, which condensed to form a planet. The second theory, the 'planetismal hypothesis' dates to the 1920s. In this, the gravitation of a large star pulled on the Sun and caused it to eject filaments of plasma that condensed into tiny bodies, which eventually accreted into planets. The current theory is that as the Sun formed, a broad disk of dust and gas condensed around it. Material within this disk began to clump together and eventually accreted into the nine planets. One way of estimating the Earth's age involves calculating how long it would take for the Moon to acquire the number of craters it has.

FACT FILE

No one has ever proved that life exists on other planets. However, as there are billions of stars, some with planets, it seems unlikely that Earth is the only place with the right conditions for life. Astronomers use radio telescopes to search for messages from other civilizations.

HOW BIG IS THE UNIVERSE?

Astronomers think that the universe formed about 13 billion years ago, but calculations of its size are too mind-numbing for most of us.

The Earth is only a tiny member our solar system. The light from the brightest star in the sky, Sirius, takes over 8½ years to get here. The solar system lies in a quiet backwater of an average galaxy that contains perhaps 100,000,000 stars. It is part of a local group of 40-odd galaxies, some members of which are almost 2,500,000 lightyears away. Beyond vast empty tracts of space, larger clusters of galaxies can be detected. The Virgo supercluster contains more than 3,000 galaxies. and as far as the universe goes, that is just in our backyard.

FACT FILE

More than two-thirds of the Earth's surface is covered by seas and oceans. About 72 per cent of the Earth's surface is water. This water is either in the oceans, locked away as ice at the poles, or held as water vapour in the atmosphere. All the Earth's water is known as the hydrosphere.

WHAT IS THE EARTH MADE OF ?

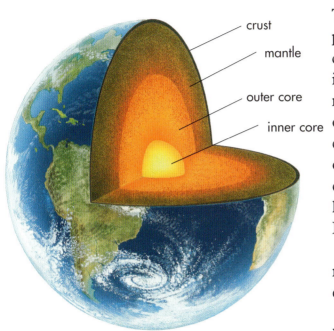

crust

mantle

outer core

inner core

The Earth is an almost spherical planet, and is made up of several distinct layers. The solid inner core is thought to consist mainly of nickel and iron, and the liquid outer core has a similar composition. The relative motions of the solid and liquid parts of the core and movements within the latter are thought to produce the Earth's protective magnetic field.

Above the outer core is the mantle, which is slowly moving, even though it is solid rock.

Above the mantle lies the lithosphere, the outer layer of which is the crust. The high parts of this crust are the continents, and the low parts of it hold the waters of the oceans, seas and lakes.

The heat radiating out from the centre of the planet and the currents in the mantle drive the forces that give us volcanoes and replenish the gases in the atmosphere. Without them, there would be no atmosphere, no oceans and no life on our planet.

FACT FILE

Volcanoes are openings in the Ear s crust through which molten lava, red-hot rocks, steam and fumes pour out. Most volcanoes have a single central pipe through which lava reaches the surface, building up into a cone as it cools. This consists of layers of lava and volcanic ash with a crater at the centre. Active volcanoes smoke and spit out lava.

HOW ARE STARS FORMED?

A star is a huge ball of bright, hot ionized gas called plasma. The main source of fuel for most of a star's life is hydrogen, which they convert into helium. They also contain other chemical elements such as nitrogen, oxygen, iron, nickel and zinc.

Stars come into existence in the vast, cold clouds of dust and gas that astronomers refer to as stellar nurseries. They are not particularly dense, but are a lot denser than the vacuum of space. If there is a disturbance in a bit of the cloud, perhaps as the result of a nearby star exploding, some of the particles might clump together. As they do, they will spin together and slowly attract more particles. As the group gradually gets larger and larger, its spins faster and its gravitational attraction becomes greater.

Pressure also builds up within the ball, which increases its heat. Eventually, when the pressure and temperature inside the ball become very high, about 15 million°C, nuclear reactions take place in the core and the gas ball becomes a star. The larger a star, the faster it will use up its hydrogen and some massive stars last only tens of thousands of years before exploding. Small stars like our Sun, last for tens of millions of years.

FACT FILE

A nebula is an enormous mass of gas and material that appears to be solid. However, it is mostly composed of dust and gas, which slowly condenses into stars.

HOW FAR AWAY ARE THE STARS?

The Sun is about 93,000,000 miles (149,699,000 km) from Earth and as light travels at the rate of 186,000 mps (299,792,458 kms) it takes eight minutes for the light to reach us. The next closest stars to Earth are Proxima Centauri and Alpha Centauri. They are 270,000 times farther away from the Earth than the Sun, so this means that it would take their light 4½ years to reach the Earth. Others are unimaginably far away: Betelgeuse, the red star in Orion's shoulder is approximately 427 light-years away.

To measure the distance of very nearby stars, astronomers use a form of geometry. Close stars appear to move very slightly against the background stars over the Earth's annual orbit, and if measurements are taken at each extreme, perhaps in December and June, the angle between the two points can be used to calculate its distance.

Other techniques are used for measuring the distances to more remote stars and galaxies, involving the use of spectroscopy, the analysis of the chemistry of stars through their light.

FACT FILE

The Milky Way is a huge mass of gas and stars that can be clearly seen as a band of light across the night sky. The Earth, and everything else in the solar system, is part of the Milky Way.

HOW FAST DOES THE EARTH MOVE?

The Earth has two main motions – it spins on its axis once every 23 hours, 56 minutes and 4.091 seconds and it moves in an orbit around the Sun once every 365¼ days.

It was believed that the speed of the rotation never changed, but there are tiny variations and our day is getting longer by about one-thousandth of a second per century.

Like all of the planets, the Earth moves faster when it is closer to the Sun (perihelion) than it does when farther out (aphelion). At aphelion the Earth orbits the Sun at 18.2 mps (29.12 kms) and at perihelion it is travelling at a speed of 18.8 mps (30.8 kms).

FACT FILE

Humans have a built-in body clock and normally have a good idea of the time even without the use of clocks, because our body is aware of the amount of time that has passed since daybreak.

Prehistory

· ·

HOW ARE PREHISTORIC TIMES CATEGORIZED?

Geological time covers many millions of years and it has been divided up into eras, which are periods of time identified by the fossilized forms of life from that period. The oldest era, called the Palaeozoic, contains fossils ranging from many primitive life forms up to some of the earliest land-dwelling animals. During this era fishes, amphibians and early reptiles appeared.

The Mesozoic era was the age of giant reptiles, when dinosaurs stalked the world. The Cenozoic era in which we still live is the age of mammals and birds. All fossils can be placed in these eras, which are subdivided further into smaller periods as shown on the chart here.

FACT FILE

Now the habits of dinosaurs are becoming better understood, museums are able to mount their fossilized remains in realistic poses that show people how they lived.

Era	Period	
Cenozoic	Quaternary	
	Tertiary	65
Mesozoic	Cretaceous	14
	Jurassic	208
	Triassic	245
Paleozoic	Permian	290
	Carboniferous	362
	Devonian	408
	Silurian	439
	Ordovician	510
	Cambrian	570

WHAT HAVE WE LEARNT FROM PREHISTORY?

Almost everything that we know about the living things on Earth before humans evolved has been learnt from fossils. Fossils are the remains of dead animals and plants that have been turned to stone over millions of years.

By studying these remains scientists have been able to come up with the type of animals that existed both on land and in water and also details of the type of food they needed to exist.

Records of prehistory and examples of fossils can be found in many of our modern museums.

million years ago

million years ago

million years ago

million years ago

million years ago

million years ago

million years ago

million years ago

million years ago

million years ago

million years ago

FACT FILE

This particular shark, called Carcharocles, lived about 15 million years ago, and was about the size of a bus. Only its huge teeth have survived and so scientists were only able to estimate its actual size.

When an organism dies, the soft parts rot away.

The hard shell is covered with a layer of silt.

A hard mineral fossil is gradually formed.

HOW ARE FOSSILS FORMED?

Fossils result from the death of an animal that took place millions of years ago. The soft parts of the animal rot quickly, and the bones or shell are scattered by scavenging animals.

Some of these remains are buried in mud or sand. If they are not disturbed in any way, more mud is deposited until the remains are deeply buried. Under great pressure from deposits above, the mud eventually compacts into sedimentary rock.

Sometimes a fossil will retain the shape and structure of the hard parts of an animal, such as fossilized dinosaur bones. These are not the original bones because minerals have replaced them over the years, but they retain the same shape. Other fossils are just the impression of an animal or plant created when it was buried.

FACT FILE

Trilobites were once among the most abundant animals on Earth. They lived only in the sea and survived for millions of years, evolving into some strangely shaped forms before they suddenly became extinct.

HOW ARE FOSSILS FOUND?

Every year fossils are found that add to our knowledge of prehistoric life. Very often they are discovered by ordinary people walking in the countryside. Places where soil is frequently being washed away from rocks, such as at the bottom of cliffs, are good places to look.

Fossils have been found accidentally by people working in mines or quarries. Sometimes they become exposed by erosion and can be seen sticking out of cliff faces.

Geologists are now able to identify those rock formations that are likely to contain fossils. More and more fossils are being found by properly organized expeditions.

Large numbers of new types of fossil are now being found in Mongolia and China. There, fossil hunters have unearthed what are probably the ancestors of modern birds. Palaeontology is the scientific name for the study of fossils.

TELL ME ABOUT THE WORLD : PREHISTORY

HOW DID LIFE BEGIN ON LAND?

Plants were the first living things on our planet, starting with very simple plants such as algae. Then mosses and liverworts developed, followed by ferns and other larger plants. Animals did not leave the sea until plants had become fully established, otherwise there would have been no food for them.

Next were relatives of the spiders and scorpions, which were probably the first creatures to leave the sea and actually colonize on land. Later they evolved into larger and more complex forms of life. Amphibians multiplied rapidly, and the word actually means 'living on land and in water'.

FACT FILE

The first mammals lived alongside the dinosaurs, but in comparison with reptiles they were tiny and insignificant, like the Glyptodon below.

WHY DID SOME FISH BECOME LAND-DWELLERS?

Around 400 million years ago fish began to creep out of the water onto land. The main reasons for an animal to change its habits would be to obtain fresh food supplies and to escape from its predators. Many fish were able to just wriggle along on land, but in order to lift their body clear of the ground ordinary fins were not strong enough. One of these fish is the coelacanth, a large fish up to 3 ft (1 m) long with strange leg-like fins. It was found to contain bones that were very like those of land-living vertebrate animals. Relatives of the coelacanth had leg-like fins reinforced with bones, which allowed them to slither along like a modern crocodile. Many ancient fish developed simple lungs, which they used instead of their gills when they were out of the water.

FACT FILE

Baryonix is the only known fish-eating dinosaur, and uniquely it had huge claws on its front limbs.

HOW DO WE KNOW WHAT DINOSAURS WERE LIKE?

Although dinosaur remains are few, we know we can deduce quite a lot about them from their fossilized skeletons. We can calculate a dinosaur's weight by studying its bones. Heavy animals have massive bones to support their weight, while swift-moving hunters have very light, hollow bones. Muscles are firmly attached to bones, and although no trace of the muscles are left in the fossils, the points at which they attach can still be seen on the bones. These facts tell scientists how big the muscles must have been.

We know that a large digestive system is necessary to digest vegetable matter. The herbivores would have had massive barrel-shaped bodies, while carnivores would be slimmer. The shape of the teeth tells scientists what type of food the dinosaurs ate.

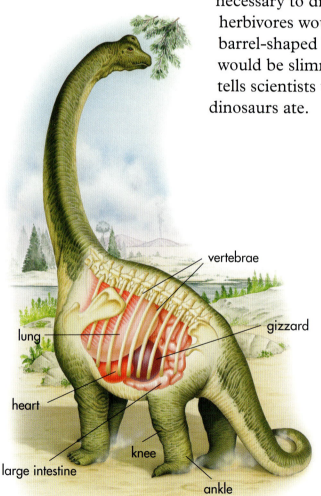

vertebrae

gizzard

lung

heart

large intestine

knee

ankle

FACT FILE

Much is presumed and guessed about dinosaurs. Looking at the Carnotaurus, it had weak jaws and was not well equipped for hunting, so it was assumed that it only fed on small prey.

HOW DID DINOSAURS EVOLVE?

Dinosaurs were reptiles that evolved into the most varied kinds of any living creature. They ranged from tiny bird-like animals to monstrous beasts that were the largest animals to ever live on land.

The dinosaurs survived for about 150 million years. They were not all meat-eating killers as often portrayed in books and films. Most dinosaurs were peaceful, browsing animals about the size of modern farm livestock.

The main thing that distinguishes dinosaurs from other reptiles is the way their body is supported by their legs. The legs of ancient and existing reptiles stick out sideways, so the body drags on the ground for most of the time. It is raised briefly when the animal runs. The skeletons of dinosaurs developed so the legs were beneath the body, raising the whole body off the ground.

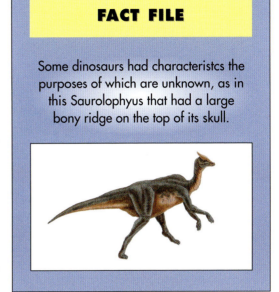

FACT FILE

Some dinosaurs had characteristcs the purposes of which are unknown, as in this Saurolophyus that had a large bony ridge on the top of its skull.

HOW MANY DIFFERENT TYPES OF DINOSAUR WERE THERE?

Pachycephalosaurus

There were thousands of different species of dinosaur and we have only discovered a small proportion of them. It is important at this stage to realise how rare fossils are. There were a few dinosaur species that must have been very common, like Iguanodon, which left many fossils. Others were probably scarce when they were alive, or lived in regions where fossilization was unlikely, and so there are few remains of these dinosaurs.

Herbivores often lived in groups or herds, but carnivores were usually more solitary and their fossils are therefore more rare. Many of the interesting dinosaurs are known from a single fossil, or one or two bones, and scientists must deduce the shape and size from these.

FACT FILE

Although in many ways the Ouranosaurus was a typical plant-eating dinosaur, it had a remarkable sail-like crest on its back and tail. Its function is not known.

124

HOW BIG WERE DINOSAURS?

Euoplocephalus

Dinosaurs vary in size enormously. Some were only about the size of a chicken, or even smaller. Compsognathus was only about 28 inches (70 cm) long and was very slightly built. It was an agile and fast-moving creature and is thought to have lived on insects and small animals. The skeleton of this dinosaur is very similar to that of a modern bird.

Scientists cannot agree on the maximum size of giant dinosaurs. But it is usually said that Brachiosaurus is the biggest, and is thought to have been about 100 ft (30 m) long and to have weighed as much as 128 tons (130 tonnes). This would make it by far the heaviest land animal to have ever existed. The Sauroposeidon has been described as being as high as 56 ft (17.2 m), making it three times the height of the tallest giraffe.

FACT FILE

The biggest mammal to have lived on Earth actually preceded dinosaurs. It was called the Indicotherium and was big enough to push over trees which were too tall for it to graze upon.

125

HOW DID CARNIVOROUS DINOSAURS CATCH THEIR PREY?

All meat-eating dinosaurs were roughly the same shape, but they all varied in size a great deal. They all belonged to a group called theropods meaning 'beast feet'.

The giant dinosaurs like Tyrannosaurus rex probably ambushed their prey, charging at them with jaws wide open. They could run at a speed of 32 mph (50 kmh), although probably for only a very short distance. The impact of seven tonnes of dinosaur hitting its prey with a jagged mouthful of teeth would likely kill most animals outright.

Many smaller dinosaurs retained powerful front limbs and claws, and could cling to their prey while biting it.

FACT FILE

Plant-eating dinosaurs had long necks to enable them to reach trees, which were their main source of food.

Saltasaurus

Tyrannosaurus rex, usually just called T-rex, was the largest and most fearsome land-living predator ever to have existed.

Tyrannosaurus rex

HOW DID PLANT-EATING DINOSAURS FIND FOOD?

Hadrosaurus

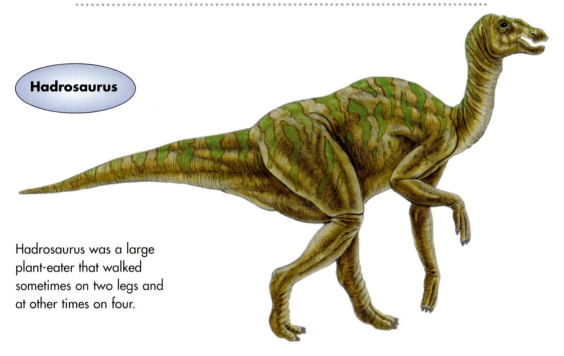

Hadrosaurus was a large plant-eater that walked sometimes on two legs and at other times on four.

The type of food that plant-eating dinosaurs fed on depended on their type of mouth. Some had broad mouths like a duck's bill and they probably grazed on a mixture of plants. Dinosaurs with narrow jaws, most likely selected particular plants to eat.

The long-necked sauropods probably grazed on leaves and shoots. Large herds of sauropods would have caused tremendous devastation by feeding in this way and may have used their great weight to push trees over so they were easier to reach.

A herd of sauropods would have cleared great areas of trees, creating large expanses of open ground where smaller dinosaurs could graze. Dinosaurs with cutting beaks would have been able to crop the vegetation short.

FACT FILE

The diets of some dinosaurs are a complete mystery. For example, the Segnosaurus could have eaten termites, fish, or plants.

127

DID DINOSAURS LOOK AFTER THEIR YOUNG?

Very large numbers of remains of Protoceratops have been found in the Gobi desert, including eggs and nestlings. These animals seem to have nested in very large groups and probably cared for their young.

It was thought at one time that dinosaurs laid their eggs in isolated places. But in 1978 a remarkable find was made in Montana, USA. Fifteen Maiasaurus babies were found scattered around a large mound-shaped structure, together with many broken eggshells. The babies were not newly hatched because their teeth were partly worn away. The nest itself was about 7 ft (2 m) across and covered with vegetation.

FACT FILE

The eggs of Orodromeus have been found broken open from the inside as the young hatched out. The baby dinosaurs are thought to have foraged for their food while being guarded by adults.

In the Gobi desert, the pig-sized dinosaur Protoceratops dug holes in the sand and buried her eggs. She left them to hatch in the heat of the sand while she guarded them from predators. The eggs were arranged in careful circles, in layers. Presumably the mother dinosaur turned herself above the nest as she laid each egg.

HOW BIG WERE DINOSAUR EGGS?

Protoceratops

Dinosaur eggs looked very much like birds' eggs and were surprisingly small. Most were about the size and shape of a large potato. Their small size means that the hatchling would also have been small and would have needed plenty of care and protection from its parents.

When Orodromeus nests were discovered, other dinosaur eggs were found between them. These eggs were smaller and were laid in straight lines. It has recently been found that they are the eggs of a small predator called the Troodon. It appears to have laid its eggs in the Orodromeus colony to gain protection from other predators. This habit is similar to that of modern cuckoos and their relatives, although they also use another species of bird to raise their young.

FACT FILE

The Oviraptor was an odd dinosaur that may have lived entirely on the eggs of other dinosaurs. It was bird-shaped, with a powerful beak for crushing eggs and did not have any teeth.

Euoplocephalus

HOW DID DINOSAURS PROTECT THEMSELVES?

Dinosaurs had various ways of protecting themselves. Firstly they might just have been too big to be brought down and eaten. Secondly, some dinosaurs could run very fast indeed, which meant they escaped their predator. Thirdly, a slow-moving dinosaur may have been covered with spikes and horns to help deter attackers.

FACT FILE

Although the sides of its body were less heavily armoured than many of its relatives, the underside of the Minmi was well protected by being covered with tough bony plates.

As well as being covered with jointed armour and defensive spines, the Euoplocephalus carried a massive club on the end of its tail, which would have crushed any predator.

HOW DID DINOSAURS USE THEIR ARMOUR?

FACT FILE

Although some dinosaurs could not run very fast at all, they had other ways of defending themselves. The Shunasaurus had a tail club that it would wield in defence.

Several theories have been put forward as to why some dinosaurs had armour on parts of their body. The plates on the back of the Stegosaurus could have been used to display to rival animals, or perhaps help to regulate body temperature. It has even been suggested that the plates could have folded flat to make a sheet of armour over the animal's back. The whole head of an Ankylosaur was covered with protective plates and this cover even extended over the eyes. Others wielded their tails in defence.

HOW DID FISH EVOLVE?

Killer fish

As fish developed jaws, they were able to hunt other animals. Soon they evolved into large creatures, sometimes with armour to protect themselves. The most fearsome fish grew to 29 ft (9 m) in length.

Fossils show that the first fish occurred in the Ordovician Period which began about 460,000,000 years ago. These fish were jawless, and the most primitive of all. Their mouths were a simple opening, suited to feeding on the tiny animals that lay hidden in the mud.

Next came fish with jaws. Jaws allowed fish to explore various food sources and to feed more efficiently. Early fish with jaws are called placoderms. The jaws actually evolved from a set of gill arches that were present in the jawless fish. Gill arches are the bony supports of the gills.

From these placoderms came our present-day fish, the sharks and bony fish.

FACT FILE

Ammonites were relatives of the modern octopus and squid. They secreted a hard shell, living in a small compartment. A new compartment was added as they grew larger, eventually producing a spiral shell.

WHAT DID MARINE REPTILES LOOK LIKE?

The ichthyosaurs looked very much like modern dolphins, but were totally aquatic reptiles that gave birth to live young.

Mesosaurus was a small ancestor of the crocodile. Its remains have been found in both North and South America.

Many reptiles returned to the sea. Some of the most familiar ones are the plesiosaurs, large animals with a barrel-like body and a long snaky neck. They did not have a flexible body, they rowed themselves along by waving their fin-like front and rear limbs up and down.

Pliosaurs were relatives of the plesiosaurs but had shorter necks and massive skulls armed with enormous teeth. They were the largest and most powerful predators ever known.

Turtles also developed at about the same time. Unlike modern ones, the early forms did not have a complete shell.

FACT FILE

Although looking at them you might think a crocodile is a dinosaur, you would be wrong. They both evolved from the same type of ancestors and crocodiles have changed very little over millions of years.

WHAT SIZE WERE PTEROSAURS?

Various reptiles have developed the ability to glide, but the pterosaurs were the only ones to develop true flight. Their arms were quite short and their wings were supported by an enormously long fourth finger, leaving the other fingers free to function as a hand. A thin, skin-like membrane was stretched from the elongated finger to the sides of the body, and sometimes to the hind legs.

The whole body was extremely light with hollow bones. Many pterosaurs lived a similar life to the modern seagull and albatross. One pterosaur discovered, the Quetzalcoatlus, had a wing span greater than 48 ft (15 m) which is larger than that of many light planes.

FACT FILE

The Pterodactylus was a very small flying reptile, smaller than a modern pigeon and much lighter in build. It had a wing span of 40cm across, which means it would have been a fast and agile flyer.

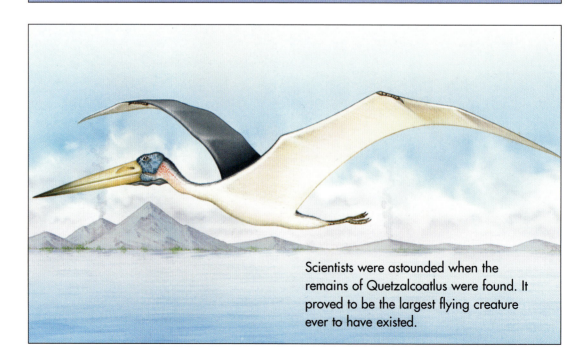

Scientists were astounded when the remains of Quetzalcoatlus were found. It proved to be the largest flying creature ever to have existed.

HOW DID PTEROSAURS FLY?

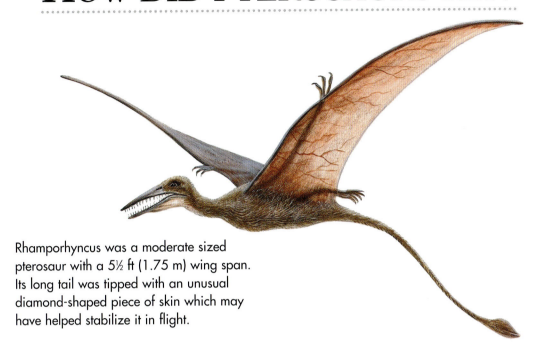

Rhamporhyncus was a moderate sized pterosaur with a 5½ ft (1.75 m) wing span. Its long tail was tipped with an unusual diamond-shaped piece of skin which may have helped stabilize it in flight.

It was believed at one time that the pterosaurs were unable to flap their wings and fly like a bird. They probably launched themselves off cliffs and glided on upward currents of air.

More recently, however, it has been suggested that pterosaurs were actually very efficient flyers. Some of the smallest types would not have been very effective gliders and must have fluttered their wings like modern birds. This would not have been possible for the giant pterosaurs, which must have been pure gliders.

Pterosaurs did not have feathers, because their large wings were more like those of a bat than a bird. However, pterosaurs did have fur! This seems to suggest that they were warm-blooded, as there would be no point in the body of a cold-blooded creature, such as a modern reptile, being insulated.

FACT FILE

The small predatory therapod dinosaur Campsognathus resembles Archaeopteryx so closely that the remains of the two animals have sometimes been confused. This seems to prove the dinosaur ancestry to birds.

WHY DID THE DINOSAURS DIE OUT?

Dinosaurs lived for a long time – some 150 million years – before they died out about 65 million years ago. During their time on the Earth they dominated the land, while other reptile relatives dominated the sea and the air. Before the dinosaurs disappeared completely there were two mass extinctions when a large number of species died out. The dinosaurs survived, however, until the end of the Cretaceous Period.

Many people believe that dinosaurs became extinct as a result of climate change after a huge meteor or a small asteroid struck the Earth.

The other theory is that it coincided with a period of high volcanic activity, which could have wiped out the whole population. However, it was not only the dinosaurs that became extinct. At the same time most marine reptiles and pterosaurs also died out as did tiny plankton whose shells form chalk deposits, ammonites and the remaining species of trilobites. It is difficult to imagine the exact causes of this extinction. For instance, how did turtles manage to survive?

High volcanic activity could have contributed to the dinosaurs' extinction.

DID CLIMATE AFFECT THE DINOSAURS' SURVIVAL?

During the late Cretaceous Period the world's continents were drifting into new positions. This constant shifting within the crust led to a huge increase in volcanic activity. Volcanoes spewed out hot lava and gases, which could have built up in the atmosphere to such high levels that they affected dinosaurs and their plant food.

Other climatic changes like an ice age may have wiped out many species of dinosaur that were unable to adapt to the extreme cold.

FACT FILE

The Earth went through some incredible climate changes during the era of the dinosaurs and one of the theories regarding their extinction would have been an extreme ice age. There are very few plants or animals that could have survived this extreme cold.

HOW DID MAMMALS EVOLVE?

A group of mammal-like reptiles preceded the appearance of the dinosaurs. These early mammals gradually disappeared, however, during the Triassic Period and were replaced by the true mammals.

It is hard to decide exactly which of these extinct animals was a reptile and which was a mammal. It is quite probable that the later reptiles had hair and other mammal-like characteristics. The first mammals were small and were vulnerable to all the fierce dinosaur predators. Once the dinosaurs died out the mammals were able to develop properly and evolve. Eventually the mammals grew into forms that were almost as gigantic as their dinosaur predecessors.

Thylacosmilus

Thylacosmilus was a typical example of the sabre-tooth cats, with long canine teeth that were used to stab its prey.

FACT FILE

Mammoths closely resembled modern elephants but were covered with thick, coarse hair and were adapted to live in the cold tundra regions. They survived in northern Arctic regions until well after the appearance of man, who hunted them to extinction.

ARE MARSUPIALS SIMILAR TO THE FIRST MAMMALS?

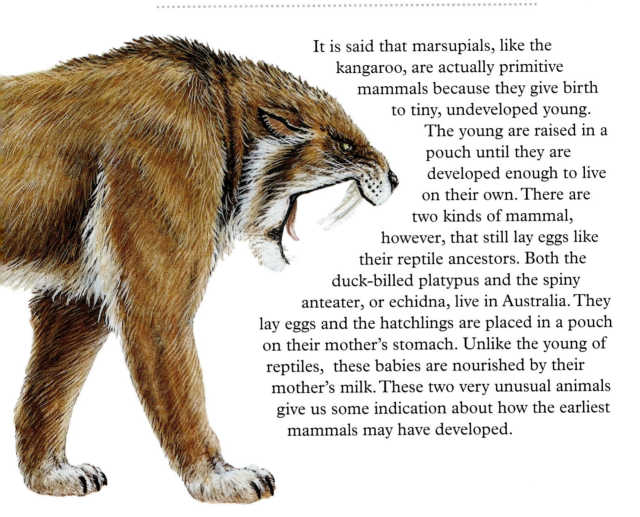

It is said that marsupials, like the kangaroo, are actually primitive mammals because they give birth to tiny, undeveloped young. The young are raised in a pouch until they are developed enough to live on their own. There are two kinds of mammal, however, that still lay eggs like their reptile ancestors. Both the duck-billed platypus and the spiny anteater, or echidna, live in Australia. They lay eggs and the hatchlings are placed in a pouch on their mother's stomach. Unlike the young of reptiles, these babies are nourished by their mother's milk. These two very unusual animals give us some indication about how the earliest mammals may have developed.

FACT FILE

Also known as Zeuglodon, Basilosaurus is the most commonly found of the ancient fossil whales. It was a predator like modern dolphins. When whales die their remains usually sink in deep water where they are unlikely to form fossils.

The Human Body

Bones & Muscles

WHICH BONES FORM THE PELVIS?

The pelvis is formed by two large symmetrical hip bones, which are joined in front as the pubic symphysis. In the back, they are attached firmly to the sacrum. In adults, each hip bone appears to be one solid bone, but in fact consists of three bones, the ilium, ischium, and pubis, that bind together as the body grows. When you put your hand on your hip, the broad, flat bone you can feel is the ilium; sitting down, your weight rests on the ischium.

Supporting the lower abdomen, the pelvis is a bony structure surrounding the urinary bladder, the last portion of the large intestine, and also, in females, the reproductive organs – hence a woman's pelvis is broader and flatter than a man's, with a larger central cavity.

FACT FILE

The pelvis is joined to the spinal column at the sacroiliac joints. The lower part of the pelvis connects wth the thigh bones, or femurs, via ball-and-socket hip joints, enabling the legs to move in various positions.

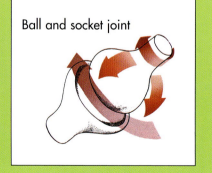

Ball and socket joint

HOW MANY MUSCLES ARE THERE IN THE HUMAN BODY?

There are over 600 major muscles in the human body, or which about 240 have particular names. These muscles are divided into two main types, skeletal muscles and smooth muscles. A third type, which shares characteristics with skeletal and smooth muscles, and is only to be found in the heart, is called a cardiac muscle.

Holding the bones of the skeleton together, skeletal muscles enable the body to move as well as giving it its shape, and they form a large part of our face, neck, abdomen, arms and legs. The larger the job, the larger the muscle is generally the rule, so they can vary in size from the thigh muscles that have to be big and strong to the eye muscles that are small and fairly weak.

FACT FILE

Cardiac muscle makes up the walls of the heart. When cardiac muscle cells contract, they push blood out of the heart and into the arteries.

WHERE ARE THE SMOOTH MUSCLES FOUND?

The smooth muscles work slowly and automatically in a natural, rhythmic way, contracting then relaxing, controlling our many body processes. For example, the steady action of these muscles in the stomach and intestines moves food along for digestion. Smooth muscles are to be found in the walls of the stomach, intestines, blood vessels and bladder, and because they are not consciously controlled by the brain, we also know them as involuntary muscles. They react instead to stimulus from particular nerves that are part of the autonomic nervous system, and also to the effect of certain body chemicals.

Cardiac muscle

Smooth muscles

Skeletal muscles

FACT FILE

Muscle cells are excitable because the membrane of each cell is electrically charged. Thus, a muscle cell is said to have electric potential.

WHAT IS BONE MADE FROM?

(A)

Blood and lymph vessels in central canal

Haversian system

Bone formation

Periosteum

Section through A

A typical bone (A) is actually made of two types of bony tissue. On the outside is a type of 'skin' called the periosteum. Below this is a thin layer of thick, dense, 'solid' bone. It is known as hard or compact bony tissue. Inside this, and forming the bulk of the middle of the bone, is a different bony tissue, more like a sponge or honeycomb. It has gaps and spaces, and it is called spongy, or alveolar, bony tissue. It is much lighter than the outer compact bone, and the spaces are filled with blood vessels, and jelly-like bone marrow for making new blood cells.

FACT FILE

There are 206 bones in the average body. However, there are a few people who have more, such as an extra pair of ribs, making 13 pairs instead of 12 and therefore 208 bones in total.

HOW DO MUSCLES WORK?

There are 639 muscles in the human body, each comprising around ten million muscle cells. Each of these cells is like a motor containing ten cylinders arranged in a row. The cylinders are tiny boxes that contain fluid and when a muscle contracts the brain sends a message to these tiny boxes. For a fraction of a second, the fluid in the tiny box congeals; then it becomes fluid again. It is this action that causes the muscle to move. When a muscle is stimulated into action, it reacts quickly – it may contract in less than one tenth of a second. But before it has time to relax, another message comes along. It contracts again and again. All these contractions take place so quickly that they become fused into one action with the result that the muscle performs one smooth, continuous action.

orbicularis oculi
(narrows eye)

sternocleido mastoid
(tilts head)

pectoral
(turns arm)

bicep
(lifts arm)

sartorius
(moves leg)

adductors
(straightens knee)

quadriceps
(bends knee)

gastrocnemius
(lifts ankle)

soleus
(holds ankle)

FACT FILE

When two muscles work against each other, they are always slightly contracted. This is called muscle tone. Active people tend to have better

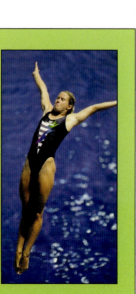

HOW DO JOINTS WORK?

The human body has more than 100 joints. Some joints move like a simple hinge, such as those in the elbows and knees. Other joints move in all directions, such as the shoulder joint or the base of the thumb. Joints in the spine allow only a small amount of movement. The ends of most bones are covered with tough rubbery cartilage, which cushions them from impact as we move. Many joints are lubricated with an oily liquid called synovial fluid so they can bend freely. Synovial fluid is held in a bladder between the layers of cartilage on the ends of the bone. These lubricated joints can move freely and without friction.

Thigh bone

Patella

Synovial fluid

Cartilage

Shin bone

The knee joint

FACT FILE

Regular exercise improves muscle strength and endurance, and keeps the body supple. It can also improve your body shape and posture as well as strengthening your heart and improving your blood flow. It will generally make you feel much better and help you to sleep soundly

Opposing muscles in the arm

biceps
relaxed

triceps
relaxed

biceps
contracted
to lift arm

triceps
contracted to
straighten arm

HOW CAN MUSCLES WORK IN PAIRS?

Muscles actually work in pairs. A muscle can only pull in one direction so it needs another muscle to pull in the opposite direction in order to return a bone to its original position. When you lift your forearm, the biceps muscle shortens to lift the bone. When you straighten your arm, the triceps muscle pulls it back again and the biceps relaxes. The same action takes place in your legs when you walk and run, and when you move your fingers and toes.

FACT FILE

Metabolism is the sum of all chemical activity in our cells which break down the food we take in. Our metabolic rate increases with exercise, which means that we use the energy we get from food much more efficiently.

HOW DO MUSCLES RESPOND TO ACTIVITY?

Muscles are made up of long, thin cells called muscle fibres. But muscles differ in what they do and how they do it. When a muscle contracts, it produces an acid known as lactic acid. This acid is like a poison, with the effect of making you feel tired, by making the muscles feel tired. If the lactic acid is removed from a tired muscle, it stops feeling tired and you can go right to work again!

But, of course, lactic acid is not removed normally when you exercise and various toxins are produced when muscles are active. They are carried by the blood through the body and cause tiredness throughout the entire body, especially in the brain. So feeling tired after exercise is really the result of a kind of internal poisoning.

However, the body needs this feeling of tiredness so that it will want to rest. During rest, waste products are removed, the cells recuperate, nerve cells of the brain recharge their batteries and the joints replace their supplies of lubricant they have used up. So while exercise is good for the body and muscles – rest is just as important!

FACT FILE

The knee is a typical load-bearing joint. The ends of the bone are cushioned by a pad of cartilage to protect them from impact. Wear and tear is minimized by a lubricant called synovial fluid.

HOW DOES A BROKEN BONE HEAL?

When mending a broken bone, we – or our doctors – are helped in amazing ways by the body itself. The core to this is bone tissue, produced by the connective tissue cells in the broken bone. When a bone is broken, bone and tissue around the break are also damaged and some of this tissue dies. The entire area around the bone ends and tissue is held together by a combination of lymph and clotted blood.

The first stage in repairing a break comes after a few hours, when young new tissue cells start to appear. The cells multiply very quickly, becoming filled with calcium, and in between 72 to 96 hours after the fracture, they form a tissue which bonds the ends of the bones. Over the next few months normal bone develops, after the calcium which has been deposited in the newly formed tissue helpd form hard bone. This is why, to keep the edges of the break in strict alignment by not allowing the bone to move while this process is taking place, a plaster cast is put on a broken limb.

The human skeleton

FACT FILE

Constant use helps to keep the bones strong. Lack of exercise is one of the main reasons why elderly people's bones can become so weak and prone to easy breakage.

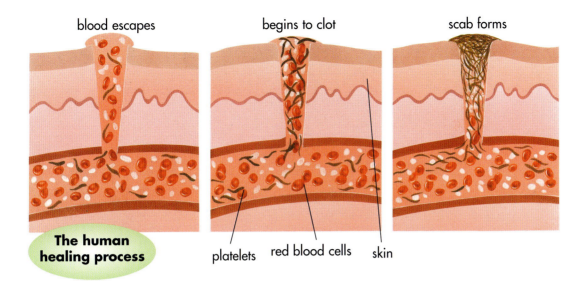

blood escapes

begins to clot

scab forms

The human healing process

platelets   red blood cells   skin

HOW DO CUTS AND GRAZES HEAL THEMSELVES?

When we cut or graze ourselves, the body is able to heal itself. When the skin incurs a wound, platelets in the blood congregate at the site of the wound to form a temporary clot. This usually happens as soon as a wound is exposed to the air. This quickly plugs the wound.

White blood cells gather around the wound site to kill invading microbes, helping to prevent infection. New cells eventually grow into the wound replacing the damaged tissue. For a small cut or graze, this usually takes a couple of days. Soon the clotted material, which has formed a scab, falls off to reveal clean, new skin underneath. Sometimes we protect our grazes and cuts with plasters whilst our bodies deal with the repair.

FACT FILE

Cells need food, oxygen and water to survive. Food and water are supplied by blood and other body fluids, which also carry away wastes. Blood also contains food and chemicals needed by the cell.

cell membrane

mitochondria

nucleus

cytoplasm

151

WHERE IS THE SMALLEST BONE IN YOUR BODY?

The smallest bone in the body is called the stirrup. It is in the middle ear and is part of the system that carries sound signals to the brain. At only 3mm long, the stirrup is about the size of a grain of rice. The footplate of the stirrup bone is attached to a membrane called the oval window, which leads to the inner ear. It is connected to two other very small bones called the hammer and anvil. All three of these bones are joined to the eardrum, where sound is collected before it is sent in the form of nerve signals to the brain.

The ear is a very important organ for keeping our sense of balance. Without a sense of balance, we could not hold our body steady, and we would stagger and fall when we tried to move.

FACT FILE

Some people suffer from motion sickness when they travel by boat, car, train, or airplane. Motion sickness is caused by excessive stimulation of the vestibular organs. But researchers do not know why some people develop motion sickness more easily than others do.

WHERE ARE THE VERTEBRAE?

The spine, which is also known as the spinal column, vertebral column, or backbone, is that part of the skeleton that extends down the middle of the back, and is made up of a column of bones called vertebrae. It plays a crucial part in our posture and movement, and also protects the all-important spinal cord.

Although some grow together later in life, the human spine basically consists of 33 vertebrae. There are 7 cervical (neck), 12 thoracic (chest region), 5 lumbar (lower back), 5 sacral (hip region), and 4 coccygeal (tailbone region) vertebrae. They are secured in place by a combination of muscles and strong connective tissue called ligaments. Most have fibrous intervertebral disks between them in order to absorb shock and enable the spine, which normally has a slight natural curve, to bend.

FACT FILE

Many people suffer from backaches. Sometimes the inter tebral disk, the tissue that lies between the vertebrae, sticks out and presses on nerves. This condition is called a slipped disk. It can cause severe pain in the lower back, thighs, and legs.

Cross-section of the spinal column

The spine

WHERE IS THE LARGEST JOINT IN THE BODY?

The knee joint is the largest and most complex joint in the body. The knee is the joint where the thighbone meets the large bone of the lower leg. The knee moves like a hinge, but it can also rotate and move a little from side to side. The knee is more likely to be damaged than most other joints because it is subject to tremendous forces during vigorous activity. Most of the knee injuries that occur in football and other sports result from twisting the joint. The knee ligaments are the strongest connections between the femur and the tibia. Ligaments keep the bones from moving out of position.

Patella

Tibia

Fibula

FACT FILE

The patella (or kneecap) is a small, flat, triangular bone in front of the joint. It is not directly connected with any other bone. Muscle attachments hold it in place.

Patella

WHERE IS THE LARGEST MUSCLE IN THE BODY?

The largest muscle in the human body is called the gluteus maximus and this is situated in the buttocks, while the smallest is the stapedius which can be found in the middle ear. A muscle is the tough, elastic tissue that makes body parts move. Muscles are found throughout the body. As a person grows, the muscles also get bigger. Muscle makes up nearly half the body weight of an adult.

Of over 600 muscles in the human body, no less than 240 have specific names. They fall into two main categories, skeletal muscles and smooth muscles, while a third type, called cardiac muscle and only to be found in the heart, has similrities to both the skeletal and smooth muscles. People use muscles to make various movements.

Gluteus maximus

FACT FILE

The longest muscle is the sartorius, which runs from the side of the waist, diagonally down across the front of the thigh to the inside of the knee. Among the most powerful muscles are the masseters, one on each side of the face.

Masseters

WHY IS EXERCISE GOOD FOR US?

Regular exercise is important because it keeps bones, joints and muscles healthy. During any physical exertion, the rate at which the heart beats increases, as it pumps more oxygenated blood around the body. How quickly the heart rate returns to normal after exercise is one way to assess how fit someone is and how exercise is actually improving their fitness.

Once almost everyone did manual work of some kind. It was essential for survival. Human bodies were not designed for the inactive lives many of us now lead. That is why exercise is important for good health.

FACT FILE

Swimming is a very good form of exercise as it uses lots of muscles without causing strain.

WHY DO MUSCLES ACHE AFTER EXERCISE?

FACT FILE

It is important to stretch your muscles before and after exercise to distribute the lactic acid.

After any kind of exercise the muscles will contract, and in doing so produce an acid called lactic acid. Acting almost like a 'poison', the immediate effect will be to make the individual tired by having a 'tiring' effect on the muscles. Once this acid disappears from a muscle, it stops feeling tired and can function normally.

But this type of body 'poisoning' serves a purpose in that by making a person tired they will want to rest, it being during periods of rest that the joints of the body are able to replace the necessary lubricants that have been used up.

WHY DO WE HAVE A SKELETON?

A skeleton is made up of a network of bones. Bones provide a framework that holds the whole body together.

Without a skeleton we would not be supported and would simply flop about like a rag doll. This would mean that we would not be able to move about.

The skeleton also gives protection to delicate organs in our bodies such as the brain, heart and lungs. It acts as a support to all the soft parts of the body. The skeleton also provides a system of levers that the muscles can work on, enabling us to carry out all our movements.

FACT FILE

At birth a baby has 300 bones, but 94 join together in early childhood. Your hand and wrist alone contain 27 bones.

skull

collarbone

breastbone

rib

backbone

Heart & Circulation

WHERE IS OUR CIRCULATORY SYSTEM?

Heart

Arteries
(red)

Veins (blue)

The aortic and pulmonic valves are in the heart. The network that carries blood throughout the body is an amazing natural device known as the circulatory system. Not only does it supply the cells of the body with the food and oxygen they need to survive, it carries carbon dioxide and other waste matter away from the cells, helps regulate the bodie's temperature and transports elements that protect the body from disease. The network also allows the movement of chemical substances called hormones, which help regulate and stabilize the functioning of various parts of the body. The blood vessels, which form a complex system of connecting tubes throughout the body, fall into three major categories. The arteries transport blood from the heart, the veins return the blood back to the heart, while the capillaries are minute vessels that connect the arteries and the veins.

FACT FILE

The three main parts of the human circulatory system are the heart, the blood vessels, and the blood. In addition a watery fluid called lymph, and the vessels that carr it, are often thought of as part of the circulatory system.

The circulatory system

Heart

WHERE ARE THE AORTIC AND PULMONIC VALVES?

The heart pumps blood on both sides at the same time. The right ventricle contracts, sending blood to the lungs, while the left ventricle contracts and squeezes blood out to the body. There are two stages in the heart's cycle of activity, called systole and diastole. The systole stage happens when the ventricles contract, and the diastole stage occurs when the ventricles relax and the atria contract. One full cycle of contraction and relaxation makes a heartbeat, and is known as the cardiac cycle. During every cardiac cycle, the heart valves open and close, and it's the closing of the valves that makes the pulsing sound of a heartbeat, which doctors listen to with a stethoscope. With the ventricles' contraction the mitral and tricuspid valves close, creating the first sound ①. As soon as the valves close, pressure in the ventricles forces the aortic and pulmonic valves to open ②. After a contraction ends, the ventricle pressure drops ③, the aortic and pulmonic valves closing and causing most of the second heart sound ④.

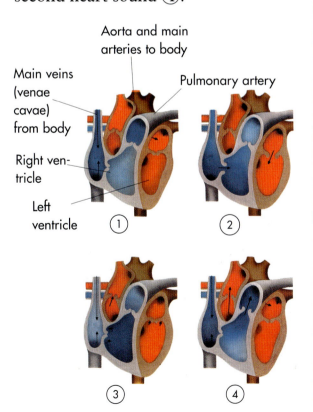

Aorta and main arteries to body

Main veins (venae cavae) from body

Pulmonary artery

Right ventricle

Left ventricle

① ②

③ ④

FACT FILE

The heart of an average person at rest beats 60 to 80 times each minute. Each beat sends about $2\frac{1}{2}$ fl oz (.75 dl) of blood out of each ventricle. This means that, at rest, the heart pumps some $2\frac{1}{2}$ gallons (9.5 litres) of blood each minute.

WHY DOESN'T BLOOD FLOW BACKWARDS?

Blood is transported to the heart by means of blood vessels called veins, part of the whole system of blood vessels via which blood circulates. The blood in your veins travels quite slowly, and many large veins have valves to stop the blood from draining backwards towards the legs and feet.

Blood flowing forwards forces the valve flaps to open ①. Blood flowing back forces them to shut ②. The valves in the heart work in exactly the same way.

Blood is also helped along by the arm and leg muscles contracting. That is why, if you stand still for a long period of time, blood can collect in your legs and make them puffy and sore.

FACT FILE

The lymphatic system is one of the body's defences against infection. Harmful particles and bacteria that have entered the body are filtered out by small masses of tissue that lie along the lymphatic vessels. These bean-shaped masses are called lymph nodes.

WHERE ARE THE JUGULAR VEINS SITUATED?

There are four large veins that return blood to the heart from the head and neck, called jugular veins. They get their name from the Latin word for collarbone, jugulus. The jugular veins are situted on either side of the neck, each side having an external and internal jugular. The external jugulars carry blood from external parts of the head and neck to the heart and are close to the surface, while the internal jugulars lie deeper, with blood from the deeper neck tissues of the neck and the interior of the skull. 'Going for the jugular' is a well-known phrase, referring to opening the much larger internal jugular vein, which usually proves fatal, because of the rapid loss of blood that invariably occurs.

FACT FILE

Whiplash is a term commonly used to describe a type of injury to the neck. This kind of injury results from a sudden blow that throws the head rapidly backward and forward.

Jugular vein

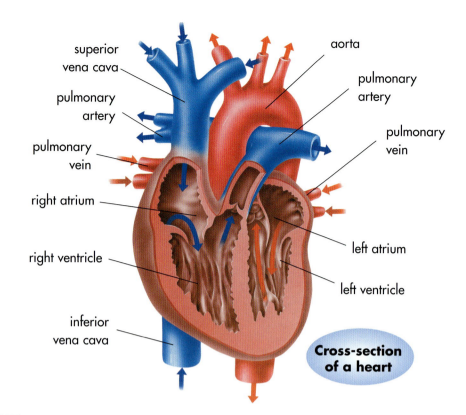

superior
vena cava

aorta

pulmonary
artery

pulmonary
artery

pulmonary
vein

pulmonary
vein

right atrium

left atrium

right ventricle

left ventricle

inferior
vena cava

Cross-section
of a heart

HOW DOES THE HEART WORK?

The heart is a fist-sized muscular organ that pumps blood around the body. It is actually two pumps that are joined together. At the top of each side of the heart is a thin-walled chamber called the atrium which receives blood that returns to the heart through the veins. Once the atrium is filled, it contracts and squeezes its blood into a much more muscular chamber called the ventricle. The ventricle contracts in turn and forces blood at high pressure along the arteries and off to the lungs or the rest of the body. A system of one way valves stops the blood from leaking back into the heart. The left side of the heart pumps blood to the lungs to collect more oxygen.

FACT FILE

An electrocardiogram, or ECG, measures the electrical signals that the heart produces as it beats. These signals change when a person suffers from certain medical conditions that affect the heart. They are measured by attaching wires to the chest near the heart. A doctor can study results as printed information.

WHAT IS BLOOD MADE FROM?

Blood components

Small and large lymphocyte

Monocyte

Platelets

Red blood cells

Blood is the fluid that is pumped around the body in the circulatory system. Blood carries oxygen, which it picks up in the lungs. It distributes this oxygen to all body parts, since every body cell needs a regular supply of oxygen to stay alive. Blood is made up of many components and has many functions. It consists of a yellow fluid, called plasma, in which red and white blood corpuscles and platelets are suspended. The capillaries allow fluid to escape from the blood. The cells and large proteins are left in the vessel and this fluid can now become the interstitial fluid (a background fluid that acts as an active support). This will either return to the capillary or join the lymphatic system. Blood amounts to about one-third of the total interstitial fluid.

The red and white blood cells are formed in the bone marrow. The plasma occupies about 55 percent of the blood volume. It is 90 percent water, 7 percent proteins, with the remaining 3 percent made up of small molecules.

FACT FILE

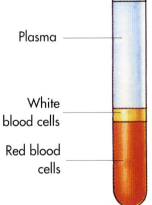

Blood is warm and works like the liquid in a central heating system. It absorbs warmth from the busy parts such as the heart and muscles and spreads it out to cooler parts like the skin.

Plasma

White blood cells

Red blood cells

WHAT IS BLOOD CLOTTING?

When you cut yourself, the blood clots to prevent the wound from bleeding. Clotting is caused by substances in the blood. Together with small particles called platelets, these substances produce masses of fine mesh when they are exposed to air. They block the wound and prevent more blood loss. New cells grow rapidly into the wound, replacing the damaged tissue. Soon the clotted material, called a scab, falls off and clean, new skin is revealed underneath.

FACT FILE

Your blood pressure can be measured by a doctor with a special blood pressure monitor. During sleep your blood pressure decreases slightly, and during exercise and emotional excitement it increases.

Tissue factor

Fibrinogen

①

Platelet

Plasma factor

Stages of blood clotting

③

②

④

Red blood cell   Fibrin

WHAT IS LYMPH?

Your body's main attack force is called the lymph system. Like the blood system, it is a set of vessels which carry liquid round the body. This liquid is called lymph. Lymph contains special white blood cells called lymphocytes. These can make substances called antibodies which fight germs and cope with poisons. It works in the following way: The fluid passes out of the capillary ① and either into the vein or into the smallest, thin-walled lymph vessel ②. These vessels join together to form large channels and finally reach the thoracic duct running next to the descending aorta. This duct joins one of the main branches of the superior vena cava ⑤. Valves ③ keep lymph flowing in one direction. Lymph glands ④ are found throughout the body and at places where lymph vessels unite ⑥.

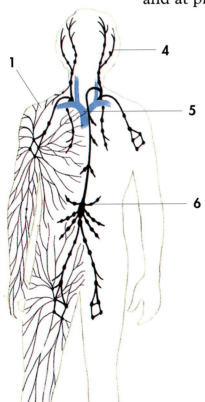

FACT FILE

Bacteria are tiny, single-celled organisms. They can measure as little as 0.001mm across and they can only be seen under a microscope. There are many different sorts of bacteria, and most of them are harmless.

167

WHEN DO PEOPLE GET HEART ATTACKS?

Your heart is a powerful muscle which pumps blood around your body. It is only the size of your fist and weighs less than half a kilogram. Each and every day it pumps about 18,000 litres of blood around your body, and yet you are not normally aware that it is even beating. Run quickly upstairs, though, and you will soon feel it thumping away inside your rib cage.

A heart attack can occur when the inability of either or both sides of the heart to pump sufficient blood to meet the needs of our body. Other prominent causes of a heart attack are abnormally high blood pressure (hypertension), coronary atherosclerosis (the presence of fatty deposits in the lining of the coronary arteries), and rheumatic heart disease.

A person with left-sided heart failure experiences shortness of breath after exertion, difficulty in breathing while lying down, spasms of breathlessness at night, and abnormally high pressure in the pulmonary veins. A person with right-sided failure experiences abnormally high pressure in the systemic veins, enlargement of the liver, and accumulation of fluid in the legs. A person with failure of both ventricles has an enlarged heart that beats in gallop rhythm – that is, in groups of three sounds rather than two.

FACT FILE

Sometimes the heart valves become stiff or leaky. They can be replaced by valves made from tissue taken from an animal, or by artificial valves made of metal and plastic.

Main veins from body

Aorta and main arteries to body

Pulmonary arteries to lungs

WHEN DOES THE HEART STOP BEATING?

The heart

— aorta
— superior vena cava

— pulmonary artery

— pulmonary valve

— pulmonary veins
— atria
— aortic valve
— mitral valve
— chordae tendineae
— tricuspid valve
— papillary muscle
— ventricles

— inferior vena cava

Your heart is a muscular pump that never stops beating. It has its own timing device that produces tiny electrical signals. These signals cause the heart muscle to contract rhythmically. The pump on the right side of the heart receives blood that has been pumped around the body. This blood is dark red and has used up most of its oxygen. The right pump sends it on a short circuit through the lungs that surround the heart. The blood comes back bright red and rich in oxygen, to the heart's left side, ready for its journey around the body. When the heart stops beating, body tissues no longer receive fresh blood carrying oxygen and nutrients. So life ends.

However, in a hospital, the cardiopulmonary machine can take over the job of heart and lungs. This means doctors can resuscitate people or carry out operations on the heart, such as replacing diseased valves.

FACT FILE

When the body is very active, the heart can pump 20 gallons (76 litres) of blood each minute. That would fill a bathtub within two minutes.

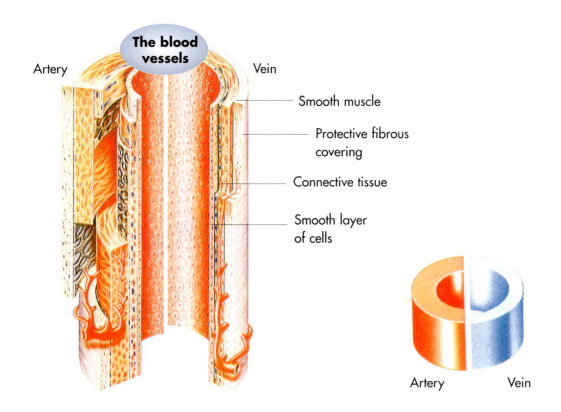

The blood vessels

Artery

Vein

Smooth muscle

Protective fibrous covering

Connective tissue

Smooth layer of cells

Artery   Vein

WHEN DOES BLOOD FLOW FROM VEINS TO ARTERIES?

Your body has an amazingly complex and delicate system of blood vessels, carrying blood to every nook and cranny, and then returning to the heart. These vessels are called arteries and veins and they are both tubes made up of four different layers. The arteries carry the blood away from the heart and the veins return it.

The veins frequently anastomose (or join together) with each other so that the blood flow can alter direction. This is caused if there is any constriction or pressure from movement of muscles or ligaments.

FACT FILE

Just over half of blood is plasma, which contains hundreds of dissolved substances, from sugars for energy, to hormones, to wastes like carbon dioxide.

WHEN DO RED AND WHITE BLOOD CELLS DIE?

Both white and red blood cells are formed in the bone marrow. Each red blood cell measure about 7.5 microns (thousandths of a milli-metre) in diameter and are shaped a little like doughnuts. They contain haemoglobin, which gives their red pigment. There are 5 to 6 million red cells per cubic mm of blood. The red cell only survives about 120 days and the damaged and old cells are removed by the spleen and liver.

A white blood cell is not really white but almost transparent. It can change shape, push out folds and finger-like projections and move along by oozing and crawling like an amoeba in a pond. These cells survive less than a week.

lymphocyte

red blood cell

stem cell

monocyte

white blood cells

Inside the bone marrow

WHEN ARE OUR BLOOD GROUPS DETERMINED?

Receptor	A	B	AB	O
Donor A				
B				
AB				
O				

Our individual blood group is determined by our parents at the time of our conception. Blood groups are determined by the presence of antigens (a substance capable of stimulating an immune response) on the surfaces of the red cells. Although the red blood cells in different people look the same they are, in fact, dissimilar. They can be divided up into four main groups: A, B, AB and O.

Blood can be transplanted from one person to another by what we call a blood transfusion. It is very important that the blood given matches the person's group, because if the wrong types of blood are mixed together the result can be serious blood clots.

FACT FILE

Blood begins to clot as soon as it is exposed to the air, plugging the wound. White blood cells gather around the wound to kill invading microbes, and new skin cells grow into the healing wound beneath the scab.

Brain & Nervous System

WHAT IS THE AUTONOMIC NERVOUS SYSTEM?

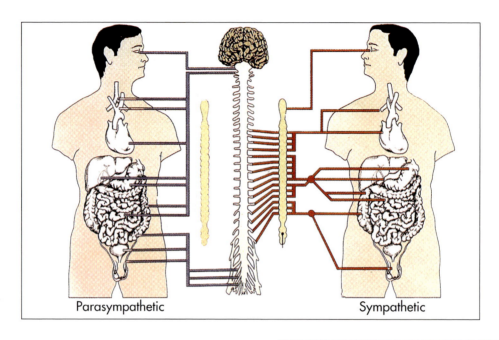

Parasympathetic

Sympathetic

There are many processes, like breathing and digestion, which it would be impossible for the body to regulate by conscious control from the brain. In order that these can function 'automatically', we have what is called an autonomic nervous system, which consists of two elements, the *sympathetic* and the *parasympathetic* system. The parasympathetic nerves tend to make the body calm and relaxed, and slow down processes such as digestion and heartbeat. The sympathetic nerves speed up all these processes and activities, so that the body is ready to spring into action. Between them, these two nerve sets fine-tune the body's internal conditions.

FACT FILE

The whole of the autonomic system is controlled by an area of the brain called the hypothalamus. This receives information about any variations in your body.

HOW DO NERVE IMPULSES WORK?

A nerve impulse is like a very simple message: either on or off. Because there are so many neurones which are connected to one another, this simple signal is enough to carry the most complicated messages throughout the whole of the body's nervous system. As a nerve impulse arrives at the junction between two nerve cells, it is carried across the gap or synapse by chemicals called neurotransmitters. These contact sensitive areas in the next nerve cell, and the nerve impulse is carried along.

nerve gap
(or synapse)

nerve
membrane

neurotransmitter

**Anatomy of a
nerve cell junction**

arriving nerve
impulse

vesicle (stores drops
of neurotransmitter)

FACT FILE

Scientists have produced maps showing how electrical activity in one part of the brain can cause a movement or other reaction. This mapping has been done during brain surgery. As there are no sense organs in the brain it is possible to operate on people who are fully conscious, without them feeling any pain. This enables doctors to know which part of the brain has been damaged after an accident.

HOW ARE MESSAGES PASSED THROUGH THE NERVOUS SYSTEM?

Nerve impulses that pass through the nervous system are able to jump from one neurone to the next. Inside the nerve fibre, the nerve impulse travels as an electrical signal. When it reaches the end of the long fibre, it jumps across to the next neurone by means of a chemical transmitter. This chemical is released from the branched ends of the fibre. As this transmitter substance contacts the next neurone, it starts another nerve impulse. This whole process is very fast, and nerve impulses travel along the largest nerve fibres at 295 ft (90m) per second.

FACT FILE

A long thread or axon extends from the body of a neurone, and it is along this that nerve impulses are carried.

brain

spinal cord

radial nerve

median nerve

sciatic nerve

tibial nerve

deep peroneal nerve

dorsal cutaneous nerve

The human nervous sytem

Cerebrum

Cross-section of the human brain

Brain stem

Cerebellum

HOW DOES THE BRAIN WORK?

FACT FILE

Each side of the brain controls the opposite side of the body. Usually the left side controls speaking, writing and logical thought, while the right controls artistic abilities. This musician is using the right side of his brain.

The brain is the body's control centre. It coordinates all the messages that pass through the nervous system, giving us the ability to learn, reason and feel. It also controls the body's automatic functions such as breathing, heartbeat, digestion, growth and blood pressure.

The brain is divided into three main regions each with a different function. The large part at the top is the cerebrum, where most of our thinking, reasoning and memory is controlled. The cerebellum is a smaller area at the back where both accurate movement and coordination are controlled. The brain stem is a small region at the base where most of our automatic body functions are processed and controlled.

Areas of the brain and their responsibilities

Movement area

Touch area

Hearing area

Vision area

Thought area

Speech area

HOW DOES MY MEMORY WORK?

Memory is the ability to store things that you experience and learn, ready for use in the future. Some things are remembered easily, such as dramatic events in our life. However, more ordinary things need to be rehearsed several times before they 'stick'.

There are three different ways of storing memory. Sensory memory, which is very brief, tells you what is happening around you and allows you to move without bumping into things. Short-term memory, which lasts for only about 30 seconds, and allows you to remember a phone number and dial it, but after a minute or so it will vanish. Finally long-term memory, for things that you have carefully memorized and learned.

FACT FILE

The sense of smell has powerful effects in retrieving memories. Often a smell, like the burning of a bonfire, can suddenly trigger a memory from many years ago.

WHERE IS THE CEREBRUM?

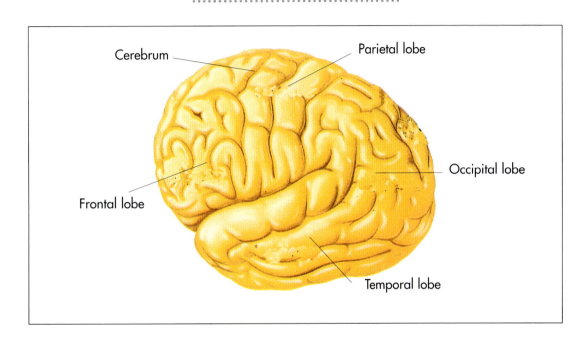

Cerebrum
Parietal lobe
Occipital lobe
Frontal lobe
Temporal lobe

FACT FILE

The brain stem is the vital control area of the brain and is concerned with maintaining all the essential regulatory mechanisms of the body: respiration, blood pressure, pulse rate, alertness and sleep.

The cerebrum is part of the brain, representing about 85 percent of its weight. It's divided into two halves, the left cerebral hemisphere and the right cerebral hemisphere, by a conspicuous groove called the longitudinal fissure.

The hemispheres themselves are joined by bundles of nerves, the largest being the corpus callosum, and are in turn divided into four lobes. The frontal lobe is at the front, the temporal lobe at the lower side, the parietal lobe in the middle and the occipital lobe at the back, each of these names being the same as the bone of the skull that it lies beneath.

WHAT ARE THE AREAS OF THE BRAIN CALLED?

Basically the brain can be divided into three different regions: hindbrain, midbrain and forebrain. Each of these regions is in turn divided into separate areas responsible for quite distinct functions, all intricately linked to other parts of the brain.

The largest structure in the hindbrain is called the cerebellum. The largest part of the entire brain is the cerebrum, which is located in the forebrain. It is more developed in humans than in any other animal. This is where the other parts of the brain send incoming messages for decision. The cerebral cortex is the thick wrinkled layer of grey matter folded over the outside of the cerebrum. This part of the brain has become so highly developed in humans that it has had to fold over and over in order to fit inside the skull. Unfolded, it would cover an area 30 times as large as when folded.

FACT FILE

Shivering is governed by four mechanisms. The hypothalamus, at the base of the brain, senses that the temperature is too low and sends messages to the thyroid gland, telling it to speed up the metabolic rate. The body muscles then alternately contract and relax rapidly, thus producing heat. The nerves then send messages to the skin and the skin pores narrow, ensuring that the heat is conserved within the body.

The human brain

Thalamus

Hypothalamus

Parietal lob

Frontal lobe

Temporal lobe

WHAT ARE THE THREE MAIN FUNCTIONS OF THE BRAIN?

The brain is the body's control centre. It keeps the body working smoothly and it looks after thoughts, feelings and memory.

Different parts of the brain have different jobs to do. The largest part is called the cerebrum, or forebrain. It looks like a huge half-walnut. The cerebrum's main job is to sort out and respond to messages sent to it from the senses. It also stores information, as memory, and it thinks. Messages from the senses are managed by the cerebrum's sensory area, while the motor area controls the muscles.

Thinking, memory and speech are managed by the parts known as the association areas. The cerebellum (or hindbrain) is below the cerebrum. It works with the cerebrum's motor area to ensure that the muscles function smoothly.

Cerebral cortex
(grey matter)

Cerebrum
(white matter)

Cerebellum

Spinal cord

FACT FILE

Although we have invented computers that can work out millions of different things in seconds, our brains can still outwork and outsmart them! Our brains control our bodies by sending out billions of tiny electrical signals every second.

WHAT CONTROLS OUR BALANCE?

The inner ear is the body's main organ of balance, but the brain also receives messages from nerve-endings in the neck, back, leg and feet muscles. The brain sifts all this information and sends messages back to the muscles, allowing us to perform incredible feats of balance such as ice-skating or gymnastics. Near the cochlea are fluid-filled tubes – the semicircular canals. As your head moves about, the fluid inside each canal swishes to and fro. When the body moves, the fluid causes hairs in a jelly-like mass to bend. These are connected to the vestibular nerve, which alerts the brain to re-balance the body.

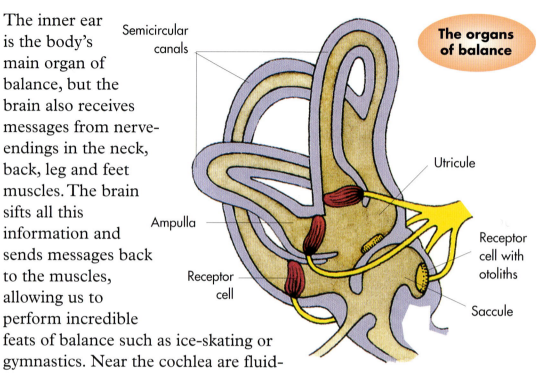

The organs of balance

Semicircular canals

Ampulla

Receptor cell

Utricule

Receptor cell with otoliths

Saccule

FACT FILE

You feel dizzy after you spin round and round because the liquid in your ears is still swirling about when you stop, and your brain can't tell where you're going! If you watch a dancer spin round, you will see that their head does not move continuously.

WHAT CONTROLS OUR TEMPERATURE?

FACT FILE

Body movements can also be homeostatic. A hot person may spread out arms and legs to increase heat loss; a cold person curls up to reduce the areas of the body losing warmth.

The name for 'constancy of the internal environment' is homeostasis. The body must regulate many body systems and processes to keep inner conditions stable. The temperature nucleus in the hypothalamus controls heat loss and production by the body through the skin. Overheating (A) causes an increased blood flow from the blood vessels (1), to radiate heat and causes sweating through the sweat glands (2), to lose heat. A fall in body temperature (B) constricts the surface blood vessels, stops sweating and makes the erector muscles (3) contract, causing the hairs (4) to stand on end, trapping air as an insulating layer. Additional heat can be produced by shivering.

Temperature control

WHEN DOES OUR SENSE OF TOUCH ALERT THE BRAIN OF DANGER?

Close your eyes and touch something, such as your clothes, a table, a car or even your own skin. Stroke it gently. What does it feel like? Is it hard or soft, hot or cold? The surface may be smooth, bumpy, gritty, furry or hairy. It could be dry, moist, or slimy. Your skin continuously passes huge amounts of information to the brain. It monitors touch, pain, temperature and other factors that tell the brain exactly how the body is being affected by its environment. Without this constant flow of information, you would keep injuring yourself accidentally, which is what happens in some rare diseases where the skin senses are lost. Senses in the skin are measured by tiny receptors at the ends of nerves. There are several different types of receptor. Each type can detect only one kind of sensation, such as pain, temperature, pressure, touch and so on.

FACT FILE

Sometimes we need drugs, or analgesics, to control a pain. Some drugs, such as aspirin, work by preventing the sensation of pain from reaching the brain.

Skin sensation

hair follicle nerve endings

WHEN DO WE USE OUR BRAIN TO SMELL?

The part of the brain that analyzes messages coming from the receiver cells in the nose is closely connected with the limbic system, that part of the brain that deals with emotions, moods and memory. It is called the primitive brain, sometimes even the 'smelling brain'. The connection explains why smells are richly supplied with emotional significance. The smell of fresh rain on a summer's day usually makes people feel happy and invigorated, and it may also evoke happy memories. The smell of fresh-baked bread may bring on instant pangs of hunger, while the scent of perfume may remind you of a loved one. On the other hand, unpleasant smells such as rotten eggs, produce revulsion and sometimes even nausea.

Certain smells will bring memories of long forgotten special occasions flooding back, as we tend to remember those things which have special emotional significance. This is because the areas of the brain which process memories are also closely linked to the limbic system, which in turn is linked to the areas in the brain that control the sense of smell.

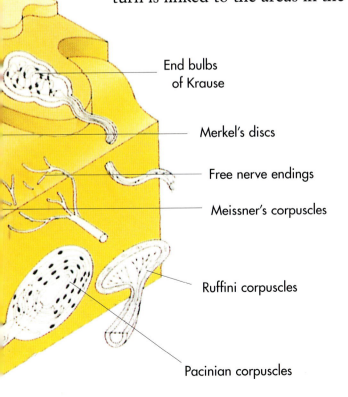

End bulbs of Krause

Merkel's discs

Free nerve endings

Meissner's corpuscles

Ruffini corpuscles

Pacinian corpuscles

FACT FILE

Aromatherapy is the art of using the perfumed essential oils of plants to treat the body and mind. The perfume passes over the nerve cells in the nasal passage and a message is sent to the brain.

WHY DO WE DREAM?

Whatever we dream, it is touched by our feelings, wishes, memories, fears and emotions. But other influences can come into play as well; if something is impacting physically, like cold or hunger, it can often be a part of our dreams. We've all heard of someone (if not ourselves) who has fallen out of bed and dreamt they were falling off a cliff just as they woke up. Psychoanalysts study the reasons for us dreaming, saying that dreams reflect wishes that didn't come true, that a dream is a form of wish fulfillment. According to this line of thought, when we are asleep our inhibitions are also asleep.

FACT FILE

Daydreaming is actually a form of dreaming, only it is done while we are awake. Night dreaming is done while we are asleep. That is the only difference between them, since both are done when the dreamer is so relaxed that he pays no attention to what goes on around him.

WHY DO WE AWAKEN FROM SLEEP?

There are some things about sleep that even scientists find hard to explain. Sometimes we 'drop off' in an instant, other times we can't get to sleep how ever hard we try. But what actually wakes us up is still something that baffles experts. Whatever mental activity we indulge in, thinking, seeing, feeling, uses up energy. Like the rest of the body, the brain and other nerve centres need a rest. When we wake up after a good sleep we feel rested. One likely reason is that when we are asleep our body might still feel hungry, or cold, or we may experience an emotion such as fear. Feelings like this can be a stimulus to the brain, the result being we wake up. On the other hand, we may be waking up because we have been asleep long enough!

FACT FILE

Even while the body sleeps, its nerve systems are active, continuously monitoring and adjusting the internal processes, and checking the outside world for danger. The heart never stops, but beats slower while at rest.

WHY DO WE GET THIRSTY?

All of us have had the experience of being thirsty at times, but can you imagine how it would feel to be thirsty for days? If a human being has absolutely nothing to drink for a long period, he or she will die. Thirst is simply our body's way of telling us to replenish its liquid supply.

The reason for this thirst is caused by a change in the salt content of our blood. There is a certain normal amount of salt and water in our blood. When this changes by having more salt in relation to water in our blood, thirst results.

There is a part of our brain called the 'thirst centre'. It responds to the amount of salt in our blood. When there is a change, it sends messages to the back of the throat. From there, messages go to the brain, and it is this combination of feelings that makes us say we are thirsty.

FACT FILE

Onions send out an irritating substance when we peel them. The onion has an oil containing sulphur which not only gives it its sharp odour, but it also irritates the eye. The eye reacts by blinking and producing tears to wash it away. That is why we cry when we peel onions.

WHY DO WE GET HUNGRY?

Have you ever wondered how your brain gets the message that makes us feel hungry? Hunger has nothing to do with an empty stomach, as most people believe.

When certain nutritive materials are missing from the blood, hunger sets in. The lack of these materials in the blood vessels results in a message being sent to a part of the brain called the 'hunger centre'. The hunger centre is a bit like a brake that works on the stomach and the intestine, if there is enough food for the blood the hunger centre slows up the action of the stomach and intestine. When food is missing from the blood, it stimulates the stomach and intestine into more anction. That is why when we are hungry we often hear our stomach rumbling.

When we are hungry, we don't want any particular kind of food, our body just needs nourishment. It depends on the individual how long we can actually live without food. A very calm person can live longer than an excitable one because the protein stored up in his body is used up more slowly.

FACT FILE

Eggs are an extremely good form of protein, which is vital for the building up and repair of muscles. Milk and dairy products are another good source of protein.

WHY ARE SOME PEOPLE LEFT-HANDED?

About four per cent of the population is left-handed. In the course of history many of the greatest geniuses have also been left-handed. Leonardo da Vinci and Michelangelo, two of the greatest artists of all time, were both left-handed.

The brain has a right half and a left half and these two do not function in the same way. It is believed that the left half of the brain is predominant over the right half.

As the left half of the brain predominates, the right half of the body is more skilled and better able to do things. We read, write, speak, and work with the left half of our brain. And this, of course, makes most of us right-handed too. But in the case of left-handed people, it works the other way around. The right half of the brain is predominant, and such a person works best with the left side of his body.

FACT FILE

Did you know that no two human beings have the same set of fingerprints? A fingerprint is the pattern formed by the ridges on the layers of skin at the tips of your fingers. If you press your finger on an ink pad and then onto a piece of paper, you should be able to see some of these patterns.

Genetics & Reproduction

WHAT HAPPENS TO A FERTILIZED EGG?

A fertilized egg (or zygote) goes through a series of changes before it reaches the uterus. In the uterus, the zygote develops into a form called the embryo, which develops rapidly. The zygote then travels through the fallopian tube toward the uterus. Along the way, the zygote begins to divide rapidly into many cells with no increase in overall size. The resulting cell mass is called a *morula*. By the third or fourth day the morula enters the uterus and the embryo

Morula

develops from the central cells of the morula. They develop into the placenta, a special organ that enables the embryo to obtain food and oxygen from the mother. After the morula enters the uterus, it continues to divide. At this stage, the ball of cells is called a *blastocyst*. The cells of the blastocyst divide as it floats in the

Blastocyst

uterus for one or two days. About the fifth or sixth day of pregnancy, the blastocyst becomes attached to the internal surface of the uterus. The

outer cells of the blastocyst, called the *trophoblast*, secrete an enzyme that breaks down the lining of the uterus. The trophoblast begins to divide rapidly, invading the uterine tissue. The process of attachment to the uterine wall is called implantation.

Trophoblast

FACT FILE

By the 11th day of the pregnancy, the blastocyst is firmly implanted in the uterus. Various structures develop in the uterus to help the embryo grow. These structures include the placenta and certain membranes.

WHAT ARE CHROMOSOMES?

The moment of conception is the most important stage of sexual reproduction. Fertilization is complete when the chromosomes of the male sperm unite with the chromosomes of the female egg. Chromosomes are threadlike structures that contain genes, the units of heredity that determine each person's unique traits. Most body cells have 46 chromosomes that occur in 23 pairs. However, as each egg or sperm develops, it undergoes a special series of cell divisions called meiosis. As a result, each sperm or egg cell contains only one member of each chromosome pair, or 23 unpaired chromosomes. During fertilization, the chromosomes pair up so that the fertilized egg has the normal number of 46 chromosomes. Only about 100 sperm survive the journey of nearly 24 hours and only one fertilizes the ovum. The sperm's acrosome disappears as it dissolves the membrane of the ovum. The tail and body are shed when the head penetrates to join its 23 chromosomes with those of the ovarian nucleus.

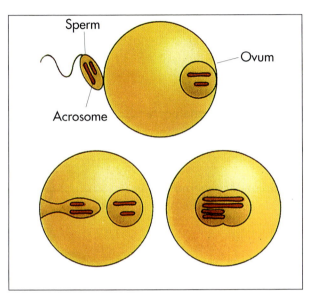

FACT FILE

Special sex chromosomes determine whether the zygote will develop into a boy or a girl. Each body cell contains a pair of sex chromosomes. In females, the two sex chromosomes are identical.

HOW DOES OUR BODY GROW?

The most important forces that cause growth lie inside a living thing from the beginning. These forces are called its heredity. The human body has stages of growth: embryo and foetus, infant, child, youth, mature adult and old age. People's bodies grow faster in the early weeks of life than at any other time. Even before the end of the first year, they are growing less rapidly. Through the whole period of childhood, they grow at a moderate rate. Then growth starts to speed up again. All human beings are much alike in their growth. But there are important differences. Boys and girls all follow the same general pathway of growth, but each individual follows it in their own way.

Growth stages of a human foetus before birth

4 weeks

8 weeks

12 weeks

20 weeks

30 weeks

fontanelle

FACT FILE

The bones of a baby's head are not fused at birth, making the skull flexible enough to pass through the mother's birth canal. The bones eventually join, but a gap in the skull, called the fontanelle, may not close up for several months.

194

Father has both blue
and brown eye genes

Mother has both blue
and brown eye genes

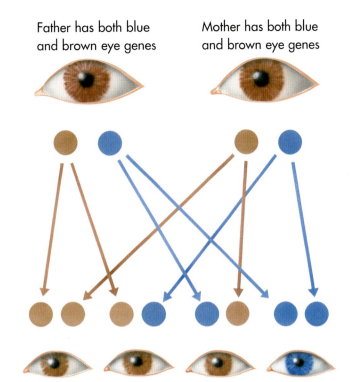

2 brown eye
genes =
brown eyes

1 brown gene
+ 1 blue =
brown eyes

1 blue gene +
1 brown =
brown eyes

2 blue eye
genes =
blue eyes

HOW DO WE GET BROWN EYES?

FACT FILE

This DNA molecule is shaped
like a ladder twisted into a spiral.
The pattern in which these are
formed is the code built into the
DNA molecule and groups of
these form genes.

Although genes from both parents
are mixed together at fertilization,
some genes have a more powerful
effect than others. These dominant
genes override the effects of others
which are called recessive genes. For
example, if a child has a gene for
brown eyes from one parent, and a
gene for blue eyes from the other, the
child will always have brown eyes.
This is because the gene for brown
eyes is a dominant gene.

However, two parents with brown
eyes may have children with blue eyes
if the parents carry the blue eyes.
This means that a child would get the
recessive blue gene from both parents.

WHEN IS A BABY'S GENETIC MAKE-UP DECIDED?

A baby's genetic make-up is decided right from the time when the egg is fertilized. A very important part of cell division involves the nucleus. Each nucleus contains two sets of genes. One came originally from the person's father and one from the mother. So before a cell divides, both sets of genes are copied. This is termed DNA replication. Each new offspring cell then receives a full double set of genes, one from the father and one from the mother.

Because each human body gets half its genes from each parent it inherits some of the features of each parent. This is why all kinds of characteristics, for example height, run in families.

However, every human body has its own unique physical circumstances, such as the food we eat, our environment and the illnesses that we catch.

We also each have our own behavioural and mental development. So we inherit a mix of physical features from our parents, but also we are all individual and unique.

Mitosis – cell reproduction

FACT FILE

A long thread or axon extends from the body of a neurone, and it is along this that the nerve impulses are carried.

WHEN DOES MITOSIS OCCUR?

As well as being packed with information, the DNA of chromosomes also has the ability to reproduce itself. Without this, the cells could not pass on information from one generation to the other. The process of cell division in which the cell duplicates itself is called mitosis, which works as follows:

1 the chromosomes become shorter and the nuclear envelope breaks,
2 the chromosomes are released, which duplicate and attach themselves to a cytoplasmic network,
3 they are then drawn apart
4–7 to form two new cells with reformed nuclear envelopes.

Mitosis is absolutely essential to life because it provides new cells for growth and for replacement of worn out cells. Mitosis may take minutes or hours, depending upon the kind of cells and species of organisms. It is influenced by time of day, temperature, and chemicals. Strictly speaking the term mitosis is used to describe the duplication and distribution of chromosomes, the structures that carry our genetic information.

FACT FILE

DNA strands look like a twisted ladder. Sections of DNA are called genes. All the instructions for growing a new human being are coded into the DNA molecule.

WHEN WERE GENES DISCOVERED?

In the 1800s a monk named Gregor Mendel experimented with characteristics in pea plants by cross-fertilizing plants with different traits. He kept a careful track of the traits displayed by the pea plants produced by cross-fertilization, discovering that the characteristics from the parent plants were inherited by the progeny plants in specific patterns.

Mendel also discovered during his experiments that certain genes seemed more dominant than others. For example if a pea with a white flower is cross-fertilized with a pea with a pink flower, the resulting flowers will all be pink.

This is obvious in human beings. For example, if a child has a gene for brown eyes from one parent and a gene for blue eyes from the other, the child will always have brown eyes. This is because the gene for brown eyes is a dominant gene.

Model of DNA

FACT FILE

Chromosomes are tiny threads that are present in all cells apart from red blood cells. They contain all the information for an entire person to develop. There are 46 chromosomes in each cell. They come in 22 pairs, plus another special pair that determine the person's sex.

WHEN DO WE LEARN TO TALK?

As air flows out of the lungs, we can use it to make the sounds of speech and other noises. At the top of the windpipe, in the sides of the voice box or larynx, are two stiff, shelf-like folds – called the vocal cords. Criss-crossed muscles in the voice box can pull them together so that air passes through a narrow slit between them and makes them vibrate, creating sounds. As the vocal cords are pulled tighter, they make higher-pitched sounds. As the vocal cords loosen, they make lower-pitched sounds. Of course, when we actually learn to talk, our speech depends on the development of the brain and its ability to copy the sounds that we hear.

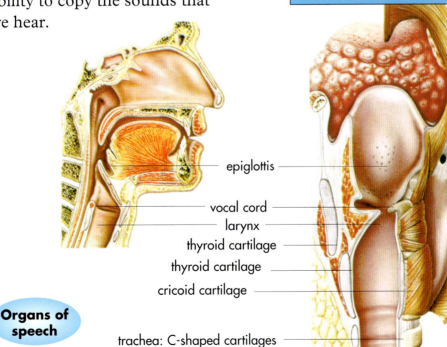

epiglottis

vocal cord

larynx

thyroid cartilage

thyroid cartilage

cricoid cartilage

Organs of speech

trachea: C-shaped cartilages

WHERE DOES A BABY DEVELOP?

A baby develops in the uterus, or womb – a hollow, muscular organ in the mother's abdomen. The period of development in the uterus lasts about nine months in most cases. During this period, development is more rapid than at any time after birth.

For a baby to develop, a sperm from the father must unite with an egg from the mother. This union of a sperm and an egg is called fertilization. It produces a single cell called a fertilized egg. By a series of remarkable changes, the fertilized egg gradually develops into a baby.

FACT FILE

The placenta is an organ composed largely of blood vessels. The placenta is attached to the wall of the uterus. A tubelike structure called the umbilical cord joins the placenta to the embryo at the abdomen. The placenta supplies everything that the embryo needs to live and grow.

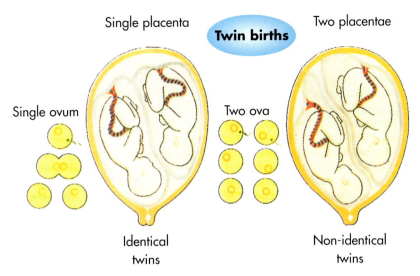

Single placenta   **Twin births**   Two placentae

Single ovum   Two ova

Identical twins   Non-identical twins

WHEN ARE TWINS CONCEIVED?

A baby begins as a fertilized egg – a pinhead-sized egg cell from the mother, which has joined an even smaller tadpole-shaped sperm cell from the father. Although thousands of these sperm cells may cluster around the egg cell, only one of these will actually fertilize the egg.

Non-identical twins are produced when two eggs are released at the same time, and both are fertilized. They can be the same sex, or brother and sister.

Identical twins are produced when the embryo splits into two in the early stages of its development. This produces two identical children of the same sex. Some identical twins look so alike that they can only be told apart by their fingerprints.

Only one in 83 pregnancies results in twins.

FACT FILE

Identical twins share the same physical traits: identical eye colour, hair colour and other characteristics. Non-identical twins are only as alike as any other pair of siblings.

WHERE IS SPERM PRODUCED?

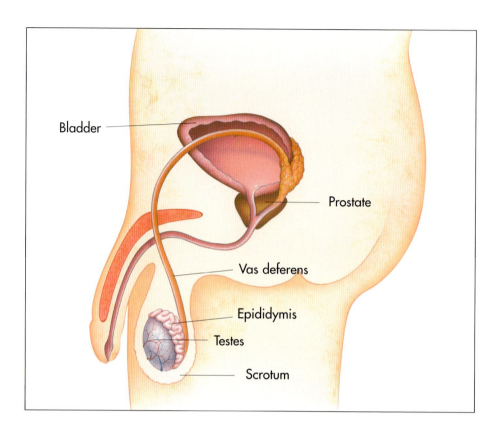

Bladder

Prostate

Vas deferens

Epididymis

Testes

Scrotum

Sperm, the male sex cells, develop in the testes. It is stored for several days until needed. The testes contain long tubes called the seminiferous tubules, which are tightly coiled. Sperm is produced continuously in these tubes, then passed to the epididymis and stored in a large duct called the vas deferens. Here liquid is added to the sperm to make a milky fluid called semen. It is stored in pouches called seminal vesicles. During sexual intercourse the seminal vesicles contract and force out the sperm.

FACT FILE

Up to 100 million sperms are produced every day by the male. If they are not released they are soon destroyed and replaced. Sperms look like tiny tadpoles with rounded heads and long lashing tails.

WHERE DOES MENSTRUATION TAKE PLACE?

Most women of child-bearing age experience menstruation, the loss of blood and cells through the vagina that takes place on a monthly basis. The uterus, or womb, is the oval-shaped organ that holds a baby during pregnancy, and each month blood and cells build up in its lining. This lining thickens in preparation for pregnancy, and pregnancy does not happen, the lining breaks down. The blood and cells are then discharged through a canal that leads from the uterus to the outside of the body; this canal is the vagina. The menstruation process can last over a period of anything from three to seven days, this time being known as the menstrual period.

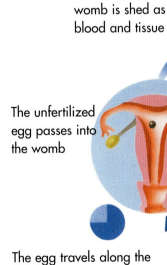

The lining of the womb is shed as blood and tissue

The unfertilized egg passes into the womb

The egg travels along the Fallopian tube. This is where fertilization would take place

A new egg is released by the ovary

WHY DO WE HAVE CHROMOSOMES?

Every cell has a nucleus which is full of information coded in the form of a chemical called deoxyribonucleic acid (or DNA). The DNA is organized into groups called genes. Every chromosome contains thousands of genes, each with enough information for the production of one protein. This protein may have a small effect within the cell and on the appearance of the body. It may make all the difference between a person having brown or blue eyes, or straight or curly hair.

At the moment the mother's egg is fertilized, the genes start issuing instructions for the moulding of a new human being. Every characteristic which we inherit from our parents is passed on to us through the coding of the genes within the chromosomes.

In rare cases, some people have 47 chromosomes. This occurs when people inherit Downs Syndrome, a genetic disorder.

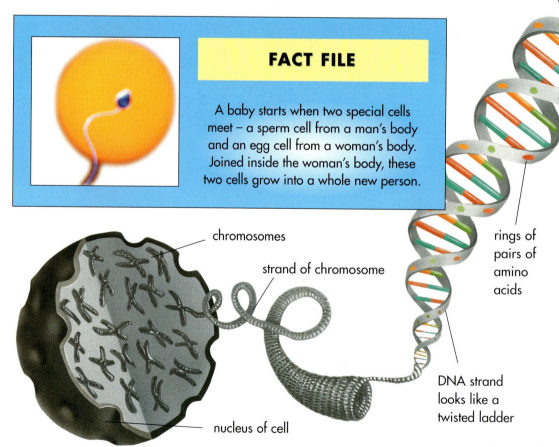

FACT FILE

A baby starts when two special cells meet – a sperm cell from a man's body and an egg cell from a woman's body. Joined inside the woman's body, these two cells grow into a whole new person.

chromosomes

strand of chromosome

nucleus of cell

rings of pairs of amino acids

DNA strand looks like a twisted ladder

WHERE DO WE INHERIT OUR TRAITS?

Living things inherit characteristics, often called traits, from their parents through heredity. Heredity is the passing on of biological characteristics from one generation to the next. The process of heredity occurs among all living things – animals, plants and even such microscopic organisms as bacteria. Heredity explains why a human mother always has a human baby and why a mother dog has puppies and not kittens. It is also the reason offspring look like their parents. You resemble your parents because you inherited your hair, nose shape and other traits from them. All organisms consist of cells. Tiny biochemical structures inside each cell called genes carry traits from one generation to the next.

FACT FILE

You may look like your parents, but you are not an exact duplicate of either of them. You inherited half your genes from your father and half from your mother.

History

Who?
· · · · · · · · · · · · · ·

WHO WERE THE FRANKS?

Frankish soldiers

The Franks emerged from the ruins of the Roman Empire in AD 476 as the dominant people of western Europe. Their leader, Clovis, enlarged his lands around the River Rhine in Germany through war. By AD 540 the Franks ruled most of the old Roman province of Gaul (France, named after the Franks).

The first Frankish ruling family is known as the Merovingian dynasty, after Clovis's grandfather Meroveus. Clovis became a Christian. He made Paris his capital city. Most of the Franks were peasant farmers, who lived on lands ruled by nobles. The peasants raised food, doing the seasonal tasks of ploughing, sowing and harvesting. They also had to fight for their lord when he went to war. The Frankish system of land-holding and service was the beginning of the feudal system in Europe.

Charlemagne was king of the Franks from 768 to 814, and created a vast empire. On Christmas Day in 800 the pope crowned Charlemagne Holy Roman Emperor. After the rule of Charlemagne the Frankish empire began to break up.

FACT FILE

The Frankish king Charlemagne introduced this writing, called 'Carolingian script', which was easier for people to read and write.

WHO WERE THE HITTITES?

Hittite charioteers

The Hittites arrived in what is now Anatolia in Turkey, from either central Europe or central Asia in about 2000 BC, and during the next 500 years, expanded their territory to parts of Syria in the south and Mesopotamia in the east. Like the Sumerians and Egyptians, they could muster huge armies, and were among the first people to use chariots in war, from which archers fired arrows, giving them an edge over enemies.

One of the first battles for which accounts remain, happened in 1282 BC at Kadesh on the Orontes River. Mutwatallis, the Hittite leader, fought a battle against Egyptian forces under Rameses II. The Hittites were winning, but Rameses managed to regroup when the Hittites stopped fighting to loot Egyptian equipment. Both sides claimed it as a victory, it was inconclusive and the two sides signed a non-aggression treaty.

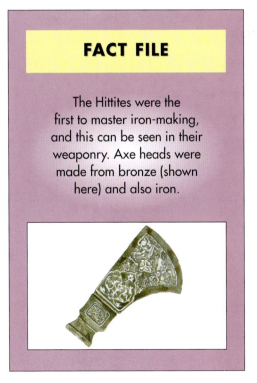

FACT FILE

The Hittites were the first to master iron-making, and this can be seen in their weaponry. Axe heads were made from bronze (shown here) and also iron.

WHO WERE THE OLMECS AND CHAVINS?

The Olmecs

Two groups developed America's earliest civilizations – in Mexico and Central America, and in Peru on the west coast of South America.

The Olmecs flourished between about 1200 and 400 BC. They made pottery and cleared the jungle to grow crops. The Olmec people constructed large stepped pyramids from earth. They also held religious ceremonies and worshipped their gods in temples built on top of these pyramids.

The Chavins were people living in the Andes foothills, who became farmers by about 1000 BC. They built the first towns in South America. They cut terraces into hillsides and became expert at irrigation to cultivate the dry land and mountain slopes.

FACT FILE

In modern Peru, craftworkers carry on the traditions of their Chavin ancestors, producing bright handwoven textiles. Designs such as these have been produced in Peru for around 3,000 years.

The Chavins

WHO DID THE PERSIANS WORSHIP?

The people of ancient Persia believed in nature gods, such as the sun and the sky. Many of their gods were adaptations of Indian gods, such as Mithra, the god of light (seen right killing a bull as a sacrifice to renew life), Varuna, Nasatyas and Indra.

Many people followed the teachings of the prophet Zoroaster (or Zarathustra) (*c.* 628 to 551 BC), who reformed the ancient religion. He taught that life was a struggle between good (light) and evil (darkness). He preached a faith based on good thoughts, words and deeds, emphasising the importance of the god, Ahura Mazda, 'the wise spirit', who had become supreme god because he was the royal family's personal protector. Zoroaster's followers gradually spread his religion through Persia as well as parts of Greece and India.

FACT FILE

Darius I ruled Persia from 521 to 486 BC. He encouraged trade through the use of coins and new canals. Darius sent an army into Greece in 490 BC, but it was defeated by Athenian forces at Marathon. Darius died in 486 BC while preparing for new attacks on Greece.

WHO WAS ASOKA?

Asoka was the third emperor of Mauryan dynasty, who ruled the first empire to unite almost all of India. The empire was founded by Asoka's grandfather, Chandragupta Maurya in about 324 BC, when he seized the throne of Magadha, a rich kingdom in the Ganges Valley. His son and grandson, Asoka, continued to expand the empire and at its height it ruled most of India and a large part of Afghanistan.

Asoka eventually became sickened by the slaughter and turned to the pacifist religion of Buddhism. He became one of its greatest supporters and sent missionaries to his neighbours. He then set out to reform his empire, instigating a new taxation system, building new cities and roads to promote trade and agriculture in the villages. Asoka made new laws and had them inscribed on stone pillars set up all across his empire. The empire broke up after his death, and the last emperor died in 185 BC.

Asoka

FACT FILE

The carved stone lions on the pillar at Sarnath have become a national emblem for India.

The Mauryan Empire

Taxila
MAGADHA
Pataliputra
Sanchi
PULINDAS
Sarnath
KALINGA

WHO WAS THE 'MAID OF ORLEANS'?

During the Hundred Years War (1337 to 1453), English kings often claimed the throne of France. In 1420, Henry V had forced the French king, Charles VI, to declare him heir to the French throne, rather than his own son Charles VII. The English controlled all of northern France, but the south of the country denied the English claim.

Jeanne d'Arc, as she is known in France, was born in 1412 at Domrémy, near Nancy. She was a devout Catholic and by the age of 13 was having visions telling her that she had been chosen by God to help King Charles VII drive the English out. In 1429 she persuaded him, and in April of that year led French troops to lift the seige of Orleans. A series of further wins took the French army to Reims, where all French coronations took place and where Charles was crowned in July.

Joan was captured in May 1430 by the Burgundian army, who sold her to the English and they burned her at the stake as a heretic at the end of May 1431. She is still revered as a national heroine in France.

FACT FILE

Medieval castles and towns were also fortified to give the citizens protection. Sieges could last for months; if attackers could not batter their way into a town, they would try to prevent any supplies of food or armaments reaching the defenders, forcing them to give up or starve.

WHO DID THE ANCIENT GREEKS WORSHIP?

Zeus

Poseidon

The Greeks believed in many different gods, chief among these were a family of supernatural beings who lived on Mount Olympus and watched over humanity. Certain gods looked after the harvest; others cared for wild animals, the sea, war and such like. King of the gods was Zeus, whom the Romans called Jupiter. The first Olympic Games, which took place in 776 BC, were held in his acclaim. Greeks believed that the universe was a sphere. The upper half was light and airy, the lower half dark and gloomy, and the Earth was a flat disc, floating between the two halves. When people died they went to the Underworld, which was ruled by Hades, the brother of Zeus. Poseidon was the Greek god of the sea, and is often shown carrying a three-pronged spear, called a trident. The Greeks believed Poseidon to be the brother of Zeus and Hades. He was also associated with earthquakes and horses, and the Greeks thought that he was the father of the winged horse, Pegasus.

FACT FILE

The ruins of Greek and Roman temples can be seen across Europe, the Near East and North Africa. Every town had its own temple, dedicated to a protector god or goddess.

WHO WAS ALFRED THE GREAT?

FACT FILE

The Alfred jewel was found near Athelney in Somerset in 1693. It may be part of a bookmark. On it are the words 'Alfred had me made' in Latin.

In the late ninth century, most of the northeastern half of England was under the control of the Danish Vikings. The West Saxons had been at war with them for years when Alfred the Great (849 to 899) came to the throne in 871. After years of war, Alfred reconquered London in 886, made peace with the Vikings and began the process of uniting the kingdoms of England under his leadership.

With more resources at his disposal, Alfred could fortify strategic points and protect the coast with a large fleet.

Alfred was an effective peacetime ruler: parts of his code of laws are still recognizable in the English legal system. He also encouraged learning and literature, as well as the translation of Christian texts into Old English to promote a cultural revival in England.

215

WHO WAS THE FIRST NORMAN KING OF ENGLAND?

The first Norman king of England was William I, the Conqueror (1027 to 1087). He was born in about 1027 in Falaise in Normandy, the son of Duke Robert I, and became duke on his father's death in 1035.

In 1066, after the death of Edward the Confessor, William claimed the English throne had been granted to him by Edward and when the latter's brother-in-law, Harold was elected to the throne by the English nobles, William had no choice but to invade. William's army won the battle known as the Battle of Hastings on October 14.

William was crowned in Westminster Abbey on Christmas Day. From the start, he ruled with an iron fist, taking lands from the Saxons. In 1086, he commissioned the great survey of every property in the country – the Domesday Survey. He started what became known as the feudal system: in return for grants of land, his followers had to swear allegiance and supply men for military service. Their followers had to do likewise, right down the social scale to the serfs (slaves).

FACT FILE

At the Battle of Hastings the English, who fought on foot, resisted as Norman cavalry charged their shield wall and fired arrows at them. When the Normans feigned retreat, the English chased them downhill and were slaughtered. This is recorded in 72 scenes on the Bayeux Tapestry.

WHO WERE THE CELTS?

The Celts came from central Europe, although their previous origins are unclear. Around 500 BC, perhaps to escape wars with their Germanic neighbours, they began to move westwards. Groups of people settled in what are now Spain, France, Britain and Ireland. Celts were warlike and their arrival usually led to fighting.

The Celts were artistic people. They loved stories and music, and they made beautiful jewellery and metalwork decorated with abstract designs and animal shapes.

They had no written language, passing on their legends of gods and heroes in stories around the fire. Most of what we know of the Celts today comes from the writings of their enemies, such as the Romans. The Celts themselves left a legacy of art and legend, and language: Welsh, Breton, Cornish, Irish and Scottish Gaelic are all Celtic languages.

FACT FILE

The Celts often constructed their settlements on hilltops, which could be easily defended. They are identified by circular defensive ditches that still survive in former Celtic areas.

An example of Celtic art

WHO FORMED THE 'NEW MODEL ARMY'?

Oliver Cromwell (1599 to 1658), led the armed forces of Parliament to victory in the English Civil War against the royalists in the 1640s.

Cromwell was a military genius. In the winter of 1644 and 1645, when the war was at a stalemate, he purged the Parliamentarian high command of those he felt were not helping their cause. Cromwell's friends persuaded Parliament to establish a full-time professional force, the New Model Army, under Sir Thomas Fairfax, with Cromwell as general. The New Model Army (or the Roundheads) was a disciplined fighting force and never lost a major battle. At the Battle of Naseby, in Northamptonshire (June 14, 1645), it destroyed the king's main field army. Cromwell earned the nickname 'Ironsides'.

FACT FILE

The term Roundhead originally referred to the parliamentary infantryman, with his hair cut short to fit his casque (steel helmet). By the end of the English Civil War, the armies of Parliament were superior in cavalry and infantry.

WHO INTRODUCED PERESTROIKA AND GLASNOST?

What are *perestroika* and *glasnost*? They formed part of the policies of Mikhail Gorbachev, the last leader of the Soviet Union. After his appointment in 1985, Gorbachev proposed reforms of the Soviet political and economic system. Everything was controlled from the centre by the Communist Party and he wished to increase the power of elected bodies and modernize the economy. This programme was called *perestroika* (restructuring). *Glasnost* means 'openness', which he wanted the Soviet Union to have internally and with other nations.

In 1990, Gorbachev received the Nobel Peace Prize for his reforms and arms limitations agreements with the United States of America, but the Soviet Union broke up in 1991.

FACT FILE

The US President Ronald Reagan was a keen supporter of Gorbachev's programme of reforms in the USSR. In 1987 the two leaders signed an agreement to dismantle many kinds of nuclear weapon.

WHO GAVE THE GETTYSBURG ADDRESS?

Abraham Lincoln (1809 to 1865) was the sixteenth president of the United States and one of the great leaders in American history. A humane, far-sighted statesman in his lifetime, he became a legend and a folk hero after his death.

Lincoln delivered the short speech that has become known as the Gettysburg address on November 19, 1863, at the site of the Civil War Battle of Gettysburg in Pennsylvania. The occasion was a dedication ceremony for a cemetery for the Union soldiers who died there in the three-day bloodbath four months earlier.

The aim of the speech was to rouse the spirits of the Union and to affirm the reasons why the Northern States were fighting the war against the Confederate states.

FACT FILE

Abraham Lincoln was against slavery, and his election convinced the leaders of the southern states that the only option to them was to leave the Union. South Carolina was the first state to leave in 1860, soon followed by Mississippi, Florida, Alabama, Georgia and Louisiana.

WHO FOUNDED FASCISM?

Fascism was a political movement founded in Italy by Benito Mussolini (1883 to 1945) in 1919. His brand of revolutionary nationalism – nationalization and putting Italy's interests first – were popular with old soldiers. In 1921, he transformed the *Fasci di Combattimento* into the National Fascist Party, and in 1922 his black-shirts marched on Rome and secured his appointment as prime minister. He imposed one-party rule with himself as dictator.

He delayed involving Italy in World War II until 1940, when a German victory seemed probable. Five years later, after Italy's defeat, he was executed by Italian partisans.

FACT FILE

Sir Oswald Mosley formed the British Union of Fascists in 1932. His views were violently anti-Semitic and his black-shirted followers rioted in areas with strong Jewish communities, such as London's East End. He was interned in World War II because of his support for Hitler.

WHO WERE THE SUMERIANS?

About 7,000 years ago, farmers began to move into an area of land between the Tigris and the Euphrates rivers. This fertile land was called Mesopotamia, in what is now called Iraq. In the south of Mesopotamia was the land known as Sumer. The Sumerians, as they became known, were a very inventive race. They developed the first form of writing and recording numbers.

The Sumerians drew pictures on soft clay with a pointed reed. The pictures were drawn downwards in lines, from the right-hand side. Later, they started to write across the tablet from left to right. The reed tip became wedge shaped, as did the marks it made.

FACT FILE

Reed houses were built using reeds cut down from the marshes around the Tigris and Euphrates rivers. The Sumerians also made canoes from these reeds.

WHO WAS ALEXANDER THE GREAT?

Alexander the Great (356 to 323 BC) was king of the Macedonians and was one of the greatest generals in history.
He came to the throne in 336 BC, and after consolidating his power in Greece, two years later began his conquest of the Persian Empire. By 328 BC he had reached India, but in 327 BC had to turn back because his soldiers were threatening to mutiny after almost ten years away from home. Alexander's conquests furthered the cross-fertilization of Greek and Persian ideas and customs in western Asia and Egypt. His empire did not last beyond his death in Babylon in 323 BC. It was split up into a number of smaller kingdoms ruled by his friends and allies.

FACT FILE

Alexander imposed a single system of money throughout his lands. He was keen to promote trade and commerce across the empire too.

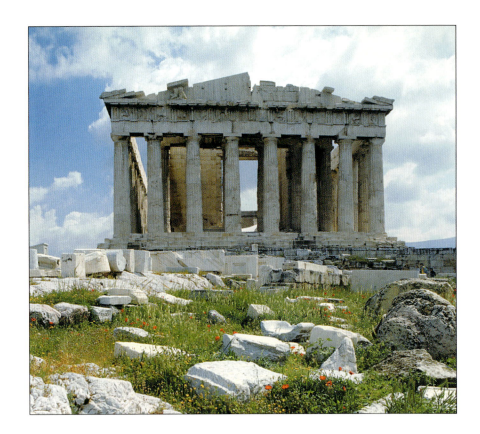

WHO BUILT THE PARTHENON?

The ancient Greeks were pioneers in medicine, mathematics and science. They looked at the world in the light of logic and reason, and made some fundamental discoveries. In the year 432 BC a building called the Parthenon was completed. The Parthenon was built in Athens to venerate the city's protector, the goddess Athene. Her gold and ivory decorated statue was inside the great hall, enclosed by columns, which supported the roof like a forest of stones.

The Greeks built many beautiful temples to their gods. Stone columns, as used in the Parthenon, were a typical feature of many Greek buildings.

FACT FILE

Greek actors wore masks to show what kind of character (comic or tragic) they played. Audiences would sit in the open air on a hillside to watch the plays.

WHO BUILT HADRIAN'S WALL?

Hadrian's Wall was built in AD 122 to defend the northern frontier of Roman Britain. It acted as a checkpoint on movement between England and Scotland. The wall took eight years to build and stretches for 73 miles (118 km).

At this time the Roman Empire was governed by the personal will of the emperor, but the emperor's power rested on his army. Weak or bad emperors were sometimes overthrown by army generals. Some emperors ruled well – Hadrian, for example, travelled widely to inspect building projects. Others, such as Nero and Caligula, were cruel or mad. The Romans were such good organizers that the empire usually kept working even when there was a fool at its heart.

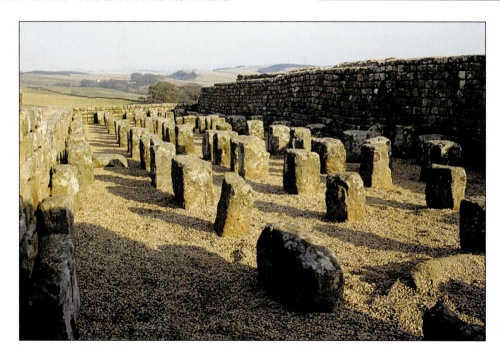

TELL ME ABOUT HISTORY : WHO?

WHO WERE THE SUFFRAGETTES?

During war time, women were brought in to fill the jobs of those men that had gone to fight in the war. The poster (shown here on the right) emphasized the important role women had to play. In 1893, New Zealand became the first country in the world to allow women to vote in national elections. Australia followed suit in 1903, and Finland in 1906. In other parts of the world, however, women were engaged in a bitter and often violent battle for the right to vote.

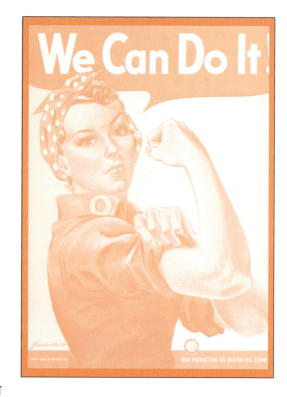

In Britain, Emmeline Pankhurst founded the Women's Social and Political Union in 1903. The WSPU believed in actions rather than words, and many of its members, known as suffragettes, were arrested and imprisoned. One suffragette called Emily Davison was killed when she threw herself beneath the king's horse at a race.

FACT FILE

The women activists were frequently arrested for their actions, including Emmeline Pankhurst, shown here. The right to vote was extended to all women over the age of 21 in 1928. Emmeline Pankhurst died a month after British women gained equal voting rights.

WHO WAS GENGHIS KHAN?

**Genghis Khan
(1167 to 1227)**

In the year 1167, a child called Temujin was born on the desolate plains of Mongolia. When the boy was nine, his father was murdered and his family was left poor and friendless. From this grim beginning Temujin grew up to become one of the world's greatest conquerors. He was hailed by the Mongols as Genghis Khan – the 'Universal Ruler'.

In 1206, Genghis Khan became leader of all the Mongol people, and began to build his astonishing empire. He was a ruthless warrior, destroying entire cities and their populations during his conquests. Yet he somehow succeeded in keeping the peace.

Genghis Khan died of a fever in 1227, but the Mongols continued to build up the empire.

FACT FILE

The Mongols lived on the flat, grassy steppes of Asia, wandering with their herds of sheep, goats and cattle. They carried their homes around with them. The Mongols were tough and violent, and splendid horse riders.

Russian peasants working the land

WHO WAS THE MOST FAMOUS TSAR OF RUSSIA?

Peter the Great was a giant figure, well over 6½ (2 m) tall, and full of violent energy. When he became tsar of Russia in 1696, he was determined to use all his energy to make Russia a strong and modern state.

After many years of civil war, invasion and bloodshed, Russia had just begun a slow progress out of its backward and primitive past. Under the new tsar, this progress became far more rapid.

Peter himself spent years touring western Europe to find out how other countries were run. He was also a great builder. He built roads, canals and introduced modern methods to mining and other industries.

FACT FILE

The beautiful city of St Petersburg lives beside the River Neva. Its magnificent Winter Palace was the winter home of the tsars. As a result of working in the difficult marshy conditions, thousands of peasants died while building Peter the Great's new city.

WHO DISCOVERED AUSTRALIA?

In 1768, the British government sent an expedition to find the mysterious southern continent. Its leader was James Cook, and his ship was a small but tough vessel called Endeavour. After visiting the island of Tahiti, Cook sailed southwards and then west until he sighted an unknown land. It turned out to be New Zealand. The Endeavour sailed on, searching for the east coast of Australia. By 1770 Cook reached the coast of what he knew to be Australia. He followed it northwards until he found a suitable place to land. He called this Botany Bay.

Cook's first meeting with the Maori people of New Zealand in 1769

WHO BUILT THE TAJ MAHAL?

The Taj Mahal is a vast mausoleum near Agra in India. It was built by the Mogul emperor Shah Jahan (1592 to 1666) in memory of his favourite wife Mumtaz Mahal, who died in 1630. It took 20,000 skilled workers more than 20 years to complete the construction and decoration. The building is intended to represent the throne of God. It is the largest Islamic tomb ever built for a woman. The building stands on a marble platform 32.5 ft (100 m) square and sits in a Persian water garden designed to represent paradise. The Shah was also responsible for part of the Red Fort at Delhi.

FACT FILE

Minarets, or towers rise from each of the four corners of the Taj Mahal. The Taj itself soars another 196 ft (60 m) into the air.

WHO FIRST USED STAMPS?

Below is an example of a postbox used in Great Britain. People post their mail in this box, which will then be collected and sorted by the Post Office.

It was in the sixteenth century that governments began to have regular postal services. They had three chief reasons for doing this. One was to enable them to inspect suspicious correspondence, the second was to produce revenue, and the third was to provide a service for the public. Henry VIII had a government postal service in England. In 1609, no one was allowed to carry letters except messengers authorized by the government. The whole system was finally changed in 1840.

Stamps were introduced, and rates made uniform for all distances within the country, varying only according to the weight of the piece of mail. All other countries were to model their postal systems on that of Great Britain.

WHO WAS BOADICEA?

Boadicea (Boudicca) was the queen of the Iceni, a tribe of Celts living in eastern England. Her husband was a governor, who worked with the Romans. After his death the Romans tried to take control. Boadicea led a rebellion, which sacked the towns of Colchester and London, until the Roman armies marched against her. The Romans defeated the Iceni and their Celtic allies. Boadicea is renowned for fighting from a chariot, and the Romans had to develop special tactics to combat these fast-moving warriors. Boadicea ended her own life by taking poison to avoid being captured.

FACT FILE

Celtic poetry:

'STORM AT SEA'
Tempest on the plain of Lir
Bursts its barriers far and near
And upon the rising tide
Wind and noisy winter ride
Winter throws a shining spear.

Queen Boadicea on her chariot

How?

HOW WAS ROME FOUNDED?

According to the legend, Rome was founded in 753 BC by twin brothers called Romulus and Remus. The babies were raised by a she-wolf, having been abandoned by their uncle on the banks of the River Tiber. They were eventually rescued by a shepherd.

By 509 BC the original Etruscan inhabitants of Rome had been driven out, and by 275 BC Rome controlled most of Italy. The Phoenicians were great rivals of Rome, and they were finally defeated by the Romans in the Punic Wars (261 to 146 BC). After this, the Romans were able to extend their empire with little organized resistance. The Celts, the Seleucid kings, the Greeks and the Egyptians all fell before Roman power. Only the Parthians in the east and the Germanic tribes in northwest Europe defied the mighty Roman army.

FACT FILE

Part of the complex of Roman baths in the city of Bath in England. Romans would visit the public baths to bathe in hot and cold pools, and also to relax and talk with their friends.

HOW VAST WAS THE ROMAN EMPIRE?

FACT FILE

The disciplined Roman armies developed special weapons and techniques to overcome the tribes they encountered as the empire expanded. This 'tortoise' formation proved impregnable against their Celtic foes.

At its peak, the Roman army extended all around the Mediterranean Sea and most of the rest of Europe. Much of what is now England and France, Belgium and the Netherlands, Spain and Portugal, Switzerland, Austria, Hungary, part of Germany, Romania, Bulgaria, Greece, Turkey, Israel, Syria, Arabia, Tunisia, Algeria, and Morocco was ruled by the Romans from their base in Italy.

A huge army was needed to maintain control over these regions, and the costs were tremendous. There were continual minor wars and skirmishes along the edges of the Empire, which meant that large garrisons of soldiers had to be maintained.

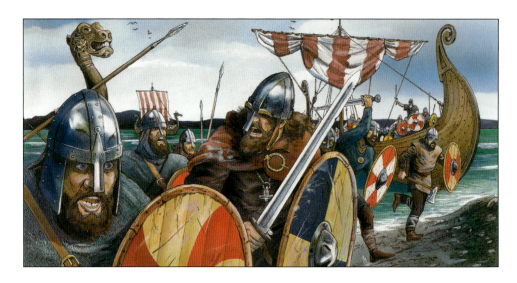

HOW SUCCESSFUL WERE VIKING ATTACKS?

The Vikings came from Scandinavia (Norway, Denmark and Sweden). Their homeland of mountains, fjords and forests offered little spare farmland for a growing population, so many Vikings went abroad in search of new lands to settle.

They were fierce warriors and their first impact on western Europe was a violent one. Norwegians and Danes began to sail across the North Sea in the late AD 700s, raiding the coasts of Britain and mainland Europe. They raided churches and towns, carrying off loot and slaves. Their raids caused panic and rulers tried to buy off the invaders with gold, known as Danegeld. This only encouraged the Vikings to come back for more.

In Britain, the Vikings were finally defeated by Alfred, the king of Wessex.

FACT FILE

Religion was important to the Vikings. Their most important gods were Odin, Thor and Grey. Odin, the god of battle, was the leader of the Norse gods, who lived in a place called Valhalla.

HOW FAR DID THE VIKINGS TRAVEL?

FACT FILE

The Viking longships were fast and strong enough to cross oceans. They had a long, slender hull with a single mast and sail.

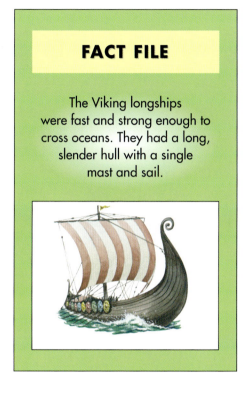

At a time when sailors dared not venture far from the coasts, the Vikings boldly sailed out far across the Atlantic in their small open longships. Viking trade routes took them throughout Europe and beyond. The Vikings travelled as far east as Baghdad and Istanbul, and as far west as Greenland and Canada. Wherever Vikings landed they mingled with local people, and they began to set up colonies in Iceland and Greenland and sailed on to North America. Traces of Viking settlements have also been found in Maine, in the United States, and in Newfoundland in Canada. However, these colonies soon vanished, together with the colony in Greenland. Other Vikings sailed around the Mediterranean, trading for goods from places as far away as China.

GREENLAND

ICELAND

LABRADOR

NORWAY

SWEDEN

Novgorod

Clontarf

DENMARK

Kiev

FRANCE GERMANY

Istanbul

SPAIN

Sicily

Baghdad

■ Danish Vikings

■ Norwegian Vikings

■ Swedish Vikings

HOW DID THE NORMANS CHANGE BRITAIN?

The Bayeux tapestry records the Norman victory over the Saxon King Harold, who is shown here receiving the fatal arrow in his eye.

FACT FILE

Knights were soldiers in the service of a Norman lord. They owed their loyalty to their lord and had to fight for him whenever asked. This meant that the knights were called upon in times of unrest.

The Normans introduced the feudal system to England. According to this system, the king owned all the land and others could hold land in exchange for providing services to the king. William the Conqueror appointed barons who were provided with estates taken from the original English earls. In return, the barons paid him taxes and supplied soldiers for his armies.

The barons, in turn, let their knights hold smaller sections of land, while the knights let part of this land to people called villeins. They were farmers who had to provide some of their produce to the local lord of the manor. In this way, the land and the whole of English society was broken into small, easily controlled units.

HOW DOES THE DOMESDAY BOOK HELP HISTORIANS?

The Domesday Book

Once the Normans had secured their hold over their new territory, they wanted to know exactly what it was worth. In AD 1085 William I ordered a survey of land in England. The findings were written down in the Domesday Book (Domesday means 'Day of Judgement'). It is the best record we have of life in England between AD 1066 and 1088, naming about 13,000 towns and villages.

This book listed every single town, village, farm, who owned what, and how much each hold was worth, so that taxes could be applied. This book is still in existence today.

FACT FILE

Conwy castle, in north Wales, is typical of the castles built by the Normans. It was built to give defending archers an uninterrupted field of fire against any attackers, and could withstand a long siege.

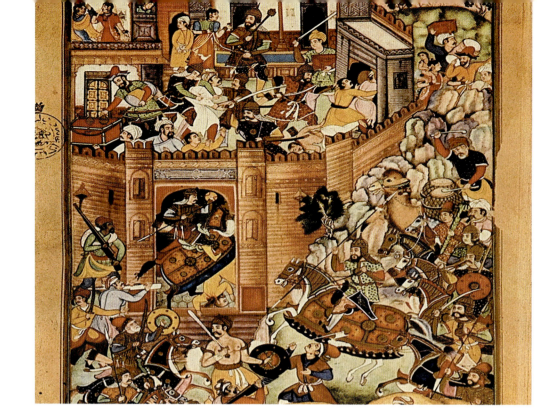

HOW DID THE MONGOLS LIVE?

The Mongols never settled permanently, but lived in large circular tent-like prefabricated homes called yurts.

These were carried with them during their migrations and invasions, and are still used today. They are made of felt, which is fastened over a light wooden frame. The whole structure can be quickly dismantled and carried by horses as the Mongol tribes migrate across the steppes, or grassy plains, following their grazing flocks.

The Mongols were feared for the ferocity of their unpredictable attacks on cities throughout Asia and the Middle East. Genghis Khan was a famous Mongol who unified the scattered tribes and began the conquest that resulted in the Mongols controlling nearly all of Asia and threatening to destroy Europe. After the death of Genghis' grandson, Kublai, the Empire proved too large to govern and began to break up.

FACT FILE

This is an example of a Mongol home called a yurt, which they carried with them during their migrations and invasions.

HOW EXTENSIVE WAS THE MONGOL EMPIRE?

Kiev

RUSSIA

MONGOLIA

Baghdad

Peking JAPAN

CHINA

KASHMIR

TIBET

INDIA

Mongol Empire

The vast Mongol empire stretched across central Asia from the sea of Japan to the Caspian Sea and occupying most of modern Russia. The Mongols succeeded against established armies because they were unpredictable. They charged into battle on horseback, relying entirely on speed and surprise, and taking no prisoners. The Mongols were remorseless fighters, developing fighting machines that enabled them to break into the cities they besieged. They were merciless towards those people who resisted them and sometimes they slaughtered entire populations. Most cities surrendered immediately, rather than risk being massacred!

FACT FILE

Marco Polo was one of the first Europeans to travel through Mongol territory. His reports helped to establish trade routes there.

HOW LONG WAS THE HUNDRED YEARS WAR?

The Hundred Years War began in 1337 and continued for more than a century. It was not a single war, but a series of skirmishes between England and France. It began when the English tried to dominate France, and the French in turn tried to confiscate lands occupied by the English.

The English invaded France and won a great battle at Crécy. The British archers with their longbows defeated a much larger army of knights, marking the beginning of the end for mounted knights. Further battles followed, but in 1396, Richard II of England married the daughter of Charles VI of France, establishing a 20-year truce that finally ended the fighting.

FACT FILE

The two branches of the Plantagenet family battled for the throne in the Wars of the Roses. The name comes from the red rose of Lancaster and the white Rose of York.

▮	1347
▮	1348
▮	1349
▮	1350

SCANDINAVIA

RUSSIA

BRITISH ISLES

POLAND

GERMANY

FRANCE

SPAIN

ITALY

GREECE

TURKEY

PERSIA

AFRICA

HOW WIDESPREAD WAS THE BLACK DEATH?

The Black Death was an epidemic that permanently changed the face of medieval Europe. It killed more than one-quarter of the population, causing thousands of villages to be abandoned and subsequently to disappear.

The Black Death probably arrived in Europe from Central Asia by way of Mongol raiders. It first caused epidemics in Italy in 1347, spreading rapidly through the rest of Europe.

The disease was spread by the bite of fleas from infected rats, but because its cause was not understood, the infection raged unchecked. The fear led to a wave of religious hysteria. A shortage of manual workers led to the collapse of the long-established feudal system.

FACT FILE

To try and ward off The Black Death, people burned incense, believing that the disease was transmitted in the air. Towns rang church bells, or fired cannons, in a futile attempt to drive the plague away

HOW DID THE SPANISH EMPIRE DEVELOP?

After the discovery of the Americas, Spanish adventurers set out to seek their fortunes. They sent expeditions to South and Central America and to Mexico in search of gold and treasure. In Mexico, a group of Spanish soldiers attacked the capital of the Aztec Empire. The Aztecs had been expecting the god Quetzalcoatl to return to Earth and believed that the leader of the raiders, Cortés, was this god. The Aztecs offered little resistance, so Cortés captured Montezuma, the Aztec emperor, and ruled in his place. In Peru, the adventurer Pizarro took advantage of a civil war to conquer the Incas, murdering their rulers.

FACT FILE

Other nations expanded their empires in the same way as the Spanish. Many British people sailed to America to establish themselves and settle on this newly discovered land.

Several factors made it easy for a small group of Spaniards to conquer these great civilizations. Though vastly outnumbered, the Spanish had horses, armour and guns, which gave them a huge advantage over the native warriors.

HOW WAS THE SPANISH ARMADA DEFEATED?

The English were envious of Spain's rich colonies in South and Central America. During the reign of Elizabeth I, the English raided Spanish ships carrying gold and silver to Spain. The Spanish suspected that the English Crown supported these privateers, which angered them. To make matters worse, an English army helped the Dutch, who were fighting against Spanish rule. In 1588 Philip II of Spain sent the Spanish Armada to invade England. The Spanish came very close to actually conquering England at this time. Their Armada, however, was scattered by storms, then harried and destroyed by English ships.

FACT FILE

Ships such as these were also responsible for the voyages of pilgrims, in search of a new life, heading from England to America. This particular ship is called The Mayflower.

HOW DID AMERICA BECOME INDEPENDENT?

Resentment against taxes imposed on the American colonies by Britain finally led to the Declaration of Independence, and in the following war, the Americans finally gained full independence of British rule.

The new American nation consisted of 13 states (this has now grown to 50). It had a president, who would be elected every four years, and was run by a Congress. This same structure exists to the present day.

FACT FILE

Eleven Confederate states (orange) broke away from the Union (green) fearing the abolition of slavery. Five slave states (red) stayed in the Union, although some of their people supported the Confederacy.

HOW DID THE AMERICAN INDIANS LOSE THEIR LAND?

FACT FILE

The American flag was originally designed with thirteen stars and thirteen stripes to represent the original colonies that signed the Declaration of Independence. With each new state, another star is added to the flag.

The Native American Indians understandably resented the numbers of settlers who swarmed onto their traditional hunting and grazing lands. As the population of the United States grew rapidly, the Indians were forced to migrate to the south and west. Soon they had nowhere left to go and began to fight back.

The US government reacted by forcing the American Indians into reservations on land that was not wanted by the settlers. Many Indians died fighting trying to save their land, or from starvation and disease.

The huge herds of buffalo on which many Indians depended were hunted by the settlers, depriving them of their main source of food, clothing and shelter.

HOW DID AFRICA BECOME COLONIZED?

FACT FILE

Powerful tribes such as the Zulus mounted strong resistance to the invading colonial armies.

The central regions of Africa were not properly explored until the middle of the 1800s. As the continent was explored, it was colonized by European countries seeking territories to exploit and bring them riches.

The British, Dutch, French and Portuguese all established colonies near the coast and later inland. The slave trade had destroyed the structure of many once-powerful African nations, and they were unable to resist the Europeans with their modern weapons. Germany, Belgium and Italy all joined in the scramble to capture new lands in Africa.

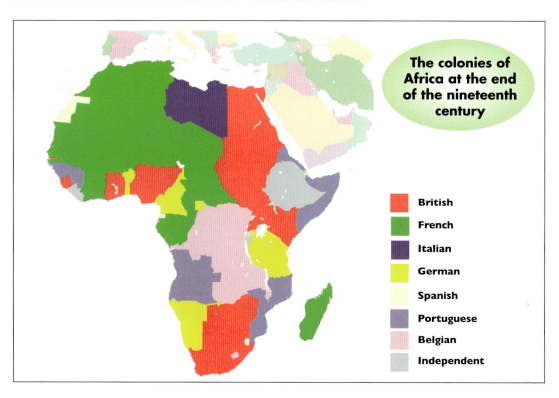

The colonies of Africa at the end of the nineteenth century

- British
- French
- Italian
- German
- Spanish
- Portuguese
- Belgian
- Independent

How did Britain gain Hong Kong?

For centuries, China was a closed country and foreigners were not encouraged to explore it. European traders smuggled huge amounts of opium into China so that people became addicted, paying for the opium with silver. The Chinese government tried to stop this opium trade and the British sent the navy to threaten them. From 1839 to 1842 the British and Chinese fought over access to the Chinese ports. The Chinese were defeated and the British forced them to grant trading rights. Five ports were opened and Hong Kong Island became a British colony. In 1898 Britain was given Hong Kong on a 99-year lease, during which time it became a hugely successful centre of finance and trade.

FACT FILE

Hong Kong was not Britain's only colony. By the middle of the eighteenth century, the British empire had reached every corner of the globe, as this map shows.

■ British Empire
■ British Protectorates

HOW DID THE FRENCH REVOLUTION BEGIN?

On July 14, 1789, a mob attacked the royal prison in Paris, the Bastille. Although only a few prisoners were released, this event marked the end of royal power in France and the beginning of the Revolution.

FACT FILE

Napoleon was a very effective military leader and politician. He ruled France for 15 years, expanding their empire abroad.

During the eighteenth century, France was not prosperous. The government was short of money and needed to raise taxes. Louis XVI could only do this by recalling a traditional assembly, which promptly demanded political reforms. He responded by trying to dismiss the assembly, but the citizens in Paris revolted in support of the assembly.

The new National Assembly showed its strength by introducing fresh laws in 1791, insisting on freedom and equality. The royal family was imprisoned for a while, then tried and executed.

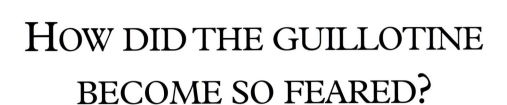

HOW DID THE GUILLOTINE BECOME SO FEARED?

The French Revolution was opposed by neighbouring countries who feared that unrest would spread across Europe. A Committee of Public Safety was set up in France to defend the revolution, and they executed any person who might oppose the committee. In fact, thousands of people who were thought to threaten this new regime were put to death by the recently invented guillotine. This period became known as the Reign of Terror. It lasted for about a year and during this time around 18,000 people were put to death. The French aristocracy was almost entirely wiped out, together with any political opponents of the regime. The Reign of Terror finally came to an end when the head of the Committee of Public Safety, Robespierre, was accused of treason.

After the revolution, anyone thought to be opposing the new regime was immediately beheaded by guillotine.

FACT FILE

Marie-Antoinette, wife of Louis XVI, was an influential woman in the court. She met a gruesome death, beheaded on the guillotine.

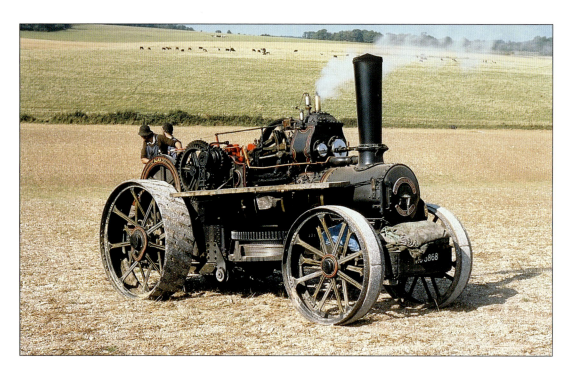

HOW DID THE INDUSTRIAL REVOLUTION CHANGE BRITAIN?

Back in the early eighteenth century, Britain was still largely an agricultural nation. The few manufactured goods were made in small workshops or at home. As a result of Britain's world trading, the cotton industry developed and everything changed. At first, water power was used to drive spinning and weaving machines, and factories and mills were set up. New towns were built to provide homes for the workers. Steam engines were adapted to provide power to factories. The railway and canal system were developed. The other key development was the smelting of iron using coke rather than wood. Britain was able to exploit the raw materials from her overseas empire to become one the world's most prosperous industrial nations.

FACT FILE

Trade with the Far East involved a long voyage around the tip of Africa. The Suez Canal provided a quick route through the Mediterranean and the Red Sea.

HOW SIGNIFICANT WAS THE INVENTION OF THE STEAM ENGINE?

The invention of practical steam engines was the most significant advance in the eighteenth century, providing power for the Industrial Revolution. The first steam engines were massive stationary devices that pumped water from flooded mines, but they were soon adapted to power vessels.

The first steam locomotives appeared in the early nineteenth century. They carried goods and allowed people to travel to factories where they worked. Trains were an important means for social change because, for the first time, people could travel quickly and visit areas that were previously too far away.

FACT FILE

Steam locomotion also made overseas trading possible. One of the most impor ant exports was tea, which was in great demand in Europe.

HOW DID WORLD WAR I BEGIN?

Continual trouble in the Balkans led to the formation of several complicated military alliances throughout Europe. The continent was eventually split into two groups. Britain, France and later Russia joined to form the Entente Cordiale, while Germany, Austria-Hungary and Italy formed the Triple Alliance. In 1914 Archduke Franz Ferdinand of Austria-Hungary was assassinated in Serbia, activating the alliance agreements. First Austria declared war on Serbia, Russia sided with Serbia, and then Germany declared war on Russia. Germany invaded Belgium, bringing the British and French into the conflict.

FACT FILE

The Versailles Treaty ended World War I, but its terms were so severe that Germany suffered economic collapse and this caused resentment that was to build up and eventually contribute to the causes of World War II.

Central Powers
Allies
Neutral nations

NORWAY
SWEDEN
IRELAND
DENMARK
BRITISH ISLES
NETHERLANDS
GERMANY
BELGIUM
RUSSIA
Paris
AUSTRO-HUNGARIAN EMPIRE
SWITZERLAND
FRANCE
PORTUGAL
ROMANIA
SPAIN
ITALY
SERBIA
BULGARIA
ALBANIA
OTTOMAN EMPIRE
Mediterranean Sea
GREECE

HOW DID NEW TECHNOLOGY INFLUENCE WORLD WAR I?

World War I was the first mechanized war in history. In the beginning, fighting was similar to wars fought in the previous century. But new and terrifying weapons were introduced, which completely changed the whole style of warfare.

Aircraft were used for the first time to observe the enemy and to locate suitable targets for the long-range artillery. Later on, fighter planes began to shoot down the spotters, introducing aerial warfare. Aircraft and Zeppelin airships were used as bombers.

The most terrifying new weapon was poison gas, which was used by both sides. It caused millions of deaths and terrible suffering. Tanks also made their first appearance.

FACT FILE

The war brought the first armoured tanks into battle. They could break through enemy lines and create openings for troops. Earlier use of tanks could have saved lives and helped shorten the war.

HOW DID WORLD WAR II BEGIN?

As in World War I, some international alliances were activated following the German invasion of Poland. As a result of this, Britain and France declared war on Germany.

When the Germans attacked Poland, the Russians also attacked the country and it was divided.

The Germans went on to invade Denmark, Norway, Belgium, The Netherlands and France in quick succession. They crushed any resistance with overwhelming armoured forces.

World War II killed more people than any other war in history. The fighting spread to nearly every part of the world and included nearly 60 nations.

The Americans entered the war in 1941 after being attacked by Germany's ally Japan. At this time a huge military build-up began in England.

Axis countries (sympathetic to Germany)

Axis occupied areas

Allies

Neutral countries

SOVIET RUSSIA
FINLAND
NORWAY
SWEDEN
EIRE
BRITISH ISLES
POLAND
GERMANY
CZECHOSLOVAKIA
SWITZERLAND
AUSTRIA
FRANCE
HUNGARY
ROMANIA
PORTUGAL
SPAIN
Black Sea
BULGARIA
ITALY
TURKEY
TUNISIA
Mediterranean Sea
LIBYA
EGYPT

HOW STRONG WAS NAZI FIGHTING POWER?

FACT FILE

The greatest military operation ever carried out was the invasion of Europe by the Allied forces in 1944, when millions of troops were ferried across the Channel and landed from floating harbours on the shores of France.

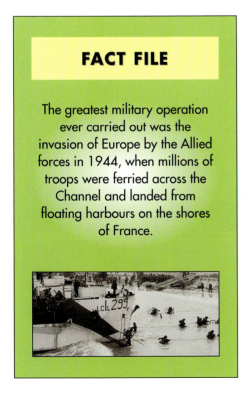

When the Germans realized that the British defences were too strong for their aircraft, they tried to destroy British industry. They hoped to damage the morale of the British population by night bombing of the cities. The German Luftwaffe, which was considered to be far superior to the RAF, set out to bomb the British airfields and shoot down their aircraft. The Luftwaffe abandoned its attempts to defeat the RAF when they realized they were flying too far from home and ran short of fuel. As part of their policy to 'purify' the German race, the Nazis had a plan to exterminate the Jews.

HOW DID THE UNITED NATIONS BEGIN?

The flag of the United Nations

During World War II, the Allied nations referred to themselves as the 'United Nations'. In 1942 they agreed that they would not make any separate peace agreements with Germany.

It was the Potsdam Conference in 1945 that really laid the ground for the foundation of the United Nations to prevent future conflict and also set out procedures for the prosecution of Nazi war criminals. Twenty-seven countries signed this first agreement and in 1945, after the war, the United Nations formally came into existence with an initial membership of fifty countries.

The United Nations (UN) is led by a powerful Security Council, which can intervene in international disputes that might lead to conflict. Today the UN is also involved in many economic aid programmes around the world.

FACT FILE

Early in 1945 the Allied leaders met in Yalta in the Crimea to decide on the post-war shape of the world. Churchill, Roosevelt and Stalin decided on how Germany was to be split up once the war was won.

What?

WHAT DID EARLY EXPLORERS USE FOR NAVIGATION?

An astrolabe

Early astronomers and navigators used astrolabes to measure the angles of celestial bodies above the horizon. A metal disk mounted on a circular frame is suspended vertically and the observer looks through the sights to line up a star and then measures its position against the marks on the frame. He can then use tables to work out his postion. The astrolabe remained in use from the time of the ancient Greeks until the seventeenth century, when it was replaced by more accurate instruments such as the sextant.

People probably made rough maps even before they began to use written language some 5,500 years ago. Over the centuries, maps became more accurate as people explored the world and developed improved ways to make maps. An early map of the world appeared in a 1482 edition of Ptolemy's eight-volume *Geography*.

FACT FILE

Ferdinand Magellan was a Portuguese sea captain who commanded the first expedition that sailed around the world. His voyage provided the first positive proof that the Earth is round. Many scholars consider it the greatest navigational feat in history.

WHAT WAS DAILY LIFE LIKE IN ANCIENT GREECE?

Much of what we know about how the Greeks lived comes from pictures on vases. The pictures not only show wars and stories from mythology, but also daily activities such as hunting, farming and fishing. Greek homes were built around a central courtyard, cool and airy, where the family slaves prepared food on an open fire. There was a small shrine to the household god. Many houses were made without windows in the outer walls. This design kept out both the hot sun and thieves. People ate with their fingers, while lying on wooden couches. Slaves brought in the dishes of food, while a musician played on pipes or a lyre. Men and women wore a *chiton*, a cloth square draped over the body and fastened by a pin at the shoulder.

FACT FILE

A portrait of a Greek woman on a fragment of pottery. Greek women spent most of their time around the home organizing the household.

WHAT IS STONEHENGE?

Stonehenge on Salisbury Plain

More than 5,000 years ago, Europeans were building spectacular stone monuments. Many of these are still standing today, as mysterious relics of a long-gone society. The huge stones that were used are called megaliths (meaning 'big stones'). Some were set up on their own, and others in groups or circles.

Stonehenge is a very famous Neolithic stone monument, which was built in several stages between 1800 and 1400 BC on Salisbury Plain. No one really knows why it was built. It is a series of concentric rings of standing stones around an altar stone at the centre. During the second stage, blue stones from the Preseli Mountains in Wales were hauled onto the site in an astonishing feat of organization and transport. The construction was highly accurate for the period. The standing stones are up to 23 ft (7m) high and weigh up to 47 tonnes each.

FACT FILE

Rock tombs, slab tombs, such as this dolmen, and stone circles and temples lie scattered across Europe, including on the island of Malta.

WHAT ARE HIEROGLYPHICS?

Egyptian picture-writing is known as hieroglyphics. This language is made up of about 750 signs, with pictures of people, animals and objects. Until hieroglyphics was deciphered in modern times, it was not known that most of the pictures represented sounds and syllables, not whole words. Scribes used a quick form of writing, which was called hieratic. The Egyptians were also good at maths, particularly geometry, which they used in architecture and surveying. They drew up an accurate 12-month calendar of 365 days, and used water clocks to measure time.

Chest from tomb of Tutankhamun

FACT FILE

The Egyptian Sun god Ra was often portrayed in picture form simply as a sun disk. He appeared in other forms too, including a cat, bird and a lion.

WHAT IS SUTTON HOO?

The most powerful ruler among the English kings was acknowledged as 'bretwalda', or supreme king.

The Sutton Hoo ship burial site in Suffolk was discovered in AD 1939. It is almost certainly the monument to King Redwald of East Anglia, who was bretwalda in the AD 620s, and who died in AD 627.

Artefacts unearthed by archaeologists at the Sutton Hoo site included a gold belt, a sword and a shield. There were also several items of jewellery. Most importantly, there was a sceptre and standard, which must have belonged to the dead King Redwald. The iron helmet (*right*) was another one of the treasures to be unearthed at Sutton Hoo.

FACT FILE

The Scots' leader Kenneth MacAlpin, was the first king to rule the land we now call Scotland. Raiders from the north, Picts and Scots, attacked northern England once the Roman army were no longer around to protect the Roman Britons of England.

264

WHAT WERE THE CRUSADES?

FACT FILE

Richard I of England and Philip II of France led the armies of the Third Crusade, setting sail for the Holy Land in 1189.

The Byzantine emperor, a Christian monarch who lived in Constantinople, needed help. He turned to the pope, who in 1095 called for all Christians to start a holy war against the Seljuk Turks.

Thousands rushed to join the Crusader armies. They crossed into Palestine and recaptured the important cities of Nicaea and Antioch. Jerusalem fell in 1099 after a desperate siege lasting six weeks, and the Crusaders took terrible revenge by slaughtering thousands of Muslims. There were to be three more crusades: one in 1147-48, another in 1189-92 and finally the Children's Crusade in 1212. Some 50,000 children set off from France and Germany for the Holy Land. Many died on the journey, many more were captured and sold as slaves in Africa.

WHAT WAS THE MAGNA CARTA?

The youngest son of Henry II, John, inherited from his brother Richard the throne of England, as well as the Plantagenet dominions of France, which he had lost to the French by 1204. John's failure to recapture these

Magna Carta

territories, his dispute with Rome over the Pope's choice of a new Archbishop of Canterbury, and a high level of taxation, had the English nobility up in arms against him.

In 1215 they forced the King to agree to the Magna Carta, guaranteeing their rights in relation to those of the crown. It was intended to protect the rights of nobles, and made sure that no-one was imprisoned without a fair trial. Copies of this document, which tried to put an end to the king's abuse of his power, were distributed across the whole of England. This led to civil war, which only ended with John's death in 1216.

Despite all these disasters, it is now known that John was a much better king than history has actually portrayed him.

John

FACT FILE

The magnificent coronation of Charles V. He became king of Spain in 1516 (he was the grandson of King Ferdinand and Queen Isabella of Spain), and three years later he was crowned Holy Roman Emperor.

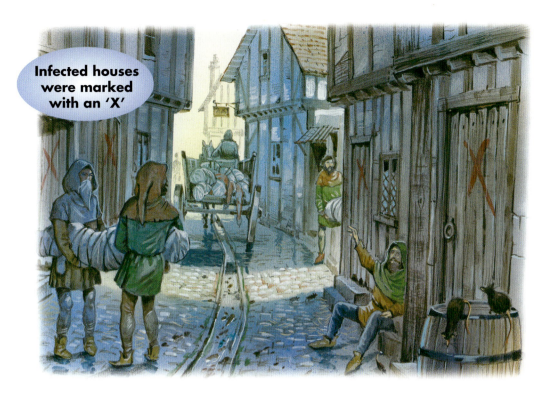

Infected houses were marked with an 'X'

WHAT WAS THE BLACK DEATH?

The bubonic plague (or 'Black Death') was a deadly disease, which brought death to most parts of Asia, North Africa and Europe. The first outbreak was recorded in 1331 in China. The plague started as a bloody swelling in the armpit or groin and quickly invaded the whole body. It was highly contagious and killed millions of people. The infection probably began on the steppes, the grassy plains of Asia. It was carried by fleas, which lived in the fur of the black rat. The rats lived close to humans and thus the disease spread rapidly. Corpses were left out in the road for people to collect, thus spreading the disease even further.

FACT FILE

Medieval paintings often depicted death as a skeleton, dancing and leading victims to their end. The epidemic killed at least 25,000,000 people in Europe and the Near East.

WHAT DO WE KNOW ABOUT THE EARLY HISTORY OF AFRICA?

FACT FILE

A view showing what the Great Enclosure inside the city of Great Zimbabwe may have looked like.

We know very little about the early history of Africa. There must have been great civilizations there, but very few of them developed writing or left any records. Some civilizations built fine communities, such as the east coast port of Kilwa or the mysterious stone complex of Great Zimbabwe. After about AD 700, Muslims from the Near East began to take over many coastal regions and trade routes. One of the wealthiest of the medieval African empires was Mali. Starting in 1240, its Islamic rulers built up a kingdom which stretched over large areas of West Africa. Much of the land was desert, but Mali grew rich from gold.

The Great Mosque, Djenne, Mali

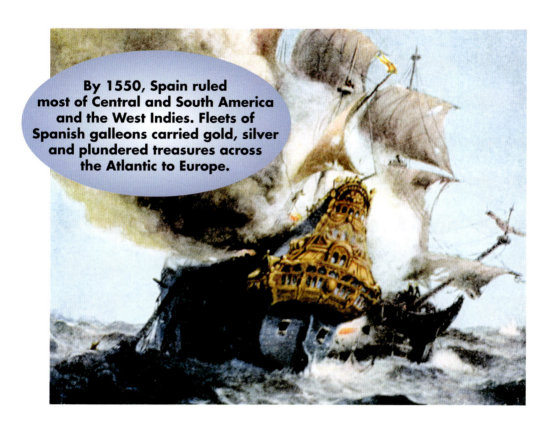

By 1550, Spain ruled most of Central and South America and the West Indies. Fleets of Spanish galleons carried gold, silver and plundered treasures across the Atlantic to Europe.

WHAT WAS THE NEW WORLD?

From 1492 onwards, European explorers sailed across the Atlantic to what they called the New World of North, Central and South America. There they discovered a treasure trove of gold and silver. They also discovered foods that only grew in the New World, such as sweetcorn, potatoes and plants that could be made into medicines.

The people that settled in the New World were traders rather than soldiers. Their first contact with the people already living there was friendly. The Native Americans showed the newcomers how to hunt, fish and farm in a land of plenty. In return they were given objects such as knives, needles, fish hooks and cloth.

FACT FILE

A modern replica of the Mayflower, the ship in which the first Pilgrims set sail from England in 1620.

WHAT WAS THE INDUSTRIAL REVOLUTION?

FACT FILE

Raw cotton, grown mainly in the USA, was very difficult and slow to clean. Whitney's cotton gin was a simple machine, which brushed out the seeds from the cotton.

One of the biggest changes in the history of the world, the Industrial Revolution, started in Britain in the late eighteenth century. As the 'Workshop of the World' Britain was the first home of new machines, new types of materials and new ways of making power. This was the age of coal and iron, of electricity and gas, of railways and factories. These factories created millions of new jobs, so people began to leave the countryside to work in the towns. Houses and factories had to be built for them. By 1850, over 60 per cent of Britons lived in towns. Factory workers led hard lives, often working 14 hours a day, 6 days a week.

Ironworks at Coalbrookdale in Shropshire

WHAT WAS HOME RULE?

In 1870, a movement calling for Home Rule was founded in Ireland. Supporters of Home Rule wanted a separate parliament to deal with Irish affairs in Dublin. Although the British government was forced to introduce many reforms, two bills to introduce Home Rule were defeated in parliament in the 1880s and 1980s. William Gladstone was Prime Minister of Britain four times during the reign of Queen Victoria. He believed that the Irish should run their own affairs and was a staunch supporter of Home Rule. But he failed to get his Home Rule Bill approved by parliament. During World War I, the issue of Home Rule continued to cause conflict in Ireland. The third Home Rule Bill had been passed by the British parliament in

William Gladstone

1914, but the outbreak of war in the same year delayed the start. Irish protestants, however, were bitterly opposed to Home Rule. They were in the majority in the northern province of Ulster, and believed that they would be treated unfairly by a Dublin parliament. They formed the Ulster Volunteer Force to protect themselves if Home Rule was introduced.

FACT FILE

Irish politician Charles Parnell addresses an audience in support of Home Rule. He became leader of the Home Rule Party in the British parliament and fought tirelessly for his beliefs.

WHAT WAS STEPHENSON'S ROCKET?

Modern rail travel owes its existence to the great engineer George Stephenson. While working as a mechanic in a coal mine, he educated himself at night school. By 1812, he was a chief mechanic and, in 1814, he built his first locomotive, the Blucher.

This locomotive propelled itself at 4 miles (6 km) per hour and could pull eight wagons loaded with coal. Stephenson refined the steam engine until, in 1829, he built the first practical steam locomotive, the Rocket.

It could travel at an amazing 36 miles (58 km) per hour.

George Stephenson

WHAT WAS THE WOMEN'S MOVEMENT?

FACT FILE

In Britain, the suffragette campaigners often went on hunger strike when imprisoned for their actions. The authorities did not want them to die, and arouse public sympathy, so they fed the women by force.

The women's movement had its roots in the late eighteenth and early nineteenth centuries. The American and French revolutions promoted ideas of 'equality' and 'liberty', yet women could not vote, and had limited access to education.

In 1792, a British writer called Mary Wollstonecraft published *A Vindication of the Rights of Women*, setting out her belief in equal rights for men and women. This idea took a firm hold during the 1800s, and many women started to campaign for reform. The suffragettes engaged in many different forms of protest, including chaining themselves to railings outside the residence of the British Prime Minister.

WHAT WERE NINETEENTH-CENTURY SLUMS LIKE?

The events of the Industrial Revolution brought great changes to towns and cities in Britain. People needed to live close to their workplace, so huge numbers of houses were put up to accommodate this new class of industrial worker. The speed with which many towns and cities expanded led to problems with overcrowding, and dirty and insanitary housing. Many workers were forced to live in slum conditions. Worse, the new factories created pollution that often contaminated both water supplies and the air. Early industrial cities were disease-ridden places with very high death rates.

FACT FILE

Life in the industrial centres revolved around the mines, mills and factories where people worked.

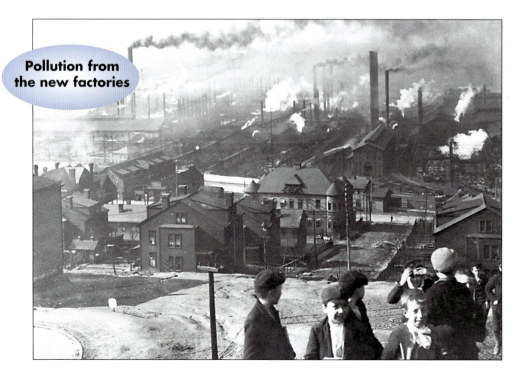

Pollution from the new factories

274

WHAT WAS THE GREAT DEPRESSION?

A disastrous stock market crash in 1929 in the USA left many people penniless overnight. The effects of the Wall Street Crash were felt all over the world. Many countries in Europe were hard hit because they had borrowed money from the USA at the end of World War I. Throughout the 1930s, unemployment soared and trade slumped in a period known as the Great Depression.

During the worst years of the Depression, many people were forced to rely on charity and government hand-outs for their most basic needs. In 1932 Franklin D. Roosevelt was elected US present. His 'New Deal' aimed to create jobs and to protect people's savings by regulating banks more closely.

FACT FILE

This is the Stock Exchange in Wall Street at the time of its collapse. You can see brokers spilling out onto the streets of the city of New York.

WHAT WAS THE TREATY OF VERSAILLES?

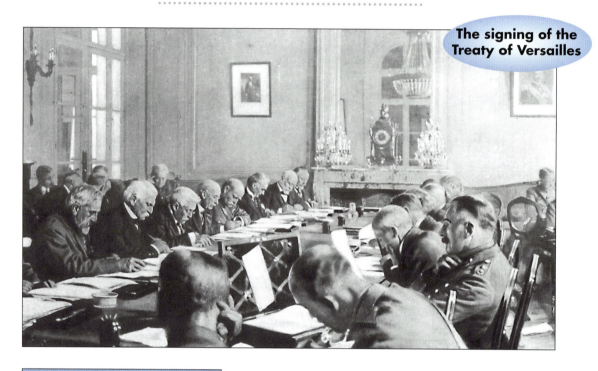

The signing of the Treaty of Versailles

FACT FILE

The signing of the Treaty of Versailles on June 28, 1919, in Paris, was the fifth anniversary of the shooting of Archduke Ferdinand in Sarajevo.

The Treaty of Versailles was a peace document signed at the end of World War I by the Allied and Associated Powers and by Germany. It took place in the Hall of Mirrors in the Palace of Versailles, France, on June 28, 1919 and actually came into force on January 10, 1920.

The treaty was drafted during the Paris Peace Conference in the spring of 1919, which was dominated by the national leaders known as the 'Big Four', David Lloyd George of Britain, Georges Clemenceau of France, Woodrow Wilson of the United States and Vittorio Orlando of Italy. They wanted to make sure that Germany would never again pose a military threat. The treaty contained a number of stipulations to guarantee this.

WHAT WAS THE EASTER RISING?

FACT FILE

The British Prime Minister, David Lloyd George, proposed that Ireland would stay under British control, but the Irish Free State would become a British dominion.

During World War I, the issue of Home Rule continued to cause conflict in Ireland. When war actually broke out in 1914, most Irish Volunteers supported Britain in its fight against the Central Powers. But a breakaway group formed the Irish Republican Brotherhood (later known as the IRA). On Easter Monday, 1916, protesters belonging to this and other nationalist movements seized buildings in Dublin and proclaimed Ireland a republic. This rebellion became known as the Easter Rising.

Easter Monday, 1916

WHAT WAS THE
BATTLE OF BRITAIN?

During World War II, the Allied forces of Britain and France became trapped by the rapid German invasion. In June 1940, the French signed a truce with Germany and Britain stood alone against the Germans.

Italy joined the war, siding with the Germans. In June 1940 Hitler made plans to invade Britain. However, he first needed to gain control of the skies. The Battle of Britain began in July 1940 between the German airforce, the Luftwaffe, and Britain's Royal Air Force (RAF). By May 1941 the RAF had gained the upper hand and Hitler stopped the bombing.

FACT FILE

Allied troops wait on a beach at Dunkerque, in northern France, in June 1940. A rescue fleet of naval ships, fishing boats, yachts and ferries sailed across the English Channel from England to carry them back to safety. In all, 300,000 soldiers were rescued.

WHAT WAS THE HOLOCAUST?

Jews held in a concentration camp

In the early 1930s, the Nazi party rose to power in Germany, led by Adolf Hitler. He set up a secret police force, banned opposing political parties and started to persecute minority groups in the German population, such as gypsies and Jews.

During World War II, concentration camps such as Belsen and Auschwitz were set up by the Nazis. Millions of Jews were imprisoned and murdered in these camps because Hitler believed they were responsible for the downfall of Germany. An estimated 6,000,000 Jews died in these camps in World War II, an event known as the Holocaust.

FACT FILE

The official flag of the United Nations consists of a map of the world circled by two olive branches. The olive branches are a symbol of peace.

What was the Blitzkrieg?

World War II was very different to the first international conflict. Trench warfare, which had claimed so many lives, was now an outdated concept. When Adolf Hitler invaded Poland in September 1939, he unleashed a new and frightening brand of warfare into the world – called 'Blitzkrieg' or lightning war.

The key to the success of Blitzkrieg was the use of tanks in very large numbers and innovative style. The tanks charged ahead independent of the troops and wreaked havoc among defenders. Bursting through defensive lines they created confusion and smashed supply lines.

FACT FILE

World War I had deadly new weaponry as well. The introduction of machine guns changed the way that they fought from the trenches. They could now easily wipe out large numbers of attacking soldiers.

Tanks used during Blitzkrieg

WHAT IS COMMUNISM?

FACT FILE

Chairman Mao and his supporters accused many people of failing to follow communist ideals. Students and young people formed groups of 'Red Guards' in support of Mao.

Communism is a system of political and economic organization in which property is owned by the state and all citizens share the common wealth, more or less according to their needs. After years of civil war, much of China was in ruins. Mao Zedong set about reforming the country according to communist ideals. Land was seized from landowners and divided up among the peasants. In Mao's 'Five-Year Plan' (1953 to 1957) new roads and railways were built, industry boosted, and health and education improved. Mao printed his ideals about his communist state in what became known as Mao's 'Little Red Book', which was read by millions of Chinese.

WHAT WAS THE CUBAN MISSILE CRISIS?

In 1949, the Western Allies formed the North Atlantic Treaty Organization (NATO) for defence against the communist presence in Europe. In the same year, the USSR exploded its first atomic bomb. With both superpowers holding nuclear weapons, fear and mistrust between the two sides increased. The Soviets constructed a wall across Berlin in 1961, separating East from West in the city. In 1962, the Cuban crisis erupted when the USA discovered that the USSR was building missile sites on the island of Cuba in the Caribbean. These sites were within range to launch an attack by nuclear weapons on American cities. The two superpowers came to the brink of war before the USSR agreed to withdraw the weapons.

Although the two superpowers never became involved in direct warfare, both sides became involved in wars elsewhere in the world. The USA fought communism and the USSR helped communist fighters.

FACT FILE

John Fitzgerald Kennedy was US president from 1961 until he was assassinated in 1963. During his presidency the Berlin Wall was built, dividing the city in two and stopping East Germans escaping communist rule.

The Vietnam War between North and South Vietnam lasted from 1957 until 1976. This is a statue of remembrance in Washington D.C.

When?

TELL ME ABOUT HISTORY : WHEN

WHEN WAS THE STONE AGE?

Stone Age man (known as Neanderthal man) lived in Europe from about 100,000 to 35,000 years ago. They sheltered in caves, made fire and hunted animals using stone tools and wooden spears.

Historians call this period of prehistory the Stone Age, because stone was the most important material used by the first tool-makers. These early stone-crafting techniques show surprising skill. They chipped or flaked off bits of stone to make shaped tools including hand axes and knives. Both the hand axe and scraper were usually made from flint, while spear heads were often shaped from wood or deer antlers.

The Stone Age hunters killed deer and other animals with spears, bows and stones, often ambushing them on the move. Although they were not as fast as the animals they hunted, they made up for it by using teamwork and accuracy with their weapons.

A skull of a Neanderthal man

Spear head

Scraper

Hand axe

FACT FILE

Stone Age people hunted with bows, spears and flint axes. On the American grasslands, groups of hunters drove to extinction large grazing animals such as mastodons and giant bison.

Ships lie beside a Viking town

WHEN DID THE VIKINGS PROGRESS THROUGH EUROPE?

The Vikings came from Scandinavia (Norway, Denmark and Sweden). Their homelands offered little spare farmland for a growing population, so many Vikings went abroad in search of new lands. The Vikings were farmers, but also fierce warriors, and their first impact on western Europe was a violent one. They began to sail across the North Sea in the late AD 700s, raiding the coasts of Britain and mainland Europe. They raided churches and towns, carrying off loot and slaves. Their raids caused panic, and rulers tried to buy off the invaders with gold. This, however, only encouraged the Vikings to come back for more.

FACT FILE

Decorative brooches such as this were used by both Viking men and women to hold their outer garments (cloaks and tunics) in place.

WHEN WAS THE HUNDRED YEARS WAR?

The 14th century was filled with wars. The longest and most exhausting of these wars was between England and France. It lasted, on and off, until the middle of the 1400s, and is known as the Hundred Years War. It actually spanned from 1337 until 1453, by which time the French, inspired by Joan of Arc, had driven the English from Maine, Gascony and Normandy and the war was finally won. The conflict was a very complicated one. The Plantagenet kings of England also ruled a large part of France, while the rest belonged to the king of France. Both kings wanted to be the sole ruler of a united country. There were plenty of other reasons for the war. The French supported the Scots in their struggle against England. The English, in turn, claimed the throne of France when Charles IV died in 1328 and left no heirs.

Edward, known as the Black Prince

FACT FILE

English troops lay siege to the French town of Troyes. The city gates have been shut and barred against them. English officials are trying to persuade the leaders of Troyes to surrender.

WHEN DID THE GREAT NATIONS OF EUROPE EMERGE?

After about 1450, the great nations of Europe began to emerge. For most of their history they had consisted of small warring states, or had been invaded by powerful neighbours. Now things were changing fast.

The connection between France and England was broken at last. Spain and Portugal grew stable enough to found their great seagoing empires. Germany (part of the Holy Roman Empire) had strong leaders from the Habsburg dynasty. The marriage in 1492 of King Ferdinand and Queen Isabella of Spain helped to unite the two strong Christian kingdoms of Aragon and Castile. Ferdinand and Isabella also completed the great 'reconquest' of Spain from Muslim control, which had begun over 400 years earlier.

FACT FILE

Unlike Spain, Italy remained a divided country, split up into several states ruled by different powers. In the north were the wealthy city-states, such as Florence, Milan and Urbino. The crest (below) belongs to the Sforza family, who ruled over Milan.

King Ferdinand and Queen Isabella

WHEN WAS THE THIRTY YEARS WAR?

The last and biggest religious war began in Germany in 1618 and continued until 1648. This very messy conflict became known as the Thirty Years' War.

The war started in a dramatic way. Protestants in Bohemia (now part of the Czech Republic) were angry with their new king, Ferdinand. He was a member of the powerful Spanish Habsburg family, and wanted to restore Bohemia to the Catholic faith. The Protestants banded together and threw some Catholic officials from an upstairs window in Prague Castle. The incident sparked off a civil war in Bohemia. In 1619 the rebels expelled Ferdinand and chose a new king, the Protestant Frederick.

FACT FILE

When the Protestants threw the Catholic officials out of the window of Prague Castle, it became known as the 'Defenestration of Prague'.

WHEN WAS THE CIVIL WAR IN BRITAIN?

In the year 1603, Britain had a new king – James I. He was the first of the Stuart monarchs, and ruled not only England and Wales, but also Scotland. James believed strongly that God had given kings their right to govern, and no one could question this authority. James's arrogant views and conduct made him very unpopular with his subjects. His son Charles I, who followed him to the throne in 1625, was even less popular. Soon Britain was split by civil wars. Charles wanted to rule without consulting parliament, but he was faced with enormous rebellion. Enraged by this, Charles tried to arrest five members of parliament for treason. The action made him hated all the more and he was forced to flee to London. By August 1642 he had declared war on the parliamentary supporters (known as 'Roundheads').

FACT FILE

A Roundhead helmet. Oliver Cromwell reorganized the Roundhead forces into a professional force known as the 'New Model Army'.

A combined force of Scots and Roundheads defeated Charles and his Royalist forces at the battle of Marston Moor, in Yorkshire, in 1644.

WHEN WAS THE SLAVE TRADE ABOLISHED IN AFRICA?

During the 1700s the slave trade brought misery to thousands of Africans, who were transported across the Atlantic Ocean and forced to work as slaves on plantations in the Americas. This trade also brought huge wealth to those who ran it – the shipbuilders, shipowners, merchants and traders.

Many people began to condemn the slave trade and to call for it to be abolished. The slave trade came to an end in the British Empire in 1807 and was finally abolished within the empire in 1833. Slavery continued elsewhere, however. It did not come to an end in the United States until after the American Civil War in 1865, and continued in Brazil until 1889.

In 1788 an association was formed in London to encourage British exploration and trade in Africa. Many British explorers set out to explore Africa along its rivers. Probably the most famous of all the expeditions was led by David Livingstone, who set out to look for the source of the River Nile. After being out of contact for almost three years, he was eventually found by the American journalist Henry Stanley.

David Livingstone

A typical colonists' hat

FACT FILE

The anti-slavery movement was strongest in Britain and the USA. Many abolitionists joined the struggle for rights for black people.

WHEN WERE THE OPIUM WARS?

The Manchus ruled China for more than 250 years, from 1644 until 1912. This time is known as the Qing dynasty. In the early 1800s, British merchants started to trade opium illegally from India to China. Despite the fact that the addictive dangers of opium were well known, the British government backed the merchants. They wanted to force China to accept more open trade.

The first Opium War broke out in 1839, and was started when Chinese officials seized 20,000 chests of opium in Guangzhou. It ended with the Treaty of Nanjing in 1842. Under the terms of this treaty, Hong Kong became a British colony and more Chinese ports were opened up to European trade. A second Opium War (1856 to 1860) extended the trading rights of European nations in China. Under Manchu rule, all Chinese males had to follow the tradition of wearing their hair in a pigtail. It was seen as a sign of loyalty to the Qing dynasty.

FACT FILE

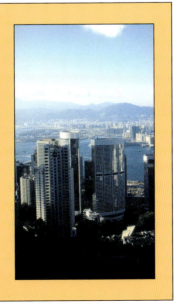

The skyline of modern Hong Kong. The island of Hong Kong came under British control in 1842, and Britain later gained part of the nearby Kowloon Peninsula. Control of Hong Kong passed back to the Chinese government in 1997.

WHEN WAS THE RUSSIAN REVOLUTION?

The last tsar, Nicholas II, ruled from 1894 until his abdication in 1917. In the early years of his reign there was increasing discontent amongst ordinary Russians. Many people, including the Bolshevik leader Vladimir Illyich Lenin, followed the teachings of Karl Marx, the founder of communism. In 1905 this discontent boiled over when troops fired on thousands of striking workers outside the tsar's Winter Palace in St Petersburg. The rebellion was quickly put down, but hundreds of workers were killed and wounded.

In early 1917 riots broke out again and this time the troops supported the rioters. Nicholas II abdicated, and a provisional government was put in place.

FACT FILE

Nicholas II and his family. Imprisoned by the Bolsheviks in 1917, they were most probably shot the following year.

WHEN DID SETTLERS FIRST ARRIVE IN JAPAN?

People from mainland Asia had settled on the islands of Japan by 7000 BC. The original inhabitants may have been the Ainu, about 15,000 of whom still live in Japan. The early Japanese lived by hunting and fishing. Farming began around 1000 to 500 BC, when the Japanese learned to grow rice, a skill brought over from China. They also began to make metal tools and to make pottery using a potter's wheel. The site in Tokyo where pottery was first found, gives this period of history its name – Yayoi.

The Yayoi farmers dug ditches to irrigate their rice fields. They built thatched homes and storehouses on stilts for their rice crop. Farmers lived together in villages, and each village was led by a chief who was often a woman shaman, or magician. The women shamans of Japan were extremely powerful figures.

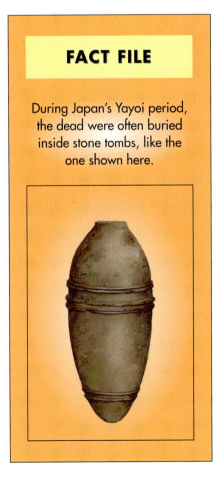

FACT FILE

During Japan's Yayoi period, the dead were often buried inside stone tombs, like the one shown here.

WHEN WAS THE WALL STREET CRASH?

In the late 1920s, the price of shares on the New York Stock Exchange increased rapidly. More and more people bought stocks and shares in the hope of selling them again when their price had gone up – therefore making a large profit. When prices dropped in October 1929, people rushed to sell their stocks and shares before it was too late, but prices fell even further. This event is known as the Wall Street Crash. Thousands of people lost all their money, many businesses and banks shut down and unemployment soared.

FACT FILE

During the worst years of the Depression, many people were forced to rely on charity and government hand-outs for their most basic needs. In 1932 Franklin D. Roosevelt was elected US present. His 'New Deal' aimed to create jobs and to protect people's savings by regulating banks more closely.

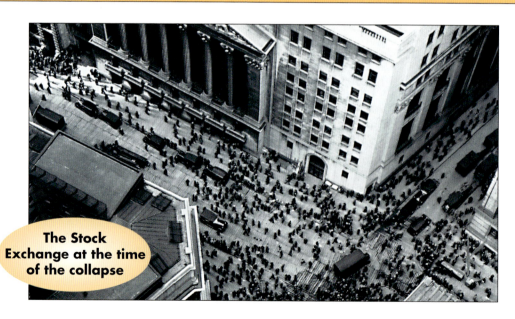

The Stock Exchange at the time of the collapse

WHEN WAS THE RISE OF FASCISM IN EUROPE?

Many people hoped that World War I was the 'war to end all wars'. However, during the 1920s and 1930s there were a lot of political changes in many countries. In 1922 these changes led to the growth of the Fascist movement. The word 'Fascism' from *fasces*, meaning a bundle of branches. Fascism promised strong leadership and to restore the national economy and pride. This was a very powerful message in the years of the Great Depression, and many people in Europe supported the various Fascist parties.

Italy was the first country to have a Fascist ruler. In 1922, Benito Mussolini marched to Rome and demanded that the Italian king, Victor Emmanuel III, make him Prime Minister.

FACT FILE

Sir Oswald Mosley knew Adolf Hitler through his wife, Diana Mitford. He was violently opposed to postwar 'non-white' immigration.

WHEN WAS THE FIRST ATOMIC BOMB EXPLOSION?

Technological advances in the machines and weapons of war were rapid during the 20th century. During World War I, inventions included the tank and the fighter aircraft. At sea, one of the major advances in military marine technology happened before the war, with the building of the battleship *Dreadnought*.

During World War II, the Germans used a new type of warfare, known as *Blitzkreig* (lightning war). But even more horrifying was the invention of the atomic bomb in the United States.

The first atomic bomb was exploded in an experiment in New Mexico, USA in July 1945. Only a month later, atomic bombs were

used to end the war. The bombs dropped on Japan killed about 130,000 people. Many more suffered terrible after effects such as radiation and burn injuries. It was this terrifying bomb that was used to bring the war against Japan to its catastrophic end.

FACT FILE

Both the British and the French armies experimented with tanks during World War I. These armoured vehicles were first used to effect at the battle of Cambrai in 1917.

WHEN DID INDIA GAIN INDEPENDENCE?

FACT FILE

Mohandas Gandhi was known as Mahatma Gandhi. He was assassinated in 1948, at the end of India's long struggle for independence.

Many Indians wanted independence from British rule, and a chance to build up industry and wealth in India itself. By the end of World War II it was clear that Britain could no longer ignore the demands of the Indian people. But negotiations were complicated by the demands of Muslims in India. Violence broke out between Hindus and Muslims, and Indians and British leaders eventually agreed to divide India into the two states of Hindu India and Muslim Pakistan.

India gained its independence in August 1947. Millions of Hindus and Muslims fled from their homes. As people tried to move to their new homes, hundreds of thousands of people were killed.

WHEN WAS THE FIRST LIGHTHOUSE BUILT?

The forerunners to the lighthouse were beacon fires kindled on hilltops, the earliest references to which are contained in the *Iliad* and the *Odyssey* (*c*. 8th century BC). The first authenticated man-made lighthouse was the *Pharos of Alexandria*, which stood some 350 feet (about 100 m) high. The Romans erected many lighthouse towers in the course of expanding their empire, and by AD 400 there were some thirty in service from the Black Sea to the Atlantic. These included lighthouses at Boulogne, France and Dover, England. A fragment of the original Roman lighthouse at Dover still survives.

FACT FILE

Early lighthouses had wood fires or roches burning in the open, sometimes protected by a roof. After the 1st century AD, candles or oil lamps were used in lanterns with panes of glass or horn.

298

WHEN DID THE EASTER EGG TRADITION BEGIN?

Many Easter customs, like Christmas customs, go back to pre-Christian traditions. For all ancient people the coming of spring represented new life. The ancient Egyptians and Persians celebrated their spring festivals by painting and eating eggs, as they still do in parts of Europe today. This is because they considered the egg as a symbol of fertility and new life. The early Christians also adopted the egg as symbolic of new life, the symbol of the Resurrection.

Until relatively recently, eggs, because they came from chickens, were forbidden food during Lent, the 40-day period before Easter. With the ending of Lent, people were so glad to see and eat eggs again that they made it a tradition to eat them on Easter Sunday.

Chocolate Easter eggs are a twentieth-century adaption of this age-old custom.

FACT FILE

In the legends of ancient Egypt and Celtic lands, the hare is associated with the Moon and became a symbol of a new period of life. The Christians therefore took it over and linked it with Easter, and exchanged it for a rabbit.

WHEN WAS HONEY FIRST USED?

Honey has been used as a sweetener since very ancient times, since, apart from dates, it was practically the only way early man could get sugar. It is mentioned in the Bible, the Koran and Homer, as well as many other Greek writers.

It is recorded as being used as a medicine in Egypt, as well as in embalming fluid and as a paste for cosmetics, such as the black kohl they used around their eyes. It was used throughout history to make a sweet, and very strong, beer called 'mead', and to sweeten wine. In ancient India, it was used to preserve and sweeten foods.

Scientists have not yet managed to recreate honey in the laboratory, and there have been concerns about future supplies of honey worldwide because of a parasitic mite called Varroa, which preys upon the bees until the hive dies, as well as the northwards sweep of killer bees in southern North America and aggressive, and less productive African bees in Europe.

FACT FILE

Honey bees tell other worker bees in the colony where good sources of food can be found, by performing a special dance, called the honey dance, on their return to the hive.

WHEN WAS THE INTERNAL COMBUSTION ENGINE DEVELOPED?

Though best known for his invention of the diesel engine, the French-born Rudolf Diesel was also an eminent thermal engineer, a connoisseur of the arts, a linguist, and a social theorist. During 1885 Diesel set up his first shop-laboratory in Paris and began his 13-year ordeal of creating his distinctive engine. At Augsburg, on August 10, 1893, Diesel's first

model, a single 10-foot (3m) iron cylinder with a flywheel at its base, ran on its own power for the first time. Diesel spent two more years on improvements and on the last day of 1896 demonstrated another model with the spectacular mechanical efficiency of 75.6 percent. His engines were used to power pipelines, electric and water plants, automobiles, trucks and marine craft. It was also later used in applications including mines, oil fields, factories, and transoceanic shipping.

FACT FILE

Diesel originally conceived the combustion engine as an alternative to the oversized, expensive, fuel-wasting steam engine, which was being widely used in industry.

301

WHEN WERE THE FIRST HOUSES BUILT?

FACT FILE

Ice Age hunters made shelters from the bones of mammoths. They made the framework of bones and filled in the gaps with skins, turf and moss.

Many early people took refuge in caves, but as they spread out through regions where there were none, they had to find alternatives. Hunters would have made tents from animal skins, while other people made huts from interwoven twigs and plastered mud in the gaps to keep the wind out, and straw on the roof to stop the rain.

The ancient Egyptians are believed to have been among the first to make sun-dried mud bricks, while in Mesopotamia people developed a way of making bricks stronger and more long-lasting, by placing them in a hot fire and firing them. At places like Babylon, such bricks have lasted for thousands of years.

WHEN WAS THE SHANG DYNASTY?

The Shang dynasty was the earliest known Chinese family of rulers. The dynasty governed from the sixteenth to eleventh centuries BC.

Its central point was in what is now known as the northern Henan Province, in the valley of the Huang He (the Yellow River). Shang society was based on agriculture, but because of their perfection of irrigation techniques the kings became wealthy and a tradition of beautiful bronze work grew up. As well as decorative vessels, they used bronze for chariot fixtures and a wide variety of weapons. Most Shang relics came from Anyang, a Shang capital, which had royal palaces, houses, temples and elaborate tombs. Beautiful marble and jade carvings have also been found by archaeologists.

Shang food vessel

FACT FILE

The Shang scribes perfected the early form of the Chinese alphabet. Their version had more than 3,000 symbols.

WHEN WERE WEDDING RINGS FIRST WORN?

The tradition of a bride wearing a wedding ring goes back so far that its origins are obscure.

We know the Egyptians wore wedding rings. In hieroglyphics, a circle is the symbol of eternity, so a wedding ring indicated an unending and indivisible bond. The wedding ring makes its first appearance in Christianity in about AD 900.

Some people see a more sinister history to the wedding ring and believe that it is a diminutive version of the slave band bracelet or neck collar that captive women wore in prehistoric times to indicate that they were someone's property. Now, the wearing of wedding rings is practised in almost all cultures, often by men as well as women.

Gold is the traditional metal for wedding rings because it does not tarnish and so is also a symbol of the hoped-for everlasting marriage.

FACT FILE

In most cultures, the ring is worn on the fourth finger of the left hand, supposedly because the ancient Greeks believed that a vein passed from this finger directly to the heart. However, it is more likely that it is simply because the fourth finger of the left hand is not used very much.

Where?

WHERE DOES THE WORD 'HISTORY' COME FROM?

History comes from a Greek word meaning 'what is known by asking'. The job of a historian is to ask questions and make sense of the answers.

The Greeks were among the first people to write history based on first-hand reporting of the facts. Herodotus (who died in 425 BC) wrote about the wars between the Greeks and the Persians. He travelled and talked to people who had taken part in the wars.

Historians work from a viewpoint. The first people to write their own history were the Chinese. We know the name of one early Chinese historian, Sima Qian, who wrote a history of China in about 100 BC. Early historians felt it was important to write down the stories and legends of the past,

FACT FILE

The word 'archaeology' comes from two Greek words and means 'the study of old things'. Many archaeological discoveries are made by digging in the ground at sites where ancient people lived.

and show how their state had come into existence. Sometimes people who made history also wrote about it. Julius Caesar, the Roman general, wrote his own book about his campaigns in Gaul.

WHERE WOULD YOU SEE A HOME OF MAMMOTH BONES?

Around 18,000 years ago, the last of a series of Ice Ages gripped much of the Northern Hemisphere. Icecaps spread southwards across Europe and North America. The sea level fell, uncovering land bridges, which animals and people crossed – between Asia and Alaska for example.

Ice Age hunters, clothed only in animal skins, adapted to living in these freezing conditions. They built shelters from the bones of mammoths. They made the framework from bones and filled in the gaps with skins, turf and moss. Groups of men drove the animals into swamps, where they became trapped and were killed with spears or rocks.

FACT FILE

Tools for scraping the skins of a hunted animal were made mostly from flint. This hard material could be chipped into tools of many different shapes and sizes. Other tools were made from bone, antlers and tusks.

Flint knife

Awl

Scraper

WHERE WAS THE WORLD'S FIRST GREAT CIVILIZATION?

The Indus Valley civilization developed out of farming and herding communities in the rich, fertile lands of the river valley, who carried on trade with each other. It appears to have been based on cooperation rather than military might.

It began to flourish about 4,500 years ago in the vast river plains of what are now Pakistan and northwestern India. Cities began to develop about 2,000 years later – Harappa in the north and Mohenjo Daro in the south. There was certainly a degree of central control because they were both carefully planned cities, laid out on a grid system. The wealth of the valley people is obvious from the amenities in the cities, which had communal water supplies and granaries, wide roads and brick houses, most of which had more than one floor. Most homes had a bathing area, which was unheard of anywhere else at that time.

FACT FILE

The farmers of the Indus Valley used wooden carts pulled by a pair of oxen. Deep grooves made by heavily laden carts have been found in the excavated streets of Mohenjo Daro.

WHERE DID KING ASHURBANIPAL RULE?

Assyria, an ancient state on the upper Tigris River in Mesopotamia, was ruled from 668 to 627 BC by a king called Ashurbanipal. It lay to the north of Babylon, with which it had many cultural similarities, and it occupied roughly the area of the northern half of Iraq. Ashurbanipal's capital was in Nineveh, where he had a magnificent palace, a library, in which he gathered a magnificent collection of Assyrian, Babylonian and Sumerian texts, and ornate gardens. Although damaged and vandalized, some of the ruins are still visible today.

Ashurbanipal was, like all Assyrian kings, an absolute ruler, as the representative on Earth of their chief god, Assur.

King Ashurbanipal

The Assyrian empire was at its height during the early part of Ashurbanipal's reign, but in 1651 BC, the Egyptians started to rebel against his rule, and then just three years later the Babylonians did the same thing, weakening his powers even further. After his death in 627 BC Babylonia invaded, and then overtook Egypt as well. This period is thought to be when the Hebrews were exiled to Babylon.

FACT FILE

Assyrian artists made wall relief sculptures showing winged spirits, hunting scenes, lions and bulls. For sport, the Assyrian king and his nobles would kill captive lions released into special enclosures.

WHERE ARE THE RUINS OF PERSEPOLIS?

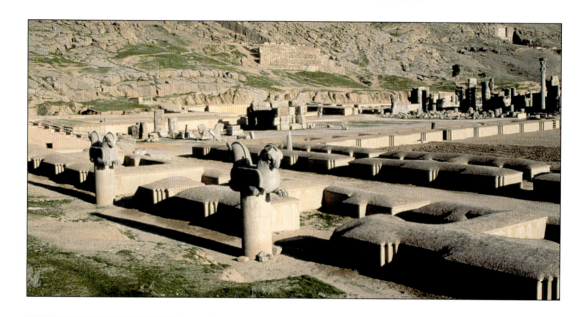

FACT FILE

Ten thousand soldiers called the Immortals formed the core of the Persian army. Each spearman or archer was instantly replaced if killed.

Persepolis lies in the southwest of what is now Iran, in a strategic position in the mountains. It was built as one of his capitals by King Darius I of Persia in around 500 BC. Large stone and mud-brick palaces were built and the city became the royal ceremonial area for the New Year's religious rituals, when Darius and his successors would renew their divine rights as kings, and expect gifts from all the client kings of the empire.

In 330 BC, having already defeated the last Persian king, another Darius, Alexander the Great seized Persepolis and the city's life came to an end. Archaeologists have uncovered many of the ruins. Some of these ruins have been restored and visitors are able to see around some of the buildings of the kings' great palace.

WHERE DOES THE NAME 'DRUID' COME FROM?

The name 'Druid' is derived from 'oak'. *Dru-wid* combines the word roots 'oak' and 'knowledge'. It was Pliny the Elder in his *Naturalis Historia* (XVI 95), who associated the Druids with mistletoe and oak groves:

> 'The Druids . . . hold nothing more sacred than the mistletoe and the tree on which it grows provided it is an oak. They choose the oak to form groves, and they do not perform any religious rites without its foliage . . .'

Celtic priests, also known as Druids, have often been identified as wizards and soothsayers. They performed mysterious rites in sacred groves of trees. The Moon, the oak and mistletoe were all magical to the Druids, and so too were many animals. However, in pre-Christian Celtic society they formed an intellectual class comprising philosophers, judges, educators, historians, doctors, seers, astronomers and astrologers. The earliest surviving classical references to Druids date to the second century BC.

FACT FILE

Around the campfire at night, Celtic poets, storytellers and musicians would pass on tales of the gods and of events in the history of the Celtic people.

WHERE WAS ETRURIA?

Etruria was an area of Italy, known today as Tuscany, Umbria and Latium. Etruria originally extended from the Arno in the north to the Tiber in the south, and from the Apennines in the east to the Tyrrhenian Sea in the west. Their origins are unclear. They were a highly organized, militaristic society, and rapidly extended their territories north across the Apennines into the Po Valley and south across the Tiber River into Latium and Campania. The civilization reached its height in the 400s BC, although the Etruscans lost control of Rome in 510 BC when the last Etruscan king, Tarquinius Superbus, was driven out, leaving Rome a republic. Rome is thought to have obtained many of her military techniques from the Etruscans as well as such customs as slavery.

FACT FILE

Part of a carved stone relief depicting a Roman funeral procession. The pallbearers carried the dead person on a raised bier, followed by the mourners.

WHERE WERE THE FIRST GLADIATOR GAMES HELD?

Records state that the first gladiator games were held to commemorate the funeral of a Roman aristocrat in a cattle market in 264 BC. There were many venues for fights, but the most famous one, the Colosseum in Rome was built between AD 72 to 81 by the emperor Vespasian. There, wild beasts fought in the morning and the gladiators fought in the afternoon.

Gladiators were highly trained, and fought using many different types of weapons – a shield and sword, a net and long trident, for example. They usually fought until one was killed, but the life of the loser could be spared if the spectators waved handkerchiefs, or the emperor gave him the thumbs-up, rather than the thumbs-down.

FACT FILE

Most gladiators were prisoners of war, slaves or criminals. Slaves wore tags advertising their skills and good character to enhance their price at auction.

WHERE DID THE
ROMANS BATHE?

Only wealthy Romans could afford to own private baths, but the city had many public ones. During the time of the emperors, the public baths became luxurious meeting places. They looked like great square-shaped swimming pools, and were surrounded by gardens, columned marble porches and libraries. The bath buildings had facilities for warm and cold baths, steam baths and massages.

The most splendid remains of baths in Rome are those of Caracalla and Diocletian. The Baths of Caracalla date from the early AD 200s, and are especially impressive. They were decorated with precious marbles, statues and mosaics. The Baths of Diocletian, completed in the early AD 300s, were the largest of all Roman baths. They could serve 3,000 people at a time. Most of the site has been built over, but some rooms can still be seen.

FACT FILE

A Roman villa was a large comfortable country home, with hot-air central heating and a courtyard for fine weather. The family had servants to run the house and slaves to work on the land.

WHERE DID CHARIOT RACES TAKE PLACE?

A Hippodrome was the place for horse and chariot races (*hippo* means 'horse'. The Greeks built hippodromes with seats in rows, or tiers, surrounding a long race course, and curved around one end of it. The course was usually from 200 to 260 yards (180 to 240 m) long and could be divided in the middle by a wall. The largest Greek hippodrome was in Constantinople (now Istanbul) and the Roman Circus Maximus, the largest of all Roman hippodromes like all the others, was a copy of the Greek originals. It seated around 250,000 spectators. The layout of one of Domitian's hippodromes can still be seen in the street plan of the Piazza Navona in Rome. The chariot races were known for their frequent violent crashes, with winning drivers becoming rich superstars. The emperor Caligula is said to have enjoyed racing, especially as he always won.

WHERE WAS THE SILK ROAD?

The Silk Road was a group of ancient trade routes that connected China and Europe, but was a concept rather than a physical road and flourished primarily from 100 BC to AD 1500. The routes stretched across about 5, 000 miles (8,050 km) from the Mediterranean, across Arabia, through India and what what is now Burma to the far edge of China.

The Silk Road was named after the vast amounts of Chinese silk carried along it, but parts of it had been trade routes for thousands of years before. Towns and cities sprang up along the route to provide facilities for food, water and recreation, as well as goods for trade. This trade made a number of countries very rich, as the merchants had to pass through to avoid being attacked by bandits. Other goods included gold, spices and jewellery. Camel caravans carried most goods across the dry, harsh regions along the Silk Road.

By AD 800, with the Ottoman empire in turmoil, traffic fell as traders started to travel by safer sea routes.

FACT FILE

The Chinese were the first to learn to make silk, and they guarded their secret. They had a monopoly until the 500s AD, when a merchant is thought to have smuggled some silk worms back in a hollow cane.

WHERE WAS THE BIGGEST GROWTH OF THE MUSLIM EMPIRE?

The advance of Islam seemed unstoppable in the late 600s. The Byzantine and Persian empires could not halt the armies of Islam, and nor could Egypt. By AD 700 Muslims controlled most of the North African coast, and ships patrolled the Mediterranean Sea and Indian Ocean. Muslims from Morocco invaded Spain, but the advance of Islam into western Europe was stopped in AD 732 by the Frankish army of Charles

Martel. Under the Ummayad family rule there were four classes of citizens: Arabian Muslims; new converts; Christians, Jews and Mandaens (a Persian sect); and slaves. The new converts included people from Egypt, Syria, Persia and Asia Minor. They adopted Arab ways, but brought to the Arabs a wealth of new learning in philosophy, medicine, art and science.

FACT FILE

The crescent moon and star became important symbols in Islam, and were often incorporated into architecture and other designs.

WHERE WAS THE BATTLE OF CRÉCY?

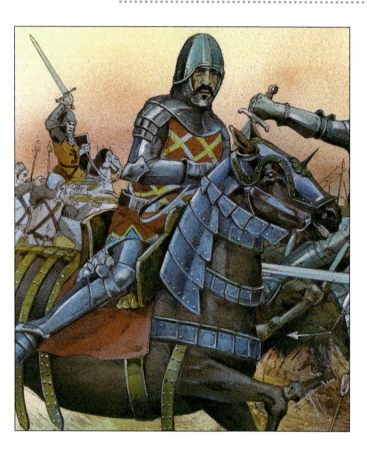

The Battle of Crécy was the first important battle of the Hundred Years War (1337 to 1453) at the site of the present village of Crécy, in northern France. The Hundred Years War began in 1337 and continued periodically for more than a century.

In this battle, English archers on foot, under Edward III, defeated Philip VI's much larger force of mounted knights, more than 1,000 of whom were killed, as was almost half of the French force in the Battle of Crécy. The hero of the battle was Edward, the Black Prince, son of Edward III of England.

FACT FILE

Knights decorated their shield or standard with the heraldic symbols of their own coat of arms. This made it easier to identify the knight in full armour. Each coat of arms had its own unique design.

WHERE ARE THE FORBIDDEN AND IMPERIAL CITIES?

The Forbidden City and the Imperial City lie within the Inner City, an area in Beijing, the capital of China. The Forbidden City includes palaces of former Chinese emperors. It was so named because only the emperor's household was allowed to enter it.

The buildings in this part of Beijing are now preserved as museums. The Imperial City surrounds the Forbidden City. It includes lakes, parks and the residences of China's Communist leaders. The Gate of Heavenly Peace stands at the southern edge of the Imperial City, overlooking Tiananmen Square.

WHERE DID THE PILGRIM FATHERS FIRST LAND?

FACT FILE

In the colonies, girls would embroider samplers – squares of cloth decorated with words and patterns of needlework. They usually added their name and age, as well as the date.

Pilgrims were the early English settlers of New England. The first group of pilgrims set sail from England in 1620 on a ship called the *Mayflower*. They landed at what is now Plymouth, Massachusetts, where they established Plymouth Colony along Cape Cod Bay.

In 1606 William Brewster helped form a small Separatist congregation in Scrooby, England. Separatist groups were illegal in England, and in 1607 the Scrooby congregation tried to flee to Amsterdam, Holland, to avoid arrest. They were caught, but most of them left England the next year. In 1609, the congregation settled in the Dutch town of Leiden.

WHERE WAS THE FIRST TRUE PRINTING PRESS BUILT?

TELL ME ABOUT HISTORY : WHERE?

FACT FILE

Another early invention was Galileo's telescope, which was more powerful than any that had been used before.

Throughout history, books have been rare and precious things, kept in libraries of monasteries or wealthy houses. Each one had to be copied out by hand with pen and ink, so very few people had the chance to learn to read. The Chinese developed a simple system of printing in the eleventh century, but it was only in about 1450 that a German named Johannes Gutenberg built the first true printing press. Using movable metal type, Gutenberg was able to make exact copies of books very cheaply.

The first books he printed were the Bible and other religious works. Soon, other printers started, and by 1500 they were producing many different sorts of literature, including poems and stories. For the first time, books were available to everyone.

WHERE DID THE CRUSADES TAKE PLACE?

FACT FILE

The word crusade comes from the Latin word crux, meaning cross. 'To take up the cross' meant to become a crusader.

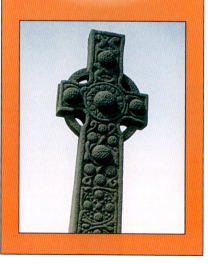

Crusades were the military expeditions organized mainly to recapture Palestine during the Middle Ages. Palestine, also called the Holy Land, was important to Christians because it was the region where Jesus Christ had lived. Palestine lay along the eastern coast of the Mediterranean Sea and Muslims had taken control of it from the Christians. The crusaders, who came from Western Europe, organized eight major expeditions between AD 1096 and 1270. This was a period when Western Europe was expanding its economy and increasing its military forces. Kings, nobles and thousands of knights, peasants and townspeople took part in the Crusades. They had two main goals: first to gain permanent control of the Holy Land and second to protect the Byzantine empire.

WHERE DID WILLIAM BUILD NORMAN CASTLES?

Conwy castle

FACT FILE

The Bayeux Tapestry was made by the Normans to celebrate their victory over the English in 1066. It is a huge series of pictures depicting incidents during the conquest.

The introduction of castles to England followed the Norman conquest of 1066. In fact, castles were the means by which William the Conqueror and his followers secured their hold on England following their victory at the battle of Hastings. William ordered castles to be built at Warwick, Nottingham, York, Lincoln, Cambridge and Huntingdon. These defensive structures helped to secure his newly acquired lands. The first Norman castles were hurriedly constructed of earth and timber.

Conwy castle, in north Wales, is typical of the castles built by the Normans to withstand a long siege. Windsor Castle, Berkshire, is perhaps England's most famous castle.

WHERE DID THE 'SALT MARCH' TAKE PLACE?

Mohandas Gandhi (1869 to 1948), known as Mahatma Gandhi, was the father of the Indian nation. He helped to free India from British control by a unique method of non-violent resistance. He is still revered as one of the foremost spiritual and political leaders of the twentieth century.

Gandhi believed that non-violence was a more effective way to get his message heard than violence, and in 1930 protested against the British government's monopoly on salt – possessing salt not bought from the government was a criminal offence – by leading his followers on a 240-mile (386-km) march to the coast, where they made salt from seawater. Gandhi spent seven years in prison in total because of his protests against British injustice, and lived to see independence in 1947.

FACT FILE

In the middle of the Indian flag is an ancient symbol of a wheel. It is known as the Dharma Chakra, which means the 'Wheel of Law'. India gained her independence from Britain on August 15, 1947.

WHERE WAS THE BATTLE OF DIEN BIEN PHU?

Vietnam is a tropical country in southeast Asia. China governed the area from about 100 BC until AD 900, when the Vietnamese established an independent state. Fighting broke out between French forces and the Vietminh in 1946. It ended in 1954, with the French defeat in the Battle of Dien Bien Phu. An international conference to arrange a peace settlement also took place at this time. In 1957, Vietminh members in the South began to rebel against the South Vietnamese government. Fighting broke out and it developed into the Vietnam War. The United States became the ally of the South.

FACT FILE

The Vietnam War showed for the first time how a small country like North Vietnam could take on and eventually defeat the military might of the US, by using superior tactics.

Science & Technology

The Earth

WHEN IS SUMMER SOLSTICE?

The Earth revolves around the Sun and at the same time it revolves on its own axis. As it moves around the Sun, it is also spinning like a top. If the axis of the Earth were at right angles to the path of the Earth around the Sun, all the days of the year would be the same length. However, the Earth is tilted at an angle of 66.5°. In June, the northern hemisphere is tilted towards the Sun and it receives more sunshine during a day. This is its warmest season called summer. On the 21 June, the Sun is directly over the Tropic of Cancer and it is midsummer in the northern hemisphere. This is the time known as the summer solstice.

FACT FILE

The Sun is the source of light and heat for the solar system. The four planets closest to the Sun are small and solid, the closest being Mercury. An asteroid belt separates these from the four larger planets, which are made up of gas.

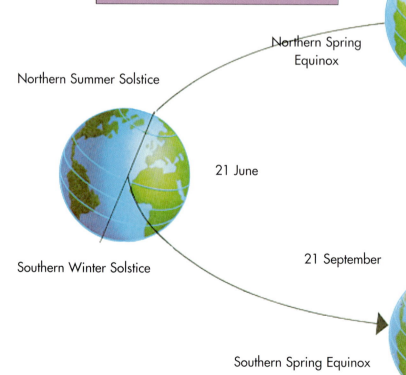

Northern Spring Equinox

Northern Summer Solstice

21 June

Southern Winter Solstice

21 September

Southern Spring Equinox

WHEN IS THE SHORTEST DAY?

FACT FILE

Mars is known as the 'Red Planet' because it is covered by a stone desert containing lots of iron oxide, making it appear red. The water and oxygen that used to exist on Mars are now locked up in these iron deposits, so the planet has hardly any atmosphere.

The shortest day of the year is in the winter solstice, which is 21 December. When the northern hemisphere is turned toward the Sun, the countries north of the equator have their summer season, and the countries south of the equator have their winter season. When the direct rays of the Sun fall on the southern hemisphere, it is their summer and it is winter in the northern hemisphere. There are two days in the year when night and day are equal all over the world. They come in the spring and fall, just halfway between the two solstices. One is the autumnal equinox in September, and the other is the spring equinox in March.

Southern Autumn Equinox

Northern Winter Solstice

21 March

SUN

21 December

Southern Summer Solstice

Northern Autumn Equinox

WHEN DO OCEANS FREEZE?

In Antarctica and the Arctic, the oceans freeze because the temperatures are so low. Seawater, unlike fresh water, continues to increase in density as its temperature decreases towards freezing point (about $-1.8°C$). In fact, Antarctica contains 90 per cent of all the ice on the Earth. Scientists have calculated that should all this ice melt, sea levels would rise by 60m causing world-wide flooding. An accumulation of sea ice can cause an iceberg, which floats in the sea because it is less dense than water.

FACT FILE

Over 360 million square kilometres of the Earth's surface area are covered by oceans and seas, with the Pacific accounting for nearly 36% of the total.

An iceberg in a frozen ocean

WHY DO WAVES BREAK?

FACT FILE

For centuries sailors have been in terror of being sucked into a whirlpool that would swallow them and their ships. Whirlpools happen when opposing currents meet.

Some sort of force or energy is needed to start a wave, and it is the wind that provides this energy in the water. Wind blows the surface layers of the sea, gradually forming a rolling movement of waves. As these waves near the coast, the sea-bed interrupts their rolling movement and they mount up and break onto the beach.

The water inside a wave moves round and round in a circle. Near the shore, the circular shape of the wave is changed and it becomes squashed. The top of the wave becomes unstable, so when it hits the beach, it topples and spills over. On beaches with a shallow slope the waves pile up to a great height before breaking, causing surf.

WHY DO EARTHQUAKES OCCUR?

Our planet is a very restless place. Every 30 seconds, the ground suddenly rumbles and trembles. Most of the movements are so slight that they are not felt. Others can be so large they cause complete disaster. Big cracks appear in the land, streets buckle and buildings simply crumble. In fact, whole towns and cities can be destroyed. These are called earthquakes and the reason they occur is because the Earth's crust is made up of moving parts called plates. When these plates slide past or into each other, the rocks jolt and send out shock waves.

FACT FILE

Both mining and tunnelling operations are known to have caused earthquakes in areas that are already under tension due to movements in the Earth's crust.

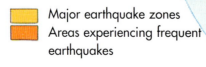

Major earthquake zones
Areas experiencing frequent earthquakes

WHAT IS A SEISMOGRAPH?

FACT FILE

The edges of the Pacific plate are surrounded by earthquakes, volcanic activity and hot springs, caused by the crust shifts and hot lava rising near the surface.

From time to time we hear news of a big earthquake that has taken place somewhere far away, and although we don't usually feel the Earth shaking, scientists can make an exact record of the earthquake from anywhere in the world. This is with instruments called seismographs, the study of earthquakes being known as seismology. The seismograph picks up the signals, which are caused by one rock mass rubbing against the other with such ferocity that the energy produced causes vibrations in the rocks, vibrations that can travel thousands of miles and still be felt.

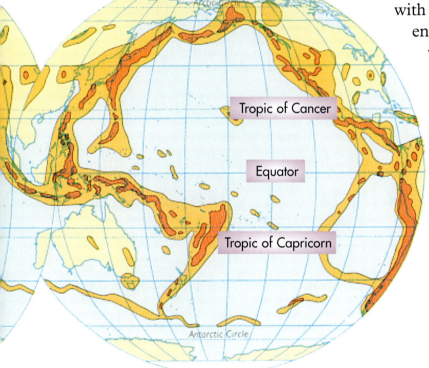

Tropic of Cancer

Equator

Tropic of Capricorn

Different types of volcanic eruption

1. Fissure eruptions release liquid lava

2. In Hawaiian eruptions the lava is less fluid and produces low cones

3. Vulcanian eruptions are more violent and eject solid lava

WHEN ARE VOLCANOES DORMANT?

FACT FILE

A major volcanic eruption can hurl boulders high into the air. These boulders, called volcanic bombs, can be very large indeed.

The word dormant actually means 'sleeping'. So when people talk about a volcano being dormant, it really means it is temporarily sleeping and might erupt at any time in the future. An extinct volcano, on the other hand, is one that will not become active again. Like earthquakes, volcanoes mainly occur along fault lines. Molten rock, gases and ash are forced out through a gap in the Earth's crust to release the pressure that has built up. When there is very little pressure, the volcano can remain in a dormant state for many, many years. On the island of Maui there is a volcano called Haleakala, which rises to a height of about 10,025 feet (3,085m). It is the world's largest inactive volcano. Its crater is about 20 miles (32km) around and some 2,720 (837m) feet deep.

4. Strombolian eruptions blow out incandescent material

5. In the Peléean type a blocked vent is cleared explosively

6. A Plinian eruption is a continuous blast of gas that rises to immense heights

WHEN WAS THE WORST VOLCANIC ERUPTION?

The island of Krakatoa, Indonesia (west of Java) was a small volcanic island. The volcano itself had laid dormant for over 200 years until August 1883. On May 20 one of the cones erupted violently and three months later the whole island blew up. It was the biggest explosion in recorded history. For two and a half days the island was in total darkness because of the amount of dust in the air. A cloud of ash rose 50 miles (80 km) into the air. The eruption caused a tidal wave, which killed 36,000 people. The explosion could be heard and felt in Australia, 2175 miles (3,500 km) away.

FACT FILE

On August 24 in the year 79AD, there was a great eruption of Mount Vesuvius, a volcano in southern Italy. The lava, stones, and ashes thrown up by the volcano completely buried two nearby towns.

HOW ARE MOUNTAINS FORMED?

Mountains can be formed in three different ways. Volcanoes form mountains when lava from deep inside the Earth cools and hardens on the surface.

Other mountains are formed when two plates move towards each other under pressure, or where an oceanic plate is pushed under a continental crust. The pressure causes the ground near the joining plate margins to fault and fold. The ground is forced upwards to form mountains. The Rockies, Alps, Andes, Urals and Himalayas were all formed in this way.

Finally, the Earth's crust can fracture and create faults, which means that large blocks of land can be moved upwards or downwards. Faults in the rocks normally occur when there is a lot of pressure on the rocks. Mountain building is a slow process and happens over centuries.

FACT FILE

Rockslides are common where forests have been destroyed on mountainsides. There are no longer any tree roots to stabilize the loose material.

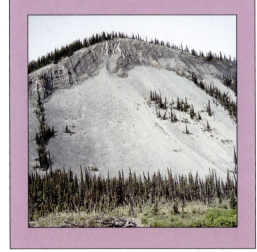

Three ways in which a mountain can form

Volcano

336

WHEN WAS THE TOP OF EVEREST FIRST REACHED?

FACT FILE

Mountain peaks are often seen to be surrounded by layers of cloud. This is because as winds laden with water are blown towards the mountains, they are forced to rise and the temperature drops. The water condenses into clouds at these higher altitudes.

Mount Everest, which is in the Himalayas, is 29,000 feet (8,863m) high. At these altitudes, mountains are always covered in snow and ice, and there is little oxygen to breathe. Mount Everest was finally conquered on May 29, 1953, when a Nepalese guide, Tenzing Norgay, and a New Zealander, Edmund Hillary, reached the highest point on the Earth's surface. Since then, many people have climbed Everest, and all the world's major peaks have now been conquered.

Fold

Fault

WHAT IS A MONSOON?

A monsoon is a season of very heavy rain falling in tropical countries. Monsoons are most common near the Equator. They occur when seasonal winds spring up carrying moist air in from the sea. Important crops such as rice depend entirely on the monsoon season to provide the right growing conditions.

If the monsoon rains fail, famine commonly follows. There are also some special winds called monsoon winds. These are winds that change their direction with the season. In India, the monsoons blow south as hot, dry winds in the wintertime, and blow north in the summer, bringing heavy rainfall.

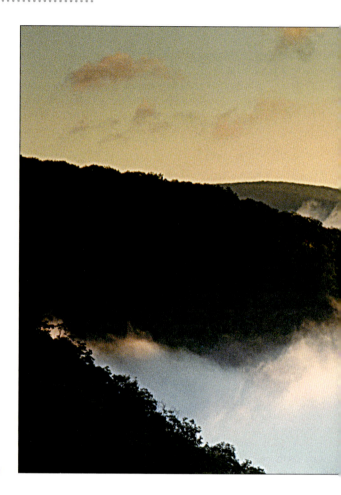

Mist over high ground

FACT FILE

The Aborigines believe that if a possum is left cooking by the water's edge, a sizzling sound is produced. This noise irritates the rainbow snake, who they believe crawls underground towards the source of the noise. As it moves along, the weather turns stormy, and the monsoon rains begin.

WHEN DO FOG AND MIST ARISE?

FACT FILE

Fog particles are small, less than 1/25,000 (1 micron) of an inch in diameter. When you have a dense fog and can't see in front of you, it is because there may be as many as 20,000 of these particles in one cubic inch (16 cubic cm).

It is tiny water droplets condensing from moist air that cause fog and mist to rise. The water droplets can occur at ground level. The air can only hold a limited amount of water. If the air suddenly cools, its capacity to hold water is reduced, which results in a mist or fog.

When fog occurs, visibility can be affected quite badly. Mist is less dense. It commonly occurs on calm, clear nights when heat rises, forming a thin layer of mist close to the ground. Mist often forms over water because a mass of warm air passes over a cold stretch of water.

Sometimes, visibility is affected in built up areas due to mist and fog, but this is sometimes mistaken for smog. Smog is a build up of exhaust fumes and factory smoke, which hangs over the area until a great amount of air movement can blow the smog away.

WHEN DO WE SEE MIRAGES?

Mirages form in hot deserts where the air is so hot it bends and distorts light rays. The shimmering images that a mirage produces have often tricked travellers in deserts. People think that they can see an oasis or town on the horizon, but in reality it is not there.

Under certain conditions, such as a stretch of pavement or desert air heated by intense sunshine, the air rapidly cools with elevation and therefore increases in density and refractive power. Sunlight reflected downward from the top of an object, for example the camel above, will be directed through the cool air in the normal way. When the sky is the object of the mirage, the land is mistaken for a lake or sheet of water.

FACT FILE

About one-third of the world's land surface is covered by desert. Deserts are found wherever there is too little water to allow much plant life to grow. Salt deserts form when shallow seas and lakes dry up, leaving a deposit of smooth salt.

WHEN WAS THE LONGEST HEATWAVE?

The longest heatwave ever recorded was in Marble Bar, Australia when the temperature stayed above 38°C. It lasted for 162 days from 23 October 1923 to 7 April 1924.

The highest mean annual temperature recorded is 34.4°C in Dallol, Ethiopia. The lowest recorded temperature (outside of the poles) was –68°C in Verkhoyansk, Siberia, on 6 February 1933. The lowest mean annual temperature of –56.6°C was recorded at the Plateau Station, in Antarctica.

FACT FILE

Some living things have adapted to survive long periods of time without water. Plants such as cacti have the ability to conserve water. They also minimize water loss as they have no leaves, and photosynthesis takes place in the stem. They have roots, which reach deep into the ground for water.

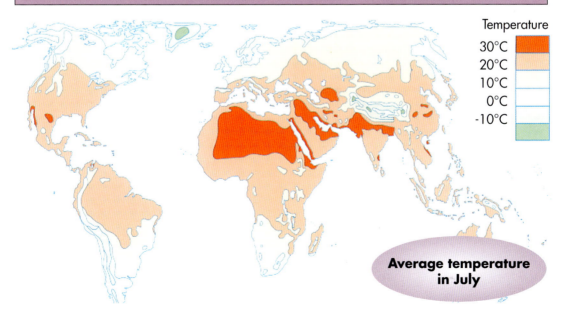

Temperature

| 30°C |
| 20°C |
| 10°C |
| 0°C |
| -10°C |

Average temperature in July

WHY DOES WATER BECOME SALTY?

FACT FILE

Lighthouses were built to warn ships at sea that they were approaching land and rocky water. Their beam of light across the waves made travelling by boat much safer.

Water becomes salty when minerals (including salts) dissolve into it. This process begins when rainwater falls on the land and erodes rock. The minerals in rock are dissolved into the rainwater.

These dissolved minerals in the rainwater enter streams and rivers, gradually working their way into the seas and oceans.

This is a process which is constantly taking place, so the level and concentration of salt in the oceans and seas is always increasing. Some of the minerals are consumed by organisms in the water, but the vast majority of them constitute the saltiness of the water.

WHEN WAS THE LONGEST DROUGHT?

The longest drought in recorded history took place in Calama, in the Atacama desert of Northern Chile. For four centuries, beginning in 1571, no rain fell in the area. It was not until 1971 that rainfall was first recorded again. The Atacama desert, which lies between the Andes and the Pacific ocean, is recognized as the driest place in the world.

The Atacama desert remains so dry because it lies in a region where there is constant high air pressure, with little air movement, and with few clouds overhead.

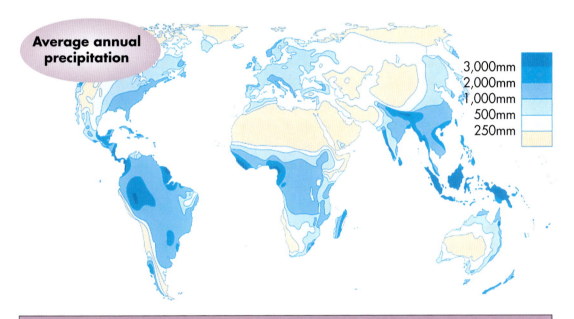

Average annual precipitation

3,000mm
2,000mm
1,000mm
500mm
250mm

FACT FILE

Some people believe that animals are good predictors of weather. One such belief is that if cows are standing in their field, then dry weather is expected. If they are lying down, however, rain is expected.

How many parts does the Earth consist of?

The Earth consists of five parts: the first, the atmosphere, is gaseous; the second, the hydrosphere, is liquid; the third, fourth, and fifth, the lithosphere, mantle and core, are largely solid. The atmosphere is the gaseous envelope that surrounds the solid body of the planet. Although it has a thickness of more than 700 miles (1100 km), about half its mass is concentrated in the lower 3.5 miles (5.6 km). The lithosphere, consisting mainly of the cold, rigid, rocky crust of the Earth, extends to depths of 60 miles (100 km). The hydrosphere is the layer of water that, in the form of the oceans, covers approximately 70.8 percent of the surface of the Earth. The mantle and core are the heavy interior of the Earth, making up most of the Earth's mass.

FACT FILE

The Earth's inner core is made up mostly of iron and nickel. It is 850 miles (1,370 km) deep and is thought to have a temperature of around 4,500°C.

WHAT WAS PANGAEA?

Some 225 million years ago all the world's land masses were joined together into one supercontinent, Pangaea, surrounded by a single universal sea, the Panthalassa. Through the upheavals that we have since come to know as plate tectonics, the shifting of the Earth's crust tore the supercontinent apart around the middle of the Mesozoic period and large bodies of land drifted across the surface of the Earth to ultimately become our present-day continents. It is now believed that the several moving plates of the Earth's crust were formed by volcanic activity. The clues to the movement of the Earth's surface can only be found on the present-day continents in rocks, fossils and structures older than about 200 million years.

FACT FILE

Certain species of terrestrial mammals became isolated, as a result, in Antarctica, South America, Africa and Australia. It was thousands of years before volcanic eruption would reunite South and North America in a land bridge.

HOW IS MINING CARRIED OUT?

The earliest forms of mining involved following seams of metal in tunnels driven into the rock. This method is still in use today, usually in deep mines where other techniques would be impossible. Tunnels are made by using explosives and with automatic machines. Some of these mines go thousands of metres into the rock face, becoming very hot and dangerous.

Today we mine minerals, diamonds, metals, coal and rock for building material. Placer mining uses huge floating dredgers to extract metals. Strip mining is used to obtain coal and minerals that lie close to the surface. Open pit mining involves blasting into the rock to produce a huge quarry from which material is removed layer by layer.

FACT FILE

The metals that are used to make coins come from mines. Pure metals (those not mixed with other substances) are called noble metals and these include gold, silver, platinum and copper.

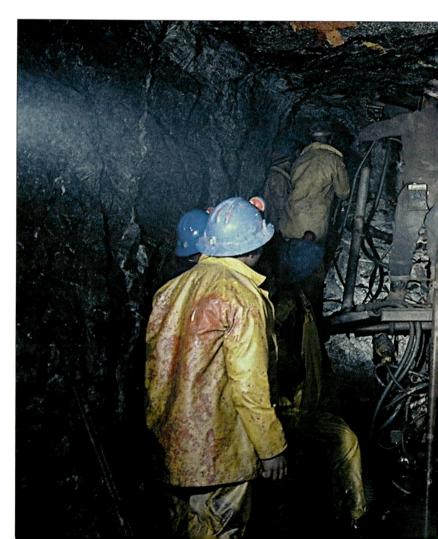

WHY DOES COAL FORM?

FACT FILE

Before we had central heating to warm our houses most people had coal fires, and matches were a quick and easy way to light them.

Coal is formed by the compressed remains of plants that lived in bogs 250–350 million years ago. This was during the Carboniferous Period when primitive animals first appeared on the land. Coal formed from the remains of tree ferns and other primitive trees, which were covered with mud and sand and buried as new rock was laid down. Very gradually, over millions of years, this material turned into coal.

A similar process is taking place today in peat bogs, where the rotting remains of heather form peat. When the peat is dried, it burns in a similar way to coal. In some parts of the world a soft shale, called brown coal, is mined. The hardest and purest form of coal is called anthracite.

HOW DO GEYSERS GET SO HOT?

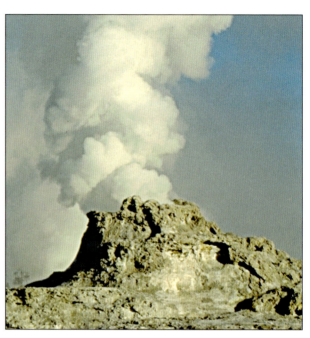

Most of the water in a geyser, which is hot when it comes to the surface, originates from rain and snow which gathers in underground reservoirs, which act like storage basins, connected to the surface by a tube.

The rock further down inside the Earth is extremely hot, and steam-like gasses from the rocks rise up through cracks in the rock, heating the water in the reservoirs to more than boiling point.

When a combination of steam and water rises freely from the depths, a continuously boiling hot spring is created.

Geysers, on the other hand, are created when the tube or passageway is not straight, as is often the case, erupting onto the surface as the water is converted into steam. Because steam needs more space than water, as this eruption takes place it pushes up through the channel of water above it, making an explosive ejection of steam thrusting into the air, causing the spectacular phenomenon of a geyser.

FACT FILE

This hotel heats water for leisure purposes. The pool is a luxury attraction and people have always found pleasure swimming in warm water.

WHEN DO WE SEE THE SPECTRUM OF LIGHT?

Sir Isaac Newton

FACT FILE

Sir Isaac Newton used his discoveries about light to build a new kind of telescope. It used a reflecting mirror instead of glass lenses to magnify images.

Sir Isaac Newton of Cambridge University first uncovered the secrets of how light is divided up. We think of ordinary light as being 'white', but really light is a mixture of red, orange, yellow, green, blue and violet. When sunlight strikes the bevelled edge of a mirror, or the edge of a glass prism, or the surface of a soap bubble, we can see the different hues in light. What actually happens is that the white light is broken up into the different wave lengths that are seen by our eyes. These wave lengths form a band of parallel stripes, each hue grading into the one next to it. This band is called a 'spectrum'. In a spectrum, the red line is always at one end and the blue and violet lines at the other.

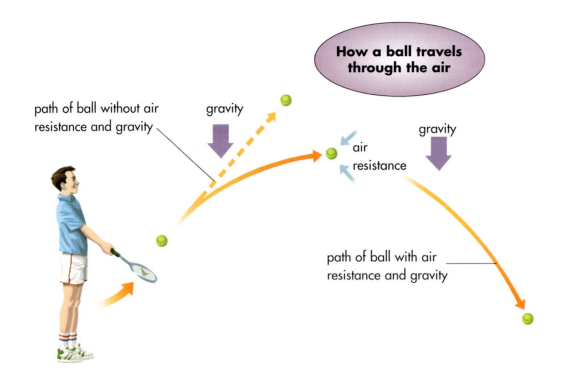

How a ball travels through the air

path of ball without air resistance and gravity

gravity

gravity

air resistance

path of ball with air resistance and gravity

WHAT IS GRAVITY?

Gravity is the force that pulls towards the centre of the Earth. It doesn't matter where you stand on the Earth's surface, the ground is always 'down'.

The force of gravity depends on the mass, or amount of material, of an object. Objects only feel heavy because of their mass.

Newton realised that gravity not only affects the Earth, but it also controls the movement of the planets and the stars, as well as the orbit of the Moon around the Earth. When you whirl something around your head on the end of a piece of string, it flies outwards and appears to defy the force of gravity. This is called centrifugal force. When you let go of the string, the centrifugal force makes the object fly away in a straight line.

FACT FILE

Sir Isaac Newton (1643–1727) was the first scientist to develop the laws of gravity. He supposedly was inspired by seeing an apple fall from a tree.

WHEN DOES LIGHTNING STRIKE?

To understand exactly what lightning is, we must recall a fact we know about electricity. We know that things become electrically charged – either positively or negatively. A positive charge has a great attraction for a negative one. As the charges become greater, this attraction becomes stronger. A point is finally reached where the strain of being kept apart becomes too great for the charges. A discharge takes place to relieve the strain and make the two bodies electrically equal. This is exactly what happens in the case of lightning. This discharge follows the path which offers the least resistance. That is the reason why lightning often zigzags. Moist air is only a fair conductor of electricity, which is why lightning often stops when it starts raining.

FACT FILE

The electrical nature of the nervous system was discovered after Italian scientist Galvani noticed how frogs' legs twitched when an electrical current was applied to the nerve.

WHEN WAS LIGHTNING FIRST UNDERSTOOD?

Ben Franklin (1706–1790) was an American with many talents. He was a printer, scientist and politician who played an important part in founding the United States.

He discovered the nature of lightning while flying a kite during a thunderstorm. Franklin noticed sparks jumping from a key tied to the end of the wet string. This could very easily have killed him, but it did not. He went on to invent the lightning conductor, a strip of copper that is run from the top of a building to the ground, in order that lightning can earth itself safely.

Lightning is a significant weather hazard and occurs at an average rate of 50 to 100 discharges per second. Lightning rods and metallic conductors can be used to protect a structure by intercepting and diverting the lightning current into the ground as harmlessly as possible. When lightning is likely to occur, people are advised to stay indoors or in a car, away from open doors and windows and to avoid contact with any electrical appliances or plumbing that might be exposed to the outside environment.

FACT FILE

A lightning conductor is a metal rod that is placed so that it points upwards above the highest point of a tall building. If lightning does strike the building, it is the conductor, not the building itself, that the spark hits.

The Natural World

WHEN DID THE FIRST PLANTS APPEAR?

Plants are organisms that use light as a source of energy and to produce the food they need in order to live and grow. The Earth's original atmosphere contained poisonous gases. The lack of oxygen meant that no animals or plants could survive on the Earth. The earliest plants or plant-like bacteria began the process of photosynthesis, which releases oxygen as well as a waste product. This gas gradually built up in the atmosphere as the plant life spread, making it possible for oxygen-dependent animals to evolve.

Coral was formed by bacteria in much the same way as plants. It is made up of a variety of invertebrate marine organisms of a stonelike, horny, or leathery consistency. They live in colonies begun by just one polyp. Each polyp builds a hard skeleton around itself.

Coral reef

FACT FILE

Lichens are a mixture of algae and fungi. Many grow like a mat over rocks or tree trunks, while others look like a small branched plant.

WHEN IS CLIMAX VEGETATION ACHIEVED?

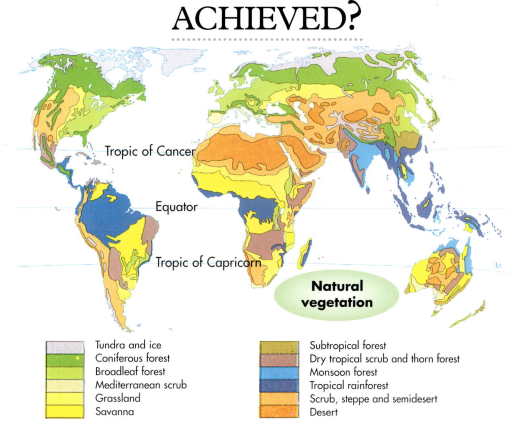

Tropic of Cancer

Equator

Tropic of Capricorn

Natural vegetation

Tundra and ice
Coniferous forest
Broadleaf forest
Mediterranean scrub
Grassland
Savanna

Subtropical forest
Dry tropical scrub and thorn forest
Monsoon forest
Tropical rainforest
Scrub, steppe and semidesert
Desert

When vegetation first starts growing in newly formed soil, it is at a disadvantage because the soil will not be nutrient-rich. As the plants die, they enrich the soil, allowing more plants to take advantage of this. As the soil gets older, it has gleaned more and more nutrients from dead plants – and more and more plants are able to grow successfully in the soil. Climax vegetation occurs when the vegetation is totally suited to the soil in the given climate. In reality, this can never last permanently due to the ever-changing environment.

FACT FILE

Rainforests have developed in areas where the soil is very fertile and where there is a great deal of rainfall. The varied vegetation suggests the soil is extremely nutrient-rich.

WHEN DID DARWIN SAIL TO THE GALAPAGOS ISLANDS?

The marine iguana

In the year 1831 Charles Darwin (1809–1882) set out on an exploratory voyage in the ship Beagle, heading for South America. The voyage lasted five years and during this time Darwin kept careful notes of everything he saw, in particular the strange animal life on the Galapagos Islands, off the western coast of Ecuador. He was disturbed by the fact that the birds and tortoises of the Galapagos Islands tended to resemble species found on the nearby continent, while inhabits of similar adjoining islands to the Galapagos had quite different animal populations. In London, Darwin later learned that the finches he had brought back belonged to a different species, not merely different varieties, as he had originally believed.

FACT FILE

When Charles Darwin first published his theories on evolution they created a sensation, but it took a while before they were accepted.

WHEN DID DARWIN PUBLISH *ON THE ORIGIN OF SPECIES?*

A Galapagos-dwelling tortoise

Upon his return from the voyage, Darwin turned over all the specimens he had brought back to cataloguing experts in Cambridge and London. In South America he had found fossils of extinct armadillos that were similar but not identical to the living animals he had seen. On November 24, 1859 Darwin published his theories in a book called *On the Origin of Species*. It caused a great sensation, but it was some time before it was accepted by the scientific world. The first edition sold out immediately and by 1872 the work had run through six editions. It became generally accepted that evolution took place along the lines that Darwin suggested. His theory on evolution of species solved many puzzles.

FACT FILE

We can see how evolution has changed living things by examining fossils. Fossils preserve the body parts of living creatures from long ago so that we can see how they have changed over millions of years.

Carl Linnaeus

WHY DID LINNAEUS DEVELOP A CLASSIFICATION SYSTEM?

Carl Linnaeus (1707–1778) was a Swedish botanist and explorer who was the first to create a uniform system for naming plants and animals. Most plants and animals have popular names that vary from place to place. Scientific names are given so that the same name is recognized everywhere. Latin is the language used for scientific names. The scientific names are in two parts. The first is the generic name, which describes a group of related living things, and the second name is the specific name, which applies only to that living thing.

FACT FILE

The Latin name of the White Water Lily is *Nymphaea alba*. They are one of a group of plants whose flowers close up for the night.

WHEN IS AN ANIMAL TERMED A VERTEBRATE?

An animal is classed as a vertebrate when it has a backbone to provide support for the muscles and protection for the spinal cord. Vertebrates include fish, amphibians, reptiles, birds and mammals. The backbone is actually a series of small bones called vertebrae. They are joined together and locked with rope-like ligaments to provide a flexible but extremely strong anchor for the back muscles. The spinal cord runs down a channel inside the vertebrae, providing protection from damage. Some primitive fish, such as sharks and rays, have a spine made of a tough rubbery material called cartilage. There are approximately 45,000 living species of vertebrates. In size, they range from minute fishes to elephants and whales (of up to 100 tons), the largest animals ever to have existed. They are adapted to life underground, on the surface, and in the air.

FACT FILE

The duck-billed platypus is a very unusual, small, semiaquatic mammal. It lives in lakes and streams of eastern Australia and Tasmania. It is notable in having a broad, flat, rubbery snout, webbed feet, and in that it lays eggs.

WHY DO ANIMALS BECOME EXTINCT?

GIANT PANDA: fewer than 1,000 remaining

YELLOW-EYED PENGUIN: about 3,000 left in the wild

RED WOLF: only 200 exist in captivity, none in the wild

According to the theory of evolution, some animal species become extinct because they are less successful than other species that gradually replace them.

These so-called 'failed' animals are also unable to adapt to changing circumstances. Humans have speeded up their extinction by changing the environment so rapidly that animals do not have the time to adapt. For example, the destruction of Indonesian rainforests has left nowhere for the orang-utan to live. It would take millions of years for the animal to evolve into a ground-living creature. Hunting is the main reason for the reduced numbers and probable extinction of animals such as the tiger, the blue whale, and the giant panda.

FACT FILE

The black rhino has been reduced to about 2,550 as a result of poaching. Most of the ones that survive today live in protected game parks.

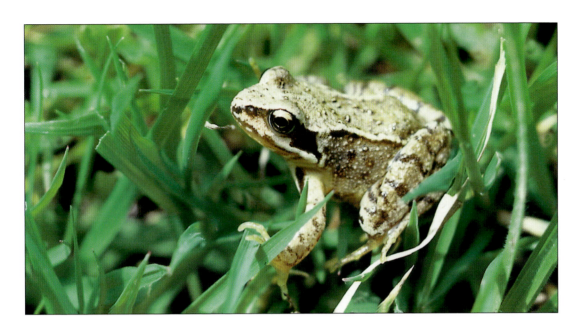

WHY DO AMPHIBIANS LEAVE THE WATER?

Although frogs and toads can live on land, they have to return to the water to breed. Common frogs can be found in many freshwater habitats. They often show up in garden ponds, but are just as happy in lakes, canals and pools. Toads usually prefer wooded ponds and lakes and can sometimes be seen in boggy pools.

Frogs and toads are amphibians, which means they are equally at home on land and water. Toads, however, spend more time away from water than most frogs. Their skin is leathery and warty and they do not lose water so easily on dry land. On land, a frog hops to escape danger, whereas a toad will walk. The bodies of some frogs and toads have adapted to survive in very dry conditions, such as in deserts.

FACT FILE

A frog's eyes are on top of its head so it can see above the water's surface. This way it can keep a watch out for predators.

WHEN ARE SEEDS FORMED?

Seeds are the main means by which flowering plants reproduce and spread. After the plant has been fertilized the egg cells develop into a seed from which a new plant can develop. The seed contains an embryo from which the new plant will grow. It also contains a food store to nourish the embryo until it has developed roots and leaves. The seed is enclosed in a tough outer coating to protect it from drying out. Many seeds can be carried by the wind. Some even have a fluffy umbrella like the dandelion seed head (above), which enables them to be carried for very long distances.

WHEN DOES POLLINATION TAKE PLACE?

FACT FILE

The flowers of orchids are highly specialized for pollination by insects. When the insect pushes into the flower to reach the nectar, the pollinia stick onto its head.

Pollination is the process of transferring pollen from the stamen to stigma. It is possible for flowers to pollinate themselves, or other flowers on the same plant – this is called self-pollination. It is, however, much better for the health of the species if cross-pollination occurs, i.e. pollen is transferred from one plant to another. The most common method involves insects that are attracted to the flowers for their nectar. Pollen grains stick to the insects' bodies and are effectively transferred from one plant to another as the insect moves from flower to flower. Other, less attractive types of flower, use wind to transport their pollen.

HOW CAN PLANTS EAT INSECTS?

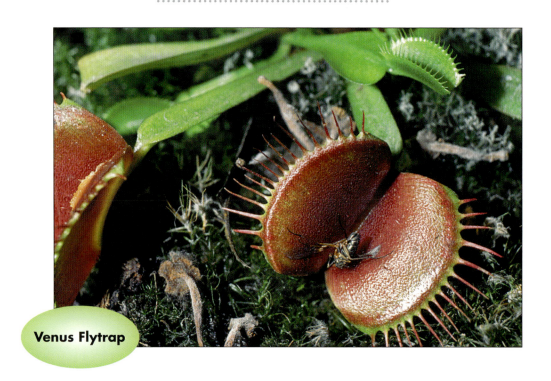

Venus Flytrap

FACT FILE

Some insects use camouflage to blend into their environment, protecting themselves from predators.

Plants growing in bogs and peaty area often need to supplement their food supply by catching insects. Bog water contains very little nitrogen, but some bog plants can obtain this substance by catching and digesting insects. They are known as insectivorous plants. Other insectivorous plants are covered with sticky tentacles that trap flies. The most remarkable is the Venus flytrap plant. It has two clawed plates that slam together when a fly walks over them and touches a trigger hair. Other insect-eating plants are aquatic, catching tiny crustaceans in bladder-shaped underwater traps. Some of the largest insectivorous plants live in the tropical rainforests.

WHEN DO DRAGONFLIES EAT?

Dragonflies are impressive insects with two pairs of powerful clear wings which enable them to catch insects on the wing. They have large eyes for spotting their prey. Dragonfly nymphs live in water and so the adults are usually seen near ponds, rivers and lakes. Some species have a feeding territory, which they guard from other dragonflies – their clattering wings can sometimes be heard as they battle. When they mate, most species fly around in tandem before they lay their eggs in the water or among the waterside vegetation. Dragonfly nymphs are active carnivores. They feed on other insects, but can catch tadpoles or even small fish. On the underside of the head is a flap called the mask. This is armed with sharp jaws and fangs. At rest it is folded, but it can shoot out to catch its prey.

Male Emperor dragonfly

Broad-bodied Libellula

FACT FILE

A dragonfly's eyes are large and give it almost all-around vision. They are sensitive to the slightest movement around them. If you look closely you will be able to see the individual facets of the eye. Each one contains its own lens; together they help form the image seen.

HOW DO BEES MAKE HONEY?

Honey is food to the bee, and bees make honey to store up this food for the whole bee colony. In order to transport the honey nectar home after visiting flowers and drinking it, the bee has a honey sac, a bag-type growth located in front of the bee's stomach, divided from the stomach by a special valve.

It is while the nectar is still in the bee's honey sac that the first stage of making honey occurs, with a chemical change taking place in the nectar's sugar. Then water is removed from the nectar by evaporation, caused by both ventilation and the heat of the hive. In fact, the honey has so much water removed, it will keep indefinitely when the bee stores it in the honeycombs.

The bee puts the honey in the honeycombs to ripen, to be stored as the future food supply for the colony. Depending on the original source of the nectar, the honey comes in a variety of different appearances and flavours.

FACT FILE

Honey is removed from the hive by various methods. It may be squeezed from the comb by presses, or it may be sold in the combs cut from the hive. Most honey, however, is removed from the combs by a machine known as 'a honey extractor'.

WHEN DO GLOW WORMS GLOW?

The glow worm is not really a worm at all. It is a firefly in an early stage of development called the larval stage. Most adult fireflies never eat because they did all their eating when they were larvae. They hide during the daytime among the vegetation. After dark, the female climbs up plant stems and the top of her abdomen glows. The light from a larva's glowing body attracts tiny flies and mosquitoes for the larva to eat.

The Waitomo Caves in New Zealand house a memorable type of glow worm. Tourists entering the Glowworm Grotto in small boats see thousands of lights on the cave ceiling. The glow worms look like stars in a night sky. If you cough or use a camera flash, the lights instantly go off. But wait quietly for a few minutes and they flicker back on, until the cave-ceiling 'sky' is again filled with 'stars'.

FACT FILE

Woodworm, the larvae of the furniture beetle, cause lots of damage to timber both in buildings and in the wild. The damage is evident from the holes they leave behind.

WHEN DO WATER-DWELLING INSECTS BREATHE?

The saucer bug

Water bugs are found in all sorts of different types of freshwater habitats. They all breathe air and have to return to the surface of the water from time to time. Ponds and lakes are the best habitats for water bugs. Only a few species live in streams and rivers, except where the current is slow-flowing. Adult water beetles have to breathe air. They do not have gills. Many have a supply of air beneath their wing cases or under the body, which they renew from time to time. Watch a beetle in a tank. Some species come to the surface tail-first, while a few come to the surface head first. Count the number of times a beetle will visit the surface in an hour.

Adult water beetle

FACT FILE

Place a needle on a piece of paper in some water. As the paper sinks, the needle floats, showing surface tension. This same process allows the water boatman to 'walk' on water. It uses its legs like oars to swim.

Discoveries & Inventions

raw ingredients are heated in a furnace

liquid glass (gob) is dropped into the mould

compressed air forces the liquid into the shape of the mould

the liquid spreads into the mould

the finished bottle is removed

molten tin

Making glass

cooling rollers

float glass

HOW WAS GLASS DISCOVERED?

It was discovered that glass forms when melted solid materials are cooled quickly, so that they do not produce crystals. The main ingredients for making glass are sand, soda ash, or potash and lime, melted together at a very high temperature. Since these materials are found in abundance in many parts of the world, the secret of glassmaking could have been discovered in many countries.

The Romans were great glassmakers and used glass as a coating for walls. By the time of the Christian era glass was already being used for windowpanes.

FACT FILE

Mercury is the only metal that is a liquid at room temperature. It is a bright shiny colour and flows rapidly when poured. This is why it used to be called 'Quicksilver'. Mercury is used today in thermometers and by dentists who mix it with silver to fill the cavities in your teeth.

HOW ARE MIRRORS MADE?

FACT FILE

Mirrors are used in lighthouses to help reflect the light a long way to guide ships out at sea. Some lighthouses have their own generators so that the light does not go out at any time.

Mirrors are pieces of glass that have been coated with a reflective material on the back, so that when a beam of light strikes the surface none of it is absorbed. The beam of light is actually reflected away from the mirror again.

The beam of light is reflected at exactly the same angle as it struck the mirror, but in the opposite direction. This can be visualized if you imagine a snooker ball striking the cushion of the table and bouncing back at an angle.

Mirrors are used in many ways, for example in telescopes, flashlights, headlights of cars and in lamps in lighthouses.

HOW DOES A BATTERY PRODUCE ELECTRICITY?

The electric current we use for power can be produced in two ways, by big machines known as dynamos and generators, and by the portable method of battery cells. Electricity is produced by the the battery cell by changing chemical energy into electrical energy, with some of the chemical energy being converted into heat and the rest into electric current. A battery contains two different conductors, or electrodes. The electrodes are separated by a conducting liquid or paste, called the electrolyte. The substances in the battery react chemically with each other to produce an electrical current. As a result of chemical activity, a positive charge builds up at one electrode and this can flow through a conductor such as a wire to the other (negative) electrode.

FACT FILE

An alternative form of power has arrived with the development of wind farms. Huge windmills situated on exposed and windy areas drive dynamos to produce electricity.

positive terminal

Dry cell

metal nail collects current

negative terminal

zinc powder

negative terminal

mercuric oxide

Button cell

positive terminal

HOW DOES AN ELECTRIC LIGHT WORK?

sealed glass bulb

filament

metal contact through which current can flow

Some of the earliest experiments that led to the electric light bulb were conducted by an English scientist, Humphrey Davey. Using a very weak version of what we would now call a battery, he first connected wires to its ends and then attached a piece of carbon to the other ends of the wires. Davey found he could produce a sparking light by touching the two pieces of carbon together and then drawing them slightly apart.

Called 'an electric arc', it was the first real evidence that light produced by electricity was possible, although the source of the power in these early bulbs was certainly not strong enough.

In a modern light bulb a current is passed through a very thin filament of metal that has a high resistance to the flow of electricity. The filament becomes white-hot and produces light. The bulb contains an inert gas so the filament will not burn.

FACT FILE

Lightning is actually electricity. A huge electrical charge can be built up in certain weather conditions, and this leads to thunderstorms when a bolt of lightning leaps between the earth and a cloud. The air is heated to a tremendous temperature, causing the explosive noise of thunder as it suddenly expands.

HOW DO LASERS WORK?

Lasers are devices that produce a narrow beam of extremely strong light. Lasers amplify light by causing photons to be bounced back and forth in a substance (which can be solid, liquid or gas), which add extra energy. The result is that intense light is emitted in a very narrow beam. The intense beam of light produced by a laser can be used to produce images for publicity or entertainment purposes.

Lasers are also used to cut metal, and for precision cuts in operations. In CD players, laser light is scanned across the CD's silvery surface, reading the tiny changes in light reflected back. They are also used in office printers and scanners. In engineering, the intense narrow beam of light is used to measure and align roads and tunnels.

Air pushing over the upper surface of an aircraft's wing reduces in pressure, allowing higher-pressure air underneath the wing to exert an upward force, thus enabling the aeroplane to fly.

airflow

propellor produces thrust

HOW DO AEROPLANES FLY?

As an aeroplane moves through the air, the air passes over the surface of its wings. These wings are shaped with a curved top surface and a flatter lower surface, which means that air passing over the top of the wing has to travel a little faster than that below the wing. This causes the pressure to lower above the wing, while the air pressure below pushes up. The end result is the lift that keeps the aeroplane in the air.

The tail surfaces of the aeroplane keep the wing at the proper angle to provide the right amount of lift. The power to propel the aeroplane along can come either from the engine, or, in the case of gliders, from rising air currents.

Jet engines propel a plane just like a rocket, with a stream of hot gases.

FACT FILE

Leonardo da Vinci (1452–1519) drew his plans for a helicopter hundreds of years before flying machines were even invented.

HOW DOES SONAR WORK?

Sound waves travel extremely well through water. They are used to detect submarines, wrecks on the seabed, or by fishermen to find shoals of fish. A sonar device under a ship sends out sound waves that travel down through the water. The sound waves are reflected back from any solid object they reach, such as shoals of fish or the seabed.

The echoes are received by the ship and can be used to 'draw' an image of the object, and its location, onto a computer screen.

FACT FILE

Supersonic aircraft actually break the sound barrier. When travelling at such very high speeds, aircraft begin to build up a huge wave of compressed air in front of them causing a sonic 'boom'.

sound waves reflected from fish

sound waves transmitted from ship

Sonar, or echo sounding is used by fishermen to detect shoals of fish. It can also be used to detect submarines or to find wrecks on the seabed.

HOW DO BATS USE SONAR?

Bats also use sonar waves to navigate. Bats are nocturnal, which means they are active at night and sleep during the day. Since bats have to hunt for their food at night, you would imagine that they need exceptionally good eyesight. But this is not the case, as bats do not depend on their eyes for getting about. When bats fly, they utter a series of very high pitched sounds, which are too high to be heard by the human ear.

The echoes from these sounds are thrown back to the bat when it is in flight, and it can tell whether the echo came from an obstacle nearby or far away. The bat can then change its course in flight to avoid hitting the obstacle!

Bats produce a continuous high-pitched squeaking in flight, and the echoes from this sound allow them to navigate in darkness and even to locate the small flying insects on which they feed.

thumb

arm bone

five-toed feet

finger bones

FACT FILE

Musical instruments produce sounds in various different ways, but they all cause air to vibrate to carry the sound to your ears. Sounds travel as waves and it is the shape of the sound wave that determines the kind of sound that will be produced. The pitch of the sound (whether high or low) depends on the frequency of the sound waves.

piccolo

pan pipes

saxophone

french horn

WHEN WAS PAPER FIRST MADE?

The first paper was made about 2,000 years ago in China, by a man called Ts'ai Lun. He took the stringy inner bark of the Mulberry tree and pounded it in water until it became a mass of flattened threads. He then placed this pulped solution onto a flat tray of fine bamboo strips.

The water was allowed to drain through the bamboo, and the threads in the bamboo were left to dry. The dried result was a flat, fibrous material considered to be the very first paper. As with all new discoveries, improvements are gradually made. One of these was to brush starch over the paper to improve it.

The secret of papermaking soon became world-wide knowledge as Chinese traders travelled to Russia and the Middle East. From there, the art of papermaking spread to Europe.

A revolutionary invention, paper-making began to be produced in mass quantities. The first continuous paper-making machine was developed in France in 1798 by Louis Robert. At the beginning of the next century, the Fourdrinier brothers in London developed the idea further.

FACT FILE

The Chinese had another secret, they were the only people who knew how to make silk. European traders would make the long journey to take silk back to Europe.

WHEN WERE THE FIRST BOOKS MADE?

The Diamond Sutta, the oldest printed book known, made in 868 AD

The first books were made about 4,000 years ago by the Egyptians who took flattened layers of papyrus stems to make sheets. The 'books' they made were collections of rolled papyrus sheets – very different to a book of today.

In the middle of the fifth century, parchment (sheep skin) replaced papyrus. Parchment sheets were placed on top of one another and bound down one side with leather tongs. But it was in the Middle Ages that books as we know them today evolved. Vellum (calf skin) was made into sheets, and each piece was folded down the middle. Four vellum sheets made eight leaves and was considered a section. Unlike parchment, vellum was thick enough to be written on both sides. Finished sections were sewn together down the back fold (the spine) and covered with wooden boards front and back. The boards and spine were then covered with leather; the result was a book similar to that of today.

FACT FILE

In about 500 AD monks would spend endless hours on illuminated handwritten books. The work was slow and painstaking, but worthwhile because it was another way to show dedication to God.

WHEN WAS FIRE DISCOVERED?

Man has been aware of fire since the most ancient times, evidence of which dates back thousands of years in charcoal and charred remnants of bone found in archeological digs.

It is most likely, and logical, that early man was able to use fire before he knew how to actually create it. A tree struck by lightning and set alight, for instance, would provide fire as long as men could keep it going.

Similarly, cavemen of old might have noticed sparks created by the movement of loose stones underfoot and such, but it was probably a long time before they realised it was the friction of two stones rubbed together that caused the sparks, and hundreds of years more before the notion was applied in practice. It goes without saying that, like with the lightening, the first fire man experienced was a creation of the natural world around him.

FACT FILE

In 1709 an ironmaster named Abraham Darby discovered that coal could be turned into coke by baking it. With this, he was able to make better-quality iron in his furnaces.

WHEN WAS BRAILLE INVENTED?

The Braille system was invented in 1829 by a blind gentleman called Louis Braille. He developed a system which would allow blind people to read and write. It is today one of the most widely used alphabets for the blind.

The basis of Braille is a system of dots. Each letter of the alphabet is represented by a combination of dots. These combinations are punched onto paper, so that they appear as raised bumps. A blind person reads the dots by moving their fingers over the bumps, recognising each letter to spell out the words.

There were earlier systems of reading for the blind. Back in the 16th century alphabetic letters were carved into blocks of wood for the blind to read. This system was good to read by, but the drawback was that the blind could not see how to form the letters when they wanted to write.

The sensitive tip of the finger 'feels' the Braille letters

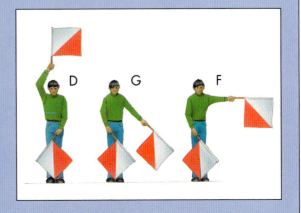

FACT FILE

Semaphore is another means of communicating by using flags. Different flag positions represent different letters and numbers. It was widely used between ships sailing near each other in the days before radio.

D   G   F

WHEN WERE FIREWORKS INTRODUCED?

Chinese crackers were probably the first fireworks to be made and this was about 2000 years ago. They are still used in China and throughout the East to celebrate weddings, births and religious festivals. They are also used to scare away evil spirits. It is probable that gunpowder was developed in China because they used potassium nitrate (saltpetre) to cure their meat, and so it was readily available.

Fireworks have also been used for centuries in ancient Indian and Siamese ceremonies. The earliest recorded use of gunpowder in England is by the Franciscan monk Roger Bacon (born 1214). He recorded his experiments with a mixture which was very inadequate by today's standards but was recognisable as gunpowder. His formula contained charcoal and sulphur because there was no natural source of saltpeter available.

FACT FILE

In January 1606 Parliament established November 5 as a day of public thanksgiving. The day, known as Guy Fawkes Day, is still celebrated with bonfires, fireworks, and the carrying of 'guys' through the streets.

WHEN WAS GUNPOWDER FIRST USED?

It was the Chinese again who first started using gunpowder in warfare. By the year 1232, the Chinese had discovered black powder (gunpowder) and had learned to use it to make explosive bombs as well as propelling forces for rockets. Drawings made in military documents later show powder rockets tied to arrows and spears.

When the Mongols laid siege to the city of K'ai-feng, the capital of Honan province, the Chinese defenders used weapons that were described as 'arrows of flying fire'. In the same battle, it is reported, the defenders dropped from the walls of the city a kind of bomb described as 'heaven-shaking thunder'.

In the same century, rockets appeared in Europe. There is indication that their first use was by the Mongols in the Battle of Legnica in 1241. The Arabs are also reported to have used rockets in 1249.

FACT FILE

Guy Fawkes is best known for his efforts to blow up the Parliament building in 1605. This became known as the 'Gunpowder Plot'. His plan, however, was foiled and he was consequently arrested on 4 November, 1605.

WHO FIRST SPLIT THE ATOM?

Ernest Rutherford (1871–1937) was a physicist who studied radioactivity. He found several different forms of radiation and also discovered that elements change as a result of radioactive decay. He received the Nobel Prize for his work. Rutherford went on to discover the nucleus of the atom, and in 1919 he finally succeeded in splitting an atom for the first time.

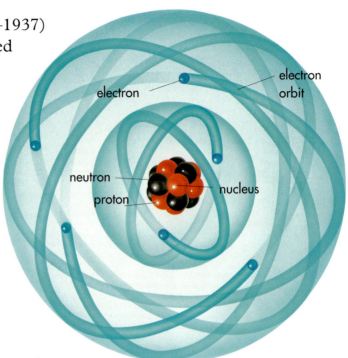

He described the atom as a tiny, dense, positively charged core called a nucleus, in which nearly all the mass is concentrated, around which the light, negative constituents, called electrons, circulate at some distance, much like planets revolving around the Sun.

FACT FILE

Atoms become linked to other atoms by electrical bonds, which work rather like chemical hooks. Some atoms only carry one of these hooks while others may have many.

WHEN WAS ATOMIC STRUCTURE DISCOVERED?

Niels Bohr was a Danish physicist. His mark on science and history was worldwide. His professional work and personal convictions were part of the larger stories of the century. Bohr studied physics at the University of Copenhagen where he began to work on the problem of the atom's structure. Ernest Rutherford had recently suggested the atom had a miniature, dense nucleus surrounded by a cloud of nearly weightless electrons. There were a few problems with the model, however. Bohr proposed adding to the model, and this proved to be a huge leap forward in making theory fit the experimental evidence that other physicists had brought to light. A few inaccuracies remained to be ironed out by others over the next few years, but his essential idea was proved correct.

He received the Nobel Prize for this work in 1922, and it is what he is most famous for. He was only 37 at the time, and went on to make many other discoveries.

FACT FILE

Niels Bohr helped to develop the atomic bomb in 1943.

WHY ARE MICROSCOPES USED?

The microscope enables us to see minute things which are otherwise invisible to the naked eye. Its name comes from the Greek 'mikros' for 'small' and skopos for 'watcher', the instrument being a 'watcher of small things'.

Things appear bigger as we bring them closer to the eye, yet when they get too close, anything less than 10 inches (25.5cm), they become blurred or out of focus. But the object can be brought nearer, and still stay in focus, with the aid of a simple convex lens that is placed between the eye and the object.

It was a Dutchman called Antonie van Leeuwenhoek (1632–1723) who discovered ground glass lenses, which he used to examine the world about him. In the 1670s he made his first crude microscope with a tiny lens. This allowed him to be the first person to see microscopic life such as bacteria, yeast and living blood cells. From his pioneering work came an instrument which is now used in every branch of science and industry.

FACT FILE

Some microscopes are so powerful they can magnify the smallest objects many thousands of times. This plant cell would be invisible to the human eye without the use of magnification.

The Solar System

WHAT IS THE MOON?

The Moon is the Earth's only satellite, and it has been orbiting our planet for at least 4,000 million years. It is a rocky sphere about 2,160 miles (3,476 km) in diameter, which is about one-quarter the size of the Earth.

Scientists believe that the Moon formed when another planet about the size of Mars collided with the Earth. The collision splashed a huge mass of molten (liquid) rock into space. This molten rock quickly formed into a sphere, and the Moon cooled into its solid form. The Moon's surface is heavily pitted by collisions with debris such as asteroids.

FACT FILE

Living things need air and water to stay alive, and neither of these is available on the Moon. The Moon also suffers extreme temperature swings between the lunar day and night.

WHAT IS THE MOON MADE OF?

The Moon is a rocky satellite, and is made of similar material to the Earth. It has an outer layer, or mantle, of rock, and a core that is probably made up mostly of iron. Unlike the Earth's liquid mantle, the interior of the Moon is cool and solid. There is little or no volcanic activity on the Moon. However, while it was cooling, early in its life, floods and streams of lava ran out across the Moon's surface. The Moon also has mountain ranges, many of which are the remains of impact craters and volcanoes that were active when the Moon was still hot. There are some huge valleys called rilles, which can be hundreds of miles in length and look a little like river-beds.

WHY DOES THE EARTH TRAVEL AROUND THE SUN?

One theory explaining the origin of our solar system is that a huge dust cloud was formed about 5 billion years ago. Spinning through space, it gradually flattened out into a disc shape, the hot centre forming the Sun. At the same time, the outer portions of the dust cloud spun off into space, breaking away from the centre in swirling masses to become the planets. The reason these planets, including the Earth, didn't just fly off into space, was the gravitational pull of the Sun.

It is this force that keeps the Earth revolving round the Sun in what we call its 'orbit'. The speed a planet moves in its orbit depends on its distance from the Sun. When closer it moves faster. The Earth moves at 18.8 miles (30 km) per second when closest to the Sun, and 18.2 miles (29 km) per second at its furthest point away.

FACT FILE

Other planets that revolve around the Sun are Mercury and Pluto. Mercury is the closest planet to the Sun and moves at an average speed of 29.8 miles (48 km) per second.

WHAT IS THE SUN MADE OF?

The Sun is a great ball of hot gases, made up of many layers. Astronomers have obtained many of their facts about the Sun by using special instruments. These instruments enable the scientists to study the glowing gases of the Sun and to see how different substances are distributed on the Sun and to take photographs of the Sun's corona without causing damage to the eyes. Finally, these instruments study radio waves that are emitted by the Sun. Because the Earth's atmosphere stops many of the Sun's radiations from reaching the Earth, scientists send instruments high up into the atmosphere. Such space probes help them learn more about the Sun.

FACT FILE

Without the Sun, life would be impossible on Earth. Among other things, the atmosphere would be frozen, no green plants would be living, and there would be no rain.

WHAT IS THE MILKY WAY?

One of the most spectacular features of the night sky that has fascinated men since ancient times is the Milky Way, which stretches from one horizon to the other. Many years ago, people imagined it was a pathway for the angels to travel to heaven, but today we know the truth about it, which is just as remarkable.

If it could be looked down upon from above, our galaxy would appear as a huge disc, round and flat like an enormous watch. But our vantage point, as part of the galaxy, is from within the 'watch' looking out towrds its edge. So it's that edge that we see, curving around us with its millions of stars twinkling in it, as the Milky Way.

FACT FILE

Containing at least 3,000,000,000 stars, the galaxy is so big we can hardly imagine its size. While the light from the Sun takes eight minutes to reach the Earth, the light from the middle of the galaxy takes about 27,000 years to reach the Sun.

WHAT IS A STAR?

Stars are huge balls of burning gas that are scattered throughout the Universe. They burn for millions of years, giving off both light and heat. Stars produce energy by a process called nuclear fusion. The coolest stars are red and dim, while the hottest stars give off blue-white light. The temperatures on their surface range from 3,500°C for cooler stars to over 40,000°C for the hottest stars.

A new star is born when gas and dust are drawn together by gravity, forming a huge clump. It heats up until nuclear fusion begins, and the new star appears in the sky.

FACT FILE

Stars die when they eventually use up all their fuel and burn out, but this process takes many millions of years. Towards the end of its life, a star starts to run out of hydrogen to power its nuclear fusion. It starts to cool, becoming a red giant.

WHY DO STARS APPEAR TO SHINE?

FACT FILE

The farthest stars in our galaxy are 80,000 light-years away. The nearest star to the Earth is our own Sun, which is 93 million miles (152 million km) away.

A star, including the Sun, is a ball of hot gas that shines with its own light. One of the things we notice about stars in the night sky is that they appear to twinkle. This 'twinkling' effect is caused by various unsteady substances in the atmosphere between Earth and space, bending the light from the star.

It is now believed that hydrogen atoms in the very core of the star burn to form helium. When this happens, it sets free energy, which flows steadily to its surface. Stars should be able to continue radiating this energy for many millions of years to come.

WHEN DO YOU SEE A SHOOTING STAR?

Shooting stars, or meteors, are streaks of light that cross the night sky, although they can only be seen for one or two seconds. They are caused when a solid piece of rock called a meteoroid plunges through the Earth's atmosphere, burning up due to air friction. If, as rarely happens, a small fragment reaches the Earth, it is called a meteorite. Sometimes these fragments of rock move through space as a meteor swarm or stream. They move in regular paths through space. The larger fragments become detached and travel through space individually.

FACT FILE

This impact crater in Arizona was caused by a huge meteorite. The amount of energy the impact released would have been equivalent to hundreds of nuclear weapons.

WHAT IS A SUPERNOVA?

Sometimes a star appears in the sky quite suddenly. This happens when there are a pair of stars rotating together. These are called binaries, and there is usually one large star called a red giant, orbiting with a smaller, hotter star. The nova takes place when gas is drawn from the red giant into the smaller star, where the heat causes a massive explosion and emits huge amounts of light. A supernova takes place when a star collapses as it begins to burn out, then suddenly explodes, producing a huge amount of light energy, and leaving behind a tiny core of neutrons, which is the heaviest substance in the Universe.

FACT FILE

Even with today's most powerful and advanced equipment, there is no visible limit to the Universe. No one is totally sure of the shape of the Universe.

WHAT IS A NEBULA?

FACT FILE

The only diffuse nebula visible to the naked eye is the beautiful Orion Nebula.

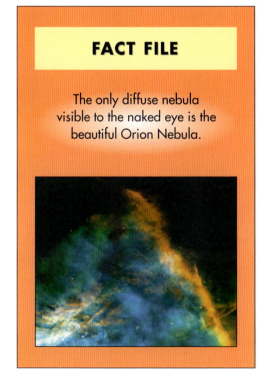

A nebula is a huge cloud of white-hot gas and solid material that whirls about in interstellar space getting smaller and hotter all the time. As the gas cloud grows smaller, it throws off rings of gas. Each of these rings condenses to become a star. Based on appearance, nebulae can be divided into two broad classes: dark nebulae and bright nebulae. Dark nebulae appear as irregularly shaped black patches in the sky and blot out the light of the stars lying beyond them. Bright nebulae appear as faintly luminous, glowing surfaces; they either emit their own light or reflect the light of nearby stars.

WHAT ARE THE PLANETS OF THE SOLAR SYSTEM?

The four planets that are nearest to the Sun are called the inner planets. In order from the Sun, they are Mercury, Venus, Earth and Mars. The inner planets are different from the outer planets, which are farther away from the Sun, because they are made of rock. Each of the inner planets has an atmosphere. However, apart from the Earth, the atmospheres of the inner planets are very thin and would be poisonous to humans. The outer planets, which are Jupiter, Saturn, Uranus, Neptune and Pluto are composed mostly of frozen gases, so although they are very large, they are comparatively light.

FACT FILE

Science fiction writers thought that life might exist beneath the thick clouds of Venus. We now know that conditions there are too extreme for life as we know it.

WHAT ARE THE RINGS OF SATURN?

FACT FILE

Pluto is the smallest and most remote planet on the edge of deep space. It was only discovered in 1930 as a result of calculations to find out why Neptune's orbit was being disturbed by an unknown body.

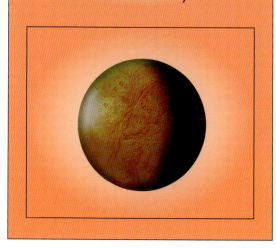

Shining rings of billions of tiny chips of ice, rock and dust surround Saturn. The rings reflect light strongly and can be clearly seen through a telescope from the Earth. It was first thought that Saturn had three wide rings, but it is now known that the rings are actually made up of thousands of narrow ringlets. The rings are only 328 ft (100 m) thick, but extend into space for 47,000 miles (76,000 km). The material in the rings was probably captured by Saturn's gravity when the Solar System was forming, or it might be the remains of a moon that has broken up. Space probes recently discovered that some of the rings are braided, or twisted.

WHY IS NEPTUNE BLUE?

Neptune is covered with a blue ocean of liquid methane. It is a very cold place – at the farthest part of its orbit it is 4,000 million km from the Sun. Its surface temperature drops to –210°C. Neptune is made of hydrogen, helium, and methane, and probably has a rocky core. It takes an amazing 164.8 years to travel just once around the Sun. Neptune was first identified in 1846 when astronomers found that an unidentified planet was disturbing the orbit of Uranus. Neptune has huge storms and one of these, the Great Dark Spot, was larger than the Earth.

FACT FILE

Mars is covered by a stony desert that contains lots of iron oxide, making it appear rusty-red. Mars has small polar ice-caps that grow larger during the Martian winter.

WHAT DOES VENUS LOOK LIKE?

Venus is often referred to as Earth's sister. The planet is a similar size to our own, but here the resemblance ends. The temperature on the surface of the planet is nearly 500°C (930°F). The air is dense enough to crush a human in seconds, and the atmosphere consists partly of acid. The dark patches that you see on the surface of Venus are a layer of cloud 19 miles (30 km) thick. If we look past the clouds, we can see that Venus is a planet once ruled by volcanoes. Scientists believe that there are at least 160 that are larger than 62 miles (100 km) in diameter and over 50,000 smaller ones. However, there is no evidence to show that these volcanoes are still active today.

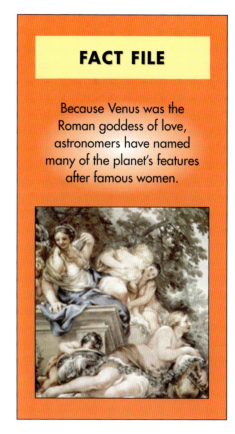

FACT FILE

Because Venus was the Roman goddess of love, astronomers have named many of the planet's features after famous women.

WHAT DOES THE EARTH LOOK LIKE FROM SPACE?

Salt Lake City, Utah

The Nile

The Mississippi

Sinai Peninsula

Earth is designated in astronomy as the third planet outward from the Sun. Its single most outstanding feature is that its near-surface environments are the only places in the universe known to maintain life. Those who have gone into space have come back with a changed perspective and reverence for the planet Earth. The effect from space is obvious. One astronaut said after his trip, 'My first view – a panorama of brilliant deep blue ocean, shot with shades of green and grey and white – was of atolls and clouds.'

FACT FILE

Pioneer 10 was the first man-made object to leave the Solar System. It carried messages about life on Earth to be read by any extraterrestrial travellers who might meet the probe.

WHERE WOULD YOU SEE BAILY'S BEADS?

A total eclipse of the Sun can be quite frightening, turning day into night in a spectacular fashion. However, as the Moon appears to eat the Sun, some incredibly beautiful 'special effects' take place. Just before the Sun disappears, a brilliant bright spot can be seen on the edge of the Moon, a little like a diamond on a ring. This is caused by the last fingers of the Sun's light filtering through valleys and mountain ranges on the Moon. Sometimes, the bright spot can appear as an arc of glowing pearls, an effect known, after the British astronomer Francis Baily, as Baily's Beads.

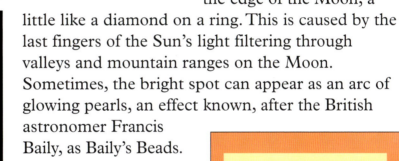

FACT FILE

It is important never to look directly at the Sun, even during an eclipse. This can cause blindness.

WHY DO COMETS HAVE TAILS?

You cannot see the nucleus of a comet with the naked eye, but you can sometimes see its tail. It appears as a smear of light that moves very gradually across the sky. As a comet moves closer to the Sun, the ice and other frozen gases in its nucleus begin to boil off, producing a long tail of gas and dust. The tail will always point away from the Sun because light and other forms of radiation from the Sun push against the minute particles that are present within the tail.

Comet tails are very different in shape and size. Some are short and stubby. Others are long and slender. As the tail grows, the comet gains in speed because it is nearing the Sun.

A comet showing its tail

FACT FILE

Halley's Comet is perhaps the most famous comet of all. It can be seen from Earth every 76 years and was even recorded in 1066 on the Bayeux Tapestry.

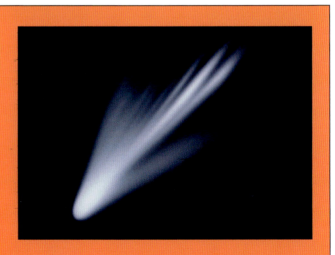

WHAT IS A BLACK HOLE?

Black holes are the monsters of the Universe. Formed from the brightest of all explosions, supernovae, they soon become the darkest objects in space, emitting no light at all. A black hole is an area in space where the force of gravity is so strong that even light cannot escape from it. Black holes are created when a burned-out star collapses. Eventually it shrinks into a tiny sphere of material. The gravity of this material is so powerful that it pulls in everything around it. Even light itself is sucked into the black hole. Nothing that goes into a black hole ever comes out. We cannot see black holes. We can sometimes identify them from the radio waves given off as a star is drawn into a black hole.

FACT FILE

Imagine space as a stretched-out sheet. If an object is placed on this sheet, it will create a dip, towards which other objects will be drawn if they come too close. A black hole creates such a steep dip that objects that enter can never escape.

WHAT WAS THE BIG BANG?

Nobody knows how the Universe began, but the most common theory is the Big Bang. According to this theory, the Universe was formed from an immense explosion 13 billion years ago. Before the Big Bang, everything in the Universe was packed into a tiny area, smaller than the nucleus of an atom. This point was called a singularity and was incredibly hot. It was released in an explosion so powerful that all of the matter in the singularity was blasted into an area larger than a galaxy in less than a fraction of a second. There is very strong evidence to support the theory of the Big Bang. The strongest 'proof' is a weak signal that has been detected in space. This is thought to be an echo from the energy released by the force of the Big Bang.

FACT FILE

According to ancient Egyptian mythology, the fundamentals of life – air (Shu) and moisture (Tefnut) – came from the spittle of their Sun God Re. From the union of Shu and Tefnut came Geb, the Earth god, and Nut, the sky goddess. The first human beings were born from Re's tears.

WHAT IS THE UNIVERSE MADE UP OF?

The Universe is everything and anything that exists. The Universe is still a mystery to scientists. It is made up almost entirely of hydrogen and helium. These are the two lightest elements. All the rest of the matter in the Universe is very rare. Elements such as silicon, carbon and others are concentrated into clouds, stars and planets. The Universe is held together by four invisible forces. Gravity and electromagnetism are the two familiar forces. The other two kinds are strong and weak nuclear forces. These operate only inside the incredibly tiny nuclei of atoms, holding the tiny particles together.

FACT FILE

Nobody knows exactly how big the Universe is, what shape it takes, where it comes from or what it is expanding into. If we could go far enough into space, maybe we could understand more.

WHICH PLANET IS ALWAYS DARK AND COLD?

On Pluto it is always dark and cold, even in the middle of the day. This is because the Sun appears 1,000 times fainter from the surface of Pluto than it does from Earth, little more than a faint star. In summer, Pluto has a slight atmosphere because the surface warms up enough to melt some of its ice, turning it to gas. As Pluto moves away from the Sun, the gas freezes and becomes ice again. This means that in winter, Pluto's weather doesn't just become worse, it completely disappears.

FACT FILE

Little is known about Pluto's atmosphere, but it probably consists primarily of nitrogen with some carbon monoxide and methane.

WHICH IS PLUTO'S COMPANION MOON?

In 1978 Pluto was found to have a companion moon, which scientists named Charon. The moon is one third the size of Pluto, making it the biggest moon in comparison to its parent planet in the entire Solar System. They are only 12,430 miles (20,000 km) apart, and are caught in a gravitational headlock, forming what scientists call a dual planet system. Nobody knows how Pluto managed to adopt so large a moon. Some believe Charon is made from ice which was chipped off Pluto during a collision.

FACT FILE

Pluto takes 248 years to orbit the Sun. Amazingly, this means that not even half a year has elapsed on the planet since its discovery in 1930! Another strange feature about Pluto is that it rotates in the opposite direction from most of the other planets.

WHAT ARE THE MAGELLANIC CLOUDS?

The two galaxies which are closest to our own galaxy the Milky Way, the Magellanic Clouds, are visible as faint areas of light in the night sky of the southern hemishere. Because the arrangement of stars within them does not follow a regular pattern, they are classified by astronomers as irregular galaxies.

They appear cloudy to the naked eye because although they include billions of stars, individual stars in these gaalxies can only be seen with the use of the most powerful telescopes.

The Magellanic Clouds also consist of an enormous quantity of gas, which is mostly composed of hydrogen, from which new stars are continually being formed. Also, much of the light that does emanate from the Magellanic Clouds originates from the young, hot blue stars that are surrounded by almost luminous clouds of this gas.

FACT FILE

Magellanic Clouds were first recorded in the early 1500s during the circumglobal voyage of the Portuguese explorer Ferdinand Magellan, after whom they were named.

410

WHAT IS THE SOLAR WIND?

Charged particles are constantly being given off by the Sun. They are known as the Solar Wind and are strongest when the sunspot activity is at its height. When the Solar Wind reaches the Earth's magnetic field, the charged particles interact with gases in the Earth's atmosphere 6 miles (10 km) above the surface. This interaction causes the particles to send out light, which is seen from Earth as an amazing lightshow, most visible within the polar circles. In the northern hemisphere this is known as the aurora borealis, and in the southern hemisphere as the aurora australis.

FACT FILE

Darker areas on the surface of the Sun are called sunspots. These areas of cooler gas occur when the Sun's magnetic field blocks the flow of heat from the core.

WHERE IS CALLISTO?

Larger than the planet Pluto and almost as big as Mercury, Callisto is a large moon of the planet Jupiter. One of the most heavily cratered bodies in the solar system, more than 4 billion years of bombardment from asteroids and comets has left its icy surface covered with craters of all sizes, the greatest impacts forming enormous bulls-eye shapes in the cracked surface.

It is also a surface covered by dark dirt, which has built up as icy crater rims and cliffs have disintegrated over the passing eons. Callisto's carbon dioxide atmosphere is not much denser than that of the near-vacuum found in outer space.

FACT FILE

Calisto was discovered by the Italian astronomer Galileo in 1610. With a diameter of 2,986 miles (4,806 km), it orbits Jupiter every 16.7 days at a distance of 1,170,000 miles (1,883,000 km).

WHAT IS THE KUIPER BELT?

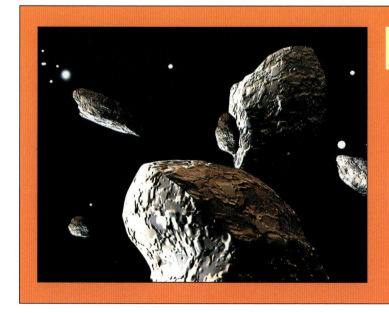

An astronomer named Gerard Kuiper suggested that beyond Neptune lay a belt of celestial bodies made up from rock and ice. Astronomers now think that there may be as many as 100,000 large, comet-like objects in the Kuiper Belt, including the planet Pluto. The icy bodies in the Kuiper Belt are called minor members, or 'Plutinos' because they act like little Plutos and are very difficult to spot from Earth, even with the most powerful telescopes. If all the objects in the Kuiper Belt joined together, they would form a planet the size of Earth.

FACT FILE

An object in space will be pulled into a spherical shape if its gravitational force is powerful enough. Because the objects in the Kuiper Belt do not have powerful gravitational pulls, they come in all sorts of shapes and sizes.

WHERE IS OLYMPUS MONS?

Mars is the only planet whose surface can be seen in detail from the Earth. Mars has one of the most striking surfaces of any planet in the solar system. Giant volcanoes tower above the landscape. The largest of these is Olympus Mons, which is 15.5 miles (25 km) tall, three times larger than Mount Everest. As well as this, Mars is home to Valles Marineris, a canyon that is 112 miles (180 km) wide, up to 4.3 miles (7 km) deep and long enough to stretch across America.

Mars does not have water on its surface now, but there is evidence to show that there were rivers and seas on Mars in the past. Probes have taken many pictures of the planet's surface and scientists have identified several channels that could only have been formed by running water. Astronomers believe that there was a great deal of liquid water on Mars billions of years ago.

FACT FILE

In 1996 scientists produced evidence they claimed, that showed living creatures inhabited Mars more than 3.6 billion years ago.

WHERE DO WE SEE METEOR SHOWERS?

At certain times of every year, the Earth meets a number of trails (also called streams) or clusters (also called showers) of tiny meteoroids, making the sky look as if it is filled with a shower of sparks. Believed to be fragments of comets, these trails and clusters have similar orbits to those of comets.

The most brilliant meteor shower ever known was one of the Leonid showers, (which occur every November, and seem to come from the direction of the constellation Leo) and took place on November 12–13, 1833.

FACT FILE

Barringer Crater is a huge depression in the earth in north-central Arizona. It measures about 4,180 ft (1,275 m) wide and 570 ft (175 m) deep. It was formed about 50,000 years ago when a meteorite struck the Earth.